IMAGES *of America*

Tulsa Movie Theaters

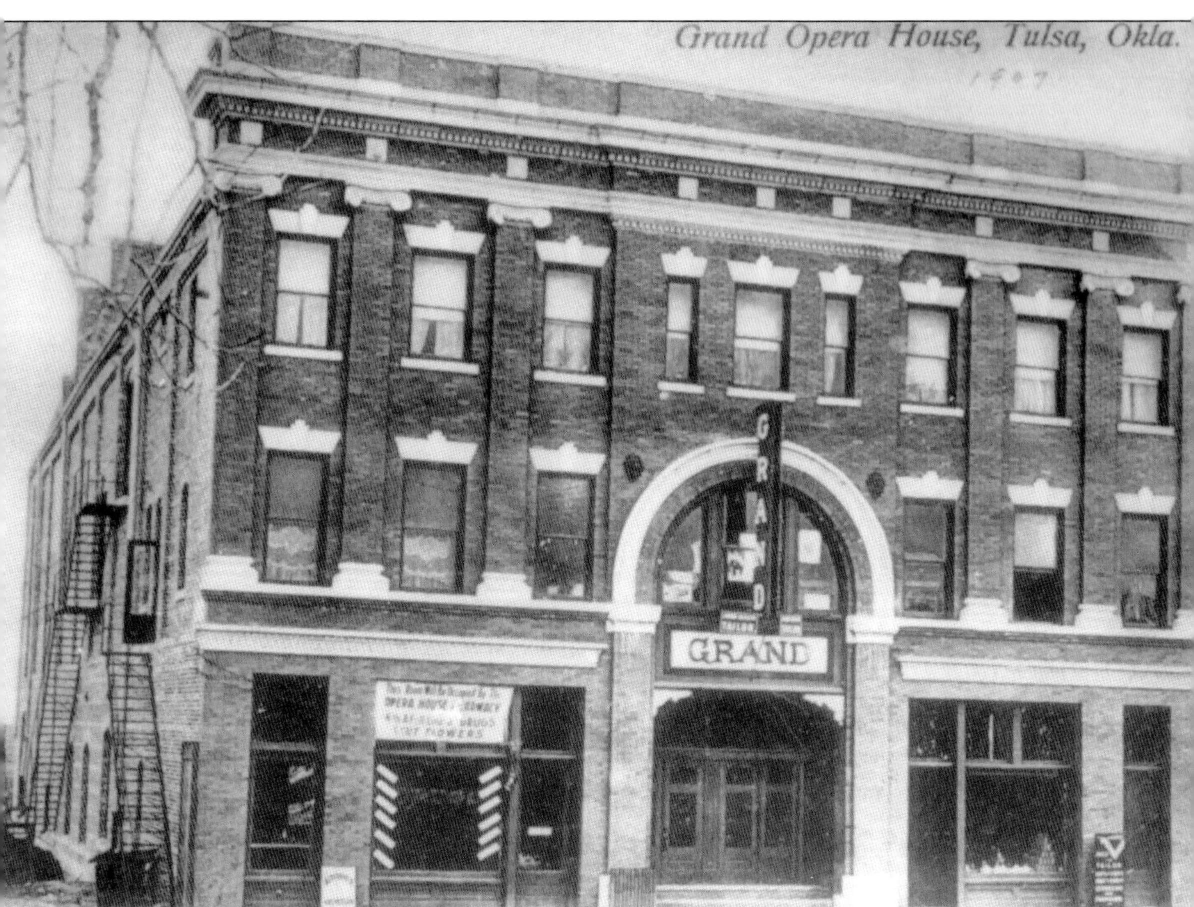

When it opened on February 1, 1906, the Grand Opera House was the first major entertainment building in the oil boomtown of Tulsa. The opera house was located on East Second Street between Boston and Cincinnati Avenues, and Tulsans gathered there to see opera stars like Lillian Russell and Otis Skinner as well as lectures and vaudeville entertainers. This impressive three-story structure opened the same year as the first tiny storefront theater, the Dreamland, displaying the novelty of moving pictures. (Courtesy of Tulsa Historical Society and Museum.)

On the Cover: The stunning neon of the Ritz and Orpheum Theaters lights up the night in downtown Tulsa. In this image looking east on Fourth Street between Boulder Avenue and Main Street, the streets are blocked off for Tulsa Day on April 18, 1949. The Ritz marquee reads "World Premiere, Walter Wanger's *Tulsa*. Stars in Person." Those stars—Susan Hayward, Robert Preston, and Chill Wills—were featured in a huge parade of Tulsa's oil industry followed by a four-theater premiere that brought an estimated 100,000 people to downtown Tulsa. (Courtesy of Tulsa Historical Society and Museum.)

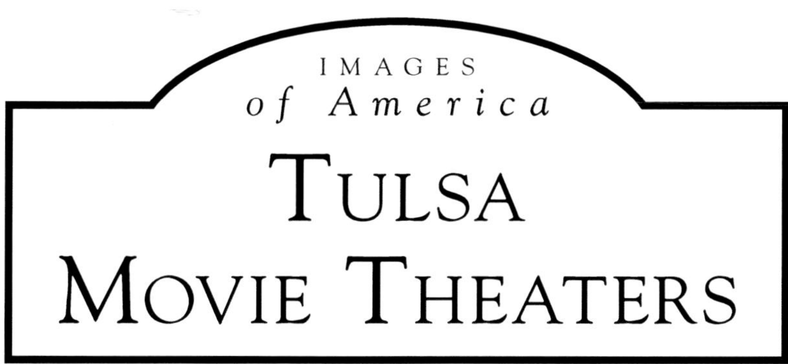

Steve Clem, Maggie Brown, and the
Tulsa Historical Society and Museum
Foreword by Gailard Sartain

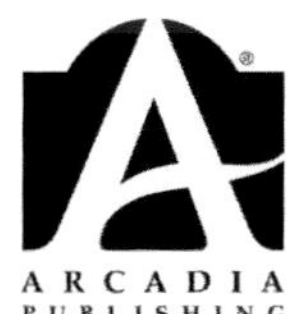

ISBN 978-1-4671-0685-6

Published by Arcadia Publishing
Charleston, South Carolina

Printed in the United States of America

Library of Congress Control Number: 2021934524

For all general information, please contact Arcadia Publishing:
Telephone 843-853-2070
Fax 843-853-0044
E-mail sales@arcadiapublishing.com
For customer service and orders:
Toll-Free 1-888-313-2665

Visit us on the Internet at www.arcadiapublishing.com

To Nancy Schallner—we stand on your shoulders, Tulsa Gal!

Steve dedicates this book to Maggie Brown, Michelle Place, and everyone at Tulsa Historical Society and Museum who makes dreams come true!

Maggie dedicates this book to Steve Clem for always coming up with great ideas, and to all those who love local history and images on film!

Contents

Foreword

With 25¢ in my pocket for a movie ticket and popcorn, I would ride my Schwinn to the Will Rogers Theatre and lose myself in the world on the screen. I would arrive hot and sweaty, park my bike in the rack, and then bask in the luxury of the "air cooled" theater.

Some of my best memories are from the Will Rogers and other theaters in Tulsa. The first movie I remember seeing was with my mother in 1948. It was *The Wake of the Red Witch*, which starred John Wayne. I saw *Julius Caesar* at the Delman, *The Song of Bernadette* every year at the Brook Theatre when I went to Cascia Hall, and a multitude of others at the Royal, the Orpheum, the Ritz, and Rialto. The names of the theaters bring back such happy memories of a childhood spent just blocks from the Will Rogers. I could just see the light on the top of the theater's tower from my bedroom window.

The interiors of the theaters were fascinating as well, most of them architectural wonders. There were murals on the walls of the Will Rogers showing Rogers on horseback, stars on the ceiling of the Ritz, and beautiful curtains in all of them that opened to reveal that silver screen. Except for the Circle Theatre, which was mercifully saved and renovated, all of these wonderful edifices are now gone.

Years ago, I was in the office of Tulsa historian Beryl Ford, whose monumental photograph collection is now part of the Tulsa Historical Society and Museum. To my amazement, I found a picture of the Will Rogers Theatre with my bike parked in the rack and *Macao* on the marquee. When I look at that photograph now, I am transported to that time of movie—and movie theater—greatness. All that is left of these theaters are memories and photographs. I hope that this beautiful book will also take you back to that wonderful time.

—Gailard Sartain

ACKNOWLEDGMENTS

Any book is a huge project and relies on the help of countless others. We specifically want to thank the people of the Tulsa area and throughout Oklahoma who have donated their movie theater memorabilia to museums and archives to be preserved for future generations.

If there is any one person to be credited with the accumulation of Tulsa's movie theater history, it is Nancy Schallner. In 2006, while volunteering for the Tulsa Historical Society and Museum, she began compiling an enormous amount of research to create a much-loved presentation about local theaters.

We are grateful for every single person who completed our information survey as we researched this book or otherwise shared their memories, information, images, and artifacts. That list includes: Jan Smith, Laura Winston Birdsong, Mary Ann Blue, Murrel Wilmoth, Dorothy McCormick, Louise Bowers, David Kimball, Russ Hembrey, Sheri Harris, Cheryl Dunlap Cassody, Pati Wilson, Monica Lamp, Cathleen Butler, Laura Ward, Bret Bradford, Karren Dunning, Marlo Holly, Randy Milligan, Bob Buchanan, Cynthia Marcoux, Stephen Walker, Janet Edwards Bull, Kaye Phelps Ellis, John McConnel, Kent Schnetzler, Connie and Barbara Fisher, Susan Yates, Gary Reynolds, Sonny Hollingshead, Mike Hardeman, John Durkee, Dennis Scott, Rodney Echohawk, Wesley Horton, and Marcia Becton Wright.

Thank you to the staff of the Tulsa Historical Society and Museum whose names are not on the cover: Britni Worley, Luke Williams, Neal Pascoe, Maggie Jewell, Michelle Place, and Grace Asher. Your help with researching, editing, digitizing, and remembering was invaluable. We also thank the many volunteers, interns, and assistants who have helped digitize and catalog artifacts.

We appreciate the organizations and historians who contributed their expertise and images to this project, including John Wooley and his book *Shot In Oklahoma: A Century of Sooner State Cinema*; Roy Heim and the Southwest Tulsa Historical Society; Rachel Mosman and the Oklahoma Historical Society; Mechelle Brown and the Greenwood Cultural Center; Mike Ransom and his website, Tulsa TV Memories; and Hilary Pittman, Tom Gilbert, and Ginnie Graham at the *Tulsa World*.

Also, thanks to Ginger Murphy and Dianna Phillips at Sand Springs Cultural and Historical Museum.

Thank you to Gailard and Mary Jo Sartain for sharing a great story that captures the experience so many Tulsans had when they visited their favorite neighborhood theaters.

The authors acknowledge the unsung heroes of the cinema experience—the local theater workers, including owners and managers, projectionists like Edward Miller, and all the young people whose first job was as a uniformed usher. Also, to the crews responsible for concessions, cleanup, and the changing of the marquee—we salute you!

We appreciate Caroline Vickerson, Sara Miller, and Arcadia Publishing for their help in allowing us to share these Tulsa movie theater memories.

Unless otherwise noted, all images appear courtesy of the Tulsa Historical Society and Museum.

INTRODUCTION

Movies changed American life. Like other major innovations that arrived in the early 1900s, such as the automobile and airplanes, movies—and the places where people gathered to view them—helped define life in the 20th century and beyond.

Tulsa and the movies grew up together. When the city's first theater, the Dreamland, opened in 1906, Tulsa, Indian Territory, was just one year into its first oil boom. With a mere 7,000 residents, Tulsa had a business district that encompassed just a few blocks of dirt streets. Oklahoma did not become a state until the following year.

The small storefront nickelodeons that appeared in Tulsa between 1906 and 1910 featured one- or two-reelers that provided between 10 and 20 minutes of entertainment. Accompanied by piano or organ, these were often featured on a bill with live vaudeville acts. These early silent movies, mainly produced by companies on the East Coast, gave little hint of the medium's true potential.

During the 1910s, both Tulsa and the movies became more fully formed. The movie industry consolidated its efforts in Hollywood, California, in a climate conducive to year-round filming. Moviemaking processes were refined, different genres of film emerged, and the first movie stars were born. Charlie Chaplin, Mary Pickford, and other early idols graced screens at Tulsa's Lyric, Idlehour, and Wonderland theaters, clustered around the 100 and 200 Blocks of South Main Street.

Tulsa experienced a second oil boom in the 1910s, and the population ballooned to 72,000 by 1920. As oil industry players from around the country came to Tulsa, city leaders worked to provide the infrastructure to make Tulsa a major oil hub.

By the time the Roaring Twenties brought a building boom to downtown, motion pictures had caught on with the public in a big way. Tulsa's emergence as "Oil Capital of the World" seemed a perfect stage for one or more of the grand movie palaces that were going up around the nation.

As it turns out, Tulsa had an "in" with one of the most prolific architects of such palaces. John Adolph Emil Eberson began designing opera houses as a young architect in Ohio. In that capacity, he designed Tulsa's Grand Opera House, the city's first major entertainment venue. It opened in 1906—coincidentally, the same year the first images flickered across a Tulsa screen.

As movies began to catch on with the public, Eberson turned his attention to theater design and moved to Chicago. He was tapped to create Tulsa's 1,200-seat Empress Theatre at 15 West Third Street, which opened in 1913. That theater later became the first Orpheum Theatre, and soon after, the Rialto. By the 1920s, Eberson was based in New York and considered one of the top theater architects in the nation. His designs were in New York, Chicago, Kansas City, Dallas, and many other cities. He was hired to design the Orpheum Theatre in Tulsa, described as Renaissance Revival in style. With 1,400 seats in an ornate auditorium and statuary looking down from the walls, it opened in 1924.

During that time, Eberson had been working on a new type of movie palace that he called "Atmospheric." Once he perfected the concept in Houston's Majestic Theatre, he brought it to Tulsa at the Ritz, which opened in 1926. The Ritz was considered the pinnacle of Tulsa's movie palaces. With elegant Italian Renaissance decor, its "ritziest" feature was the auditorium's deep-blue ceiling with pinpoint lights that simulated stars. A special machine called a Brenograph projected clouds on the ceiling to create the effect of being outdoors under a brilliant nighttime sky.

As Tulsa expanded in every direction from downtown, Art Deco became a frequent choice in theater design. Zigzag, Streamline, and Deco Moderne styles were popular for neighborhood theaters built from the 1920s through the 1940s. Noted architects designed many of those as well.

The Delman and Tower theaters featured Streamline designs by W. Scott Dunne, a Texas-based architect known for his theaters throughout the Southwest. One of his creations became instantly famous on November 22, 1963, when Lee Harvey Oswald was captured in the Texas Theatre in Dallas. Oklahoma-born Jack Corgan and his prestigious Dallas-based firm Corgan & Moore gave Tulsans the Will Rogers, with its marquee-wrapped tower, as well as the Streamline Deco designs of the Pines and Tulsa theaters. William Henry Cameron Calderwood designed the striking Deco Moderne–style Brook Theatre as well as other local businesses and residences. Noted Tulsa architect Joseph R. Koberling was responsible for the 1935 Zigzag Deco remodel of the State Theatre at 118 South Main Street, one of the city's original theater locations.

This is where the story of Tulsa movie theaters takes a turn. All of the historic theaters mentioned so far are now gone. Many, including the downtown movie palaces, were lost to urban renewal efforts in the 1960s and 1970s. The program was designed to acquire distressed or unwanted properties in order to encourage new development.

During the construction of one single project—the building of Williams Center Tower, now known as the BOK Tower—nine square blocks were razed; this area included several theaters. Those blocks contained the city's early business district and oldest buildings. Some had housed Tulsa's original storefront theaters.

Other theaters were demolished when their buildings were no longer safe or when the space they occupied was deemed ideal for parking. Historic theaters that became parking lots include the Alhambra/Plaza, Will Rogers, and the Majestic theaters.

The destruction of these and other landmarks, including the Hotel Tulsa and Akdar Shrine Temple, led local citizens to get organized in the name of historic preservation in the 1970s. The absence of these structures is a true loss for Tulsa. However, through projects such as this book, they can be learned about, celebrated, and remembered for the hours upon hours of entertainment that was enjoyed within their walls.

While this book showcases the many changes in theater architecture and decor through the years, there have also been major alterations in the way movies are presented inside the theater. Some of these changes fall into the category of preshow entertainment. There was a time when moviegoers would see a cartoon, newsreel, or other "shorts" before the feature presentation.

There was a preshow that was unique to Tulsa's Ritz Theater from the 1930s into the 1950s. Many who attended movies at the Ritz recall Wade Hamilton or Milton Schlosser at the organ. Hidden from sight, Schlosser would begin playing as he and the organ rose up from the orchestra pit illuminated by a spotlight. Bathed in different colored lights depending on each song's mood, Schlosser led audience sing-alongs in which patrons followed a bouncing ball that accompanied the lyrics on the screen. The Ritz's unique preshow entertainment utilized the same machine that projected clouds onto the ceiling, the Brenograph, to display lyrics for the sing-alongs.

Another lost art of movie-house presentation is the use of the curtains. Once upon a time, beautiful draperies adorned theater screens. Often red or gold, with some cascading like a waterfall, the curtains opened for the preshow entertainment and closed as it concluded, only to immediately open again for the feature presentation. Former projectionists have also mentioned the art of synchronizing the final closing of the curtains to the last images appearing on the screen. Baby boomers who watched movies at Tulsa's first multiplex, the Boman Twin, may recall the plush curtains there, which were identical (except for their color) in Boman's East and West auditoriums.

From a technical standpoint, the biggest change in movie presentation is completely behind the scenes. The automation of the projection process has eliminated physical reels, projectors, and personnel. In the new millennium, movies are delivered digitally.

The time of uniformed ushers, film projectionists, and preshow fun feels far removed from today's endless automated previews digitally projected onto a plain white screen. Amid all the alterations, however, there is still one aspect of going to the movies that has not changed: the excitement and anticipation of seeing a film in a theater. In those moments, as the lights come down and the first images appear on the screen, audience members fidget in their seats, settling in. They are ready for the movies to take them away!

There are a number of movie industry terms that appear in this book. Here are some definitions that may prove helpful:

Art house: There are theaters that show films that are artistic or experimental in nature. These films are generally independently made and aimed at a niche audience.

B movie: This term refers to a cheaply made film. In the mid-20th century, movie studios made low-budget B movies to accompany major film releases on a double feature. Some have compared this to the A and B sides of a 45-rpm vinyl record.

First-run theater: This describes a movie house that shows films during their initial release. Tulsa's "Big Four" theaters—the Majestic, Rialto, Ritz, and Orpheum—were all first-run theaters.

Nickelodeon: Early movie theaters were called nickelodeons due to their admission charge of 5¢.

Reel: In early movie advertising, the length was often described by the number of reels of film. One silent film reel was 10 to 15 minutes long, so a two-reeler was 20 to 30 minutes in duration.

Reverse layout: This refers to a theater design in which the lobby is on the same end as the screen. In a theater with a reverse layout, ticket-holders typically enter the auditorium on one or both sides of the screen.

Roadshow release: This is a term for a film that opened in a limited number of theaters for a specified time. Roadshow films were promoted like major events. Characteristics included reserved seats, limited showings per day, opening and closing overtures, and an intermission. They often had a printed program. Popular roadshow engagements in Tulsa included *The Sound of Music* at the Brook Theatre and *2001: A Space Odyssey* at the Continental.

Second-run theater: These theaters show films after their initial run. Typically, after a film debuted at first-run theaters, it moved on to second-run and small-town theaters. A subset of the second-run theater is the dollar theater, where second-run films are shown at a discounted price.

Serial: A serial is a multipart series shown in theaters in short episodes, usually weekly. Film serials were popular in the first half of the 20th century.

Silent film: This refers to a movie with no recorded sound. All films were silent before the late 1920s. Title cards in the film conveyed dialogue and plot points, while live accompaniment, usually featuring piano or organ, set the mood for each scene.

Todd-AO: This is a film process developed in the early 1950s that produced larger (70 mm instead of 35 mm) film prints with improved picture clarity and dynamic six-track sound. Todd-AO is closely associated with roadshow releases, as many films produced in this large format from the late 1950s to the early 1970s received roadshow exhibitions. The first two films released in Todd-AO were *Oklahoma!* and *Around the World in 80 Days*. Both played at the Rialto in roadshow engagements.

One

Silent Era

The Early Picture Shows

The silent-film era began with tiny storefront theaters displaying simple posters out front. Tulsa's first movie house, the Dreamland, began showing films in June 1906 near First and Main Streets in a space previously occupied by a cigar parlor. With the opening of the Idlehour in 1907 and Lyric in 1908, movies were off and running in the rapidly growing oil town of Tulsa.

Storefront theaters with small, unadorned interiors were dubbed "nickelodeons" by the public due to their admission price of 5¢. Many of these theaters had screens and stages as well as an organ or piano that could be used for both silent films and live shows. In silent movies, a live musician provided the soundtrack, setting the mood for each scene on the screen. Title cards within the film itself helped advance the story.

Early films were very much a novelty. By 1910, different genres emerged, including melodrama, comedy, and Westerns. Refinement of the moviemaking process allowed for more elaborate stories and produced the first silent-era movie stars, including Charlie Chaplin and Mary Pickford.

The heyday of silent film was the 20-year period between 1910 and 1930, which coincided with Tulsa's transformation from a small boomtown to the "Oil Capital of the World."

Tulsa's theaters, all clustered within a few downtown blocks, frequently changed names and locations. For example, 117 South Main Street was home to the Empire in 1910, the Yale in 1912, and the Strand in 1915. In 1911, the Lyric, Idlehour, Wonderland, and Empire were all on the same block in the heart of downtown, while the Majestic and Rialto each changed locations three times before landing in their final homes. Very few of these early theaters lasted beyond the silent era.

The Roaring Twenties brought a building boom to downtown, which led to the creation of elaborate movie palaces designed by top architects. The two most magnificent examples of this in Tulsa—the Orpheum and the Ritz—opened in 1924 and 1926, respectively.

When *The Jazz Singer*, the first talking picture, debuted in 1927, the days of silent films were numbered. By 1930, Tulsa's theaters were remodeling to accommodate movies with sound, which had quickly become the new standard.

The popularity of going to the movies brought significant changes to theaters, and the era that began in small, unadorned spaces ended in the spacious comfort of Roman and Italian palaces.

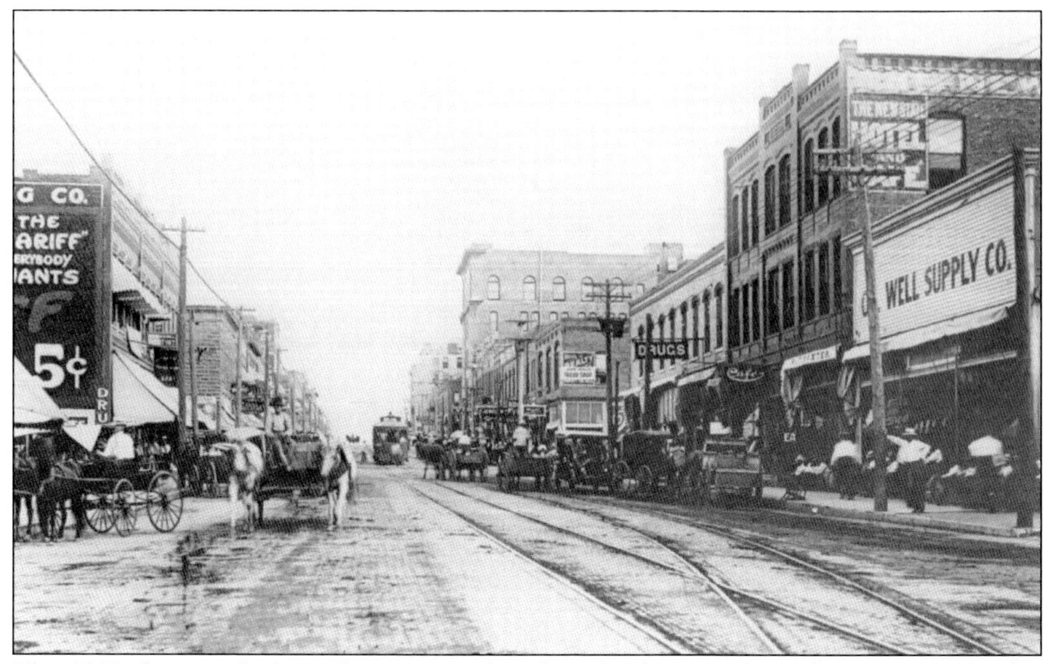

This 1909 photograph shows downtown Tulsa when the first storefront theaters opened. This view looks south along the bricked Main Street from the St. Louis–San Francisco Railway tracks toward First Street. Tulsa's first three theaters were all near this intersection. Visible at far left (next to the man on a horse and buggy facing the camera) is the sign for the Lyric Theatre in the 100 block of South Main Street. The Dreamland was around the corner to the left on First Street, and Idlehour was across from the Lyric on Main Street. A trolley is visible in the distance.

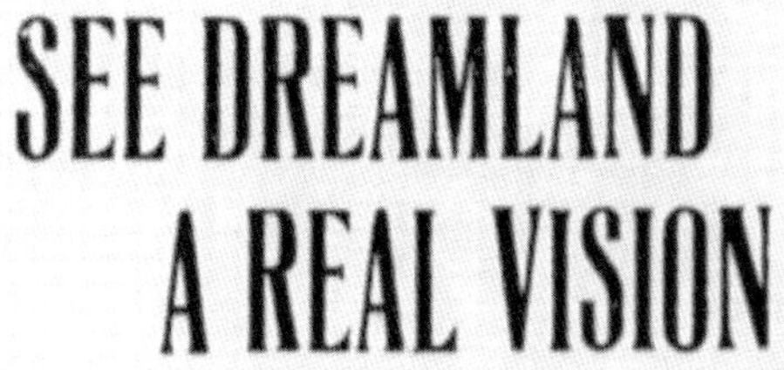

SEE DREAMLAND A REAL VISION

NOTHING LIKE IT EVER BEFORE IN TULSA.

ALL LADIES SHOULD GO

Entrancing, Delightful, Superb Films, Moving Pictures Which Don't Make the Eyes Ache.

In the young oil boomtown of Tulsa, Indian Territory, the arrival of a new form of entertainment—moving pictures—was announced in a small newspaper story on February 9, 1906. Oklahoma was still over a year away from statehood. Tulsa's business district encompassed just a few city blocks when the Dreamland, a small storefront theater, opened near First and Main Streets. There is no evidence of the Dreamland existing after 1906. It is also unrelated to the Williams Dreamland Theatre that was built a few years later on Greenwood Avenue. (Courtesy of *Tulsa World*.)

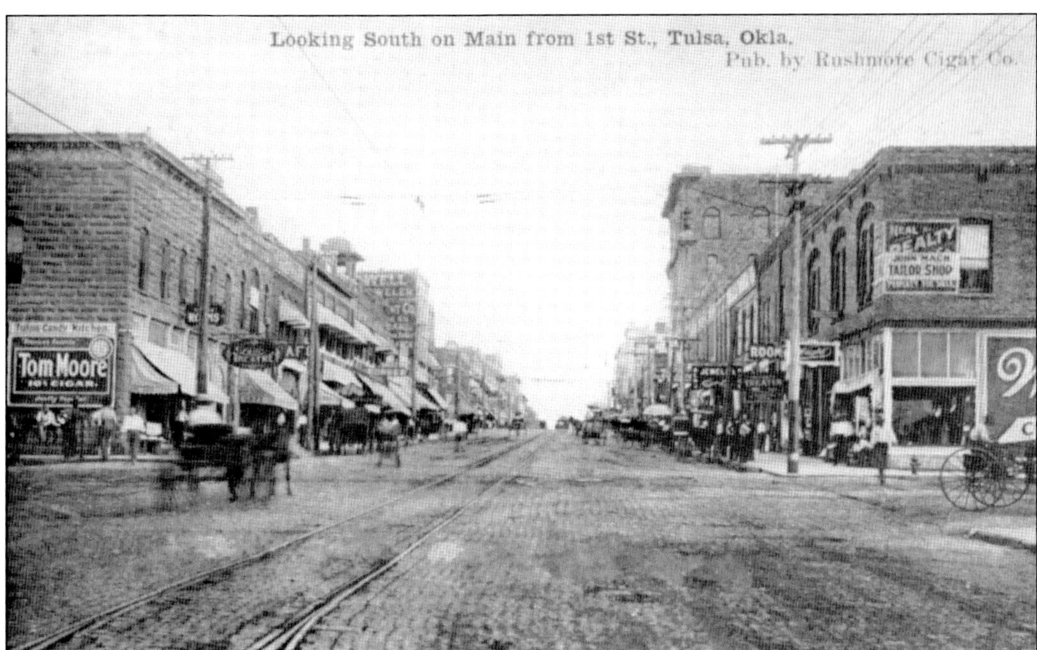

This postcard view looks south on Main Street in Tulsa's early theater district around 1910. The Lyric Theatre is visible at left, and the Idlehour is across the street with a sign that simply reads, "Theater." Horses and buggies, trolleys, and walking were the primary modes of transportation during this time.

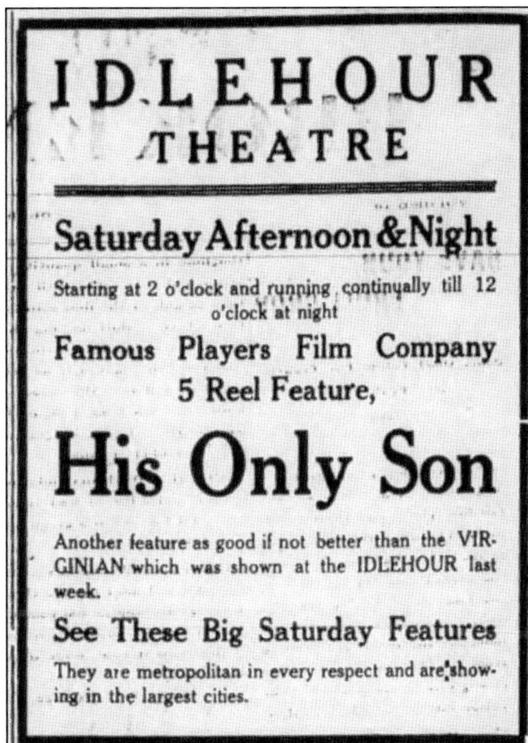
IDLEHOUR THEATRE

Saturday Afternoon & Night

Starting at 2 o'clock and running continually till 12 o'clock at night

Famous Players Film Company 5 Reel Feature,

His Only Son

Another feature as good if not better than the VIRGINIAN which was shown at the IDLEHOUR last week.

See These Big Saturday Features

They are metropolitan in every respect and are showing in the largest cities.

The Idlehour Theatre, located at 106 South Main Street, was across the street from the Lyric Theatre. This advertisement from 1915 notes a "5 Reel Feature," meaning a film with a duration of around an hour. (Courtesy of *Broken Arrow Ledger*.)

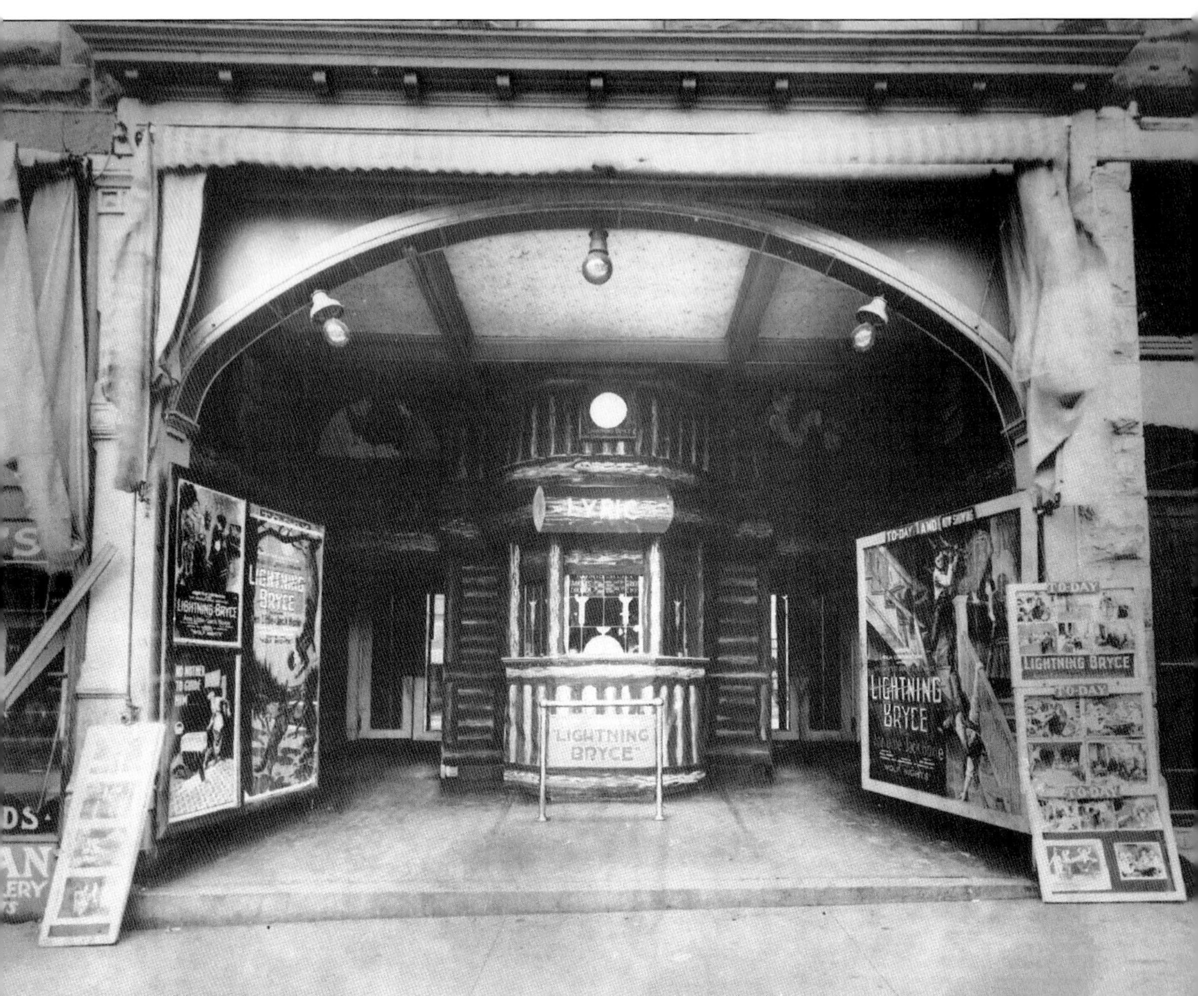

While many theaters came and went during the silent-film era, the Lyric Theatre lasted for over 40 years. Located at 103 South Main Street, the Lyric opened in February 1908 with films and live vaudeville shows. After starting with a seating capacity of 315, a 1923 remodel doubled the number of seats. This c. 1920 image features advertising for *Lightning Bryce*, a 15-chapter serial featuring Jack Hoxie and Ann Little that had audiences coming back week after week to see what would happen next in the silent adventure/romance involving found Native American treasure.

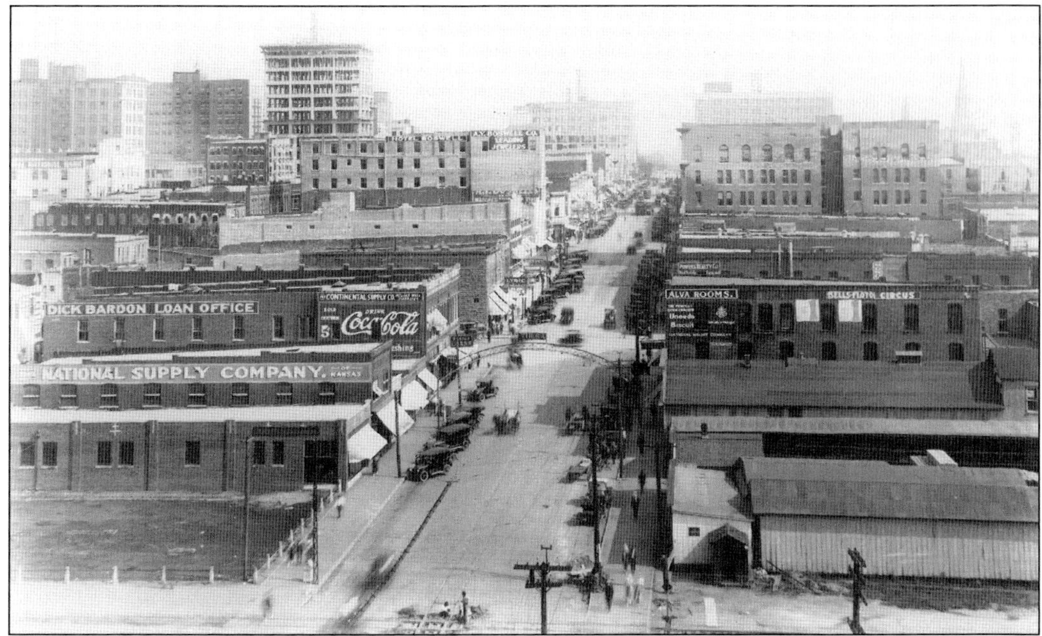

This photograph shows an aerial view of Tulsa's Main Street looking south from the railway yard near Archer Street in 1916. An arched metal sign that spans the street says "Tulsa" on the top. Just above that arch, the Lyric Theatre's sign is visible on the east side of the 100 block of South Main Street.

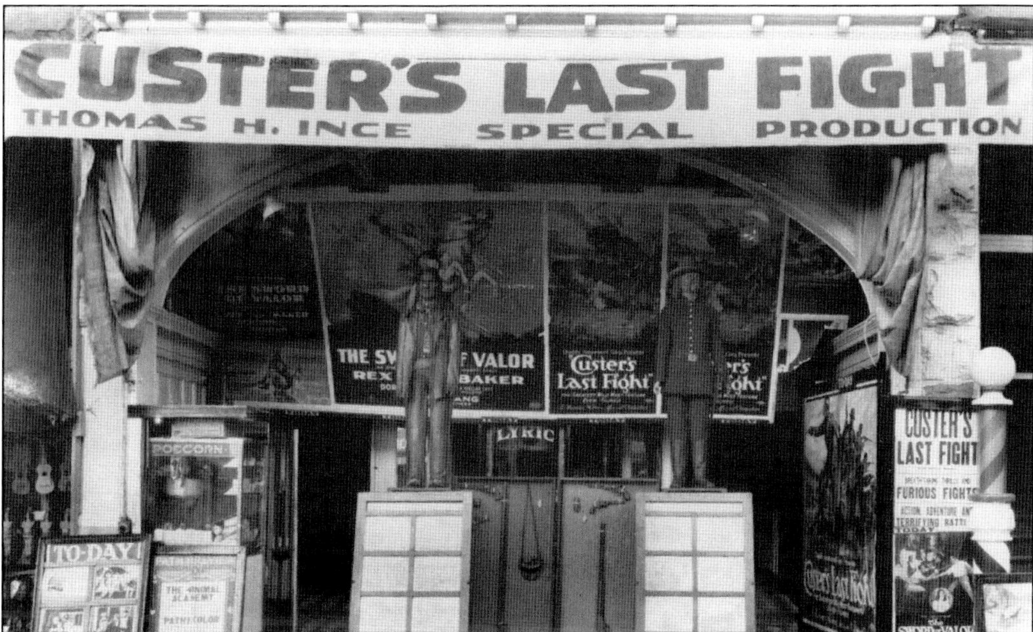

This early picture of the Lyric Theatre shows the front of the building with a banner for the 1912 film *Custer's Last Fight*, starring Francis Ford as Custer. Statues of a Native American and a cavalry soldier stand on either side of a box office display of old weapons. Thomas Harper Ince was a pioneer American director who was the first to organize production methods into a disciplined system of filmmaking. He is also considered to be the "Father of the Western."

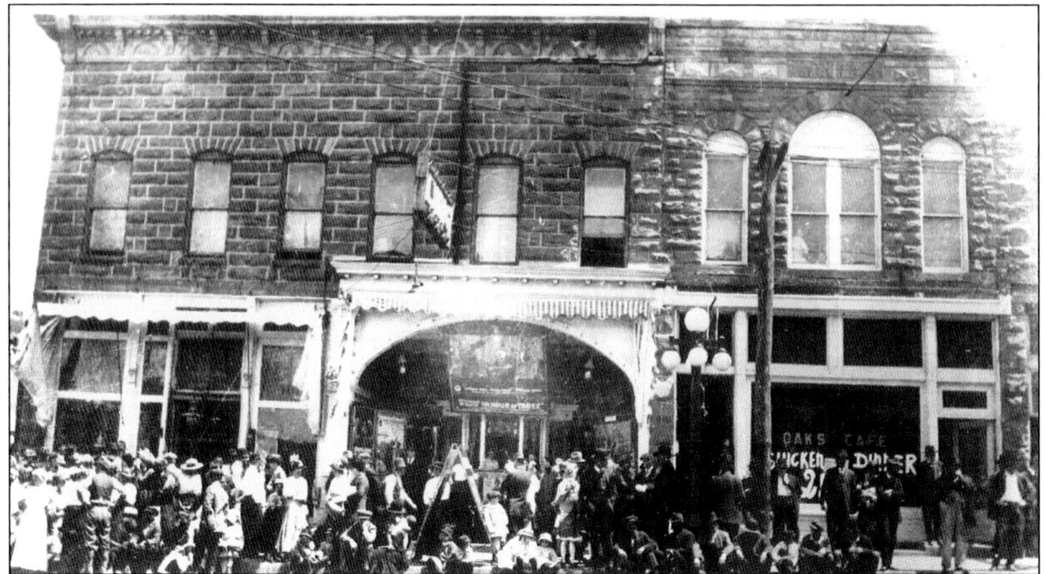

This 1915 photograph shows a sizeable crowd in front of the Lyric Theatre. A poster displayed above the box office advertises *The Hour of Three*, the latest installment in the Pathé Pictures serial *Exploits of Elaine*. The actress who played Pauline in the damsel-in-distress genre of the *Perils of Pauline*, Pearl White, also played Elaine. The series is notable for introducing the first mystery villain in a film serial, the Clutching Hand. The serial was added to the US National Film Registry in 1994 for its cultural and historic importance. The advertisement below, for the film *Abraham Lincoln's Clemency*, features the Lyric's slogan: "The Home of Pictorial Vaudeville." (Below, courtesy of *Tulsa World*.)

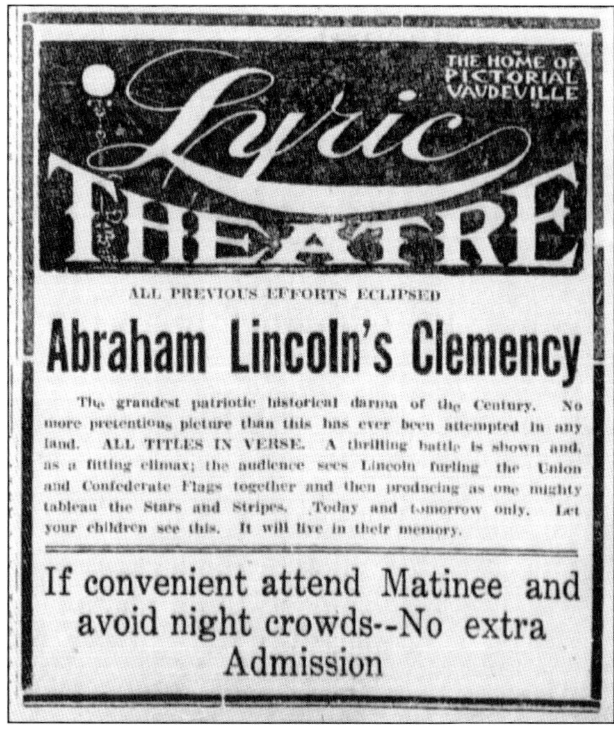

This photograph shows the Lyric Theatre in 1942. In operation for more than 30 years by this time, the Lyric had a new sign and a fresh paint job on its stone building near First and Main Streets. Bicycles were a popular way for kids—and some adults—to get to the theater during this era. (Courtesy of Oklahoma Historical Society.)

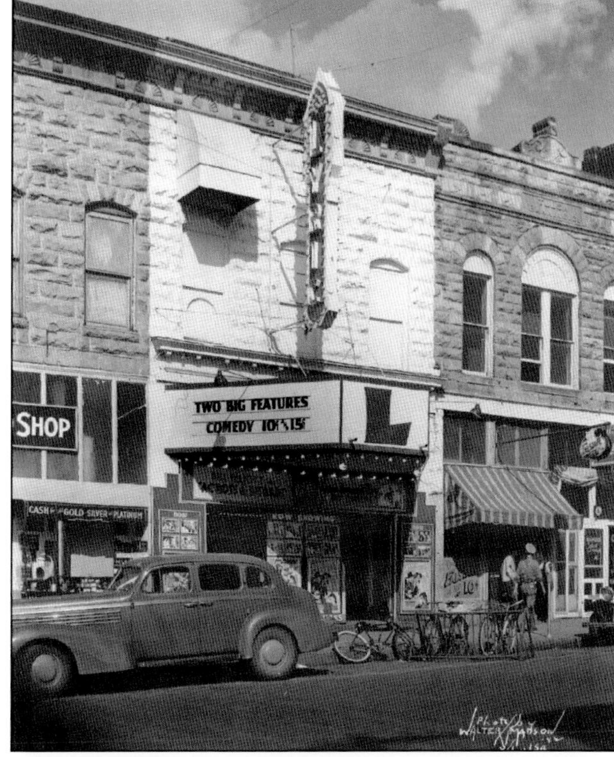

Here is a 1942 picture of the Lyric Theatre's auditorium looking toward the balcony and projection window. With the three sections of wooden seats on the floor and the balcony seating, the Lyric could accommodate 600 people. (Courtesy of Oklahoma Historical Society.)

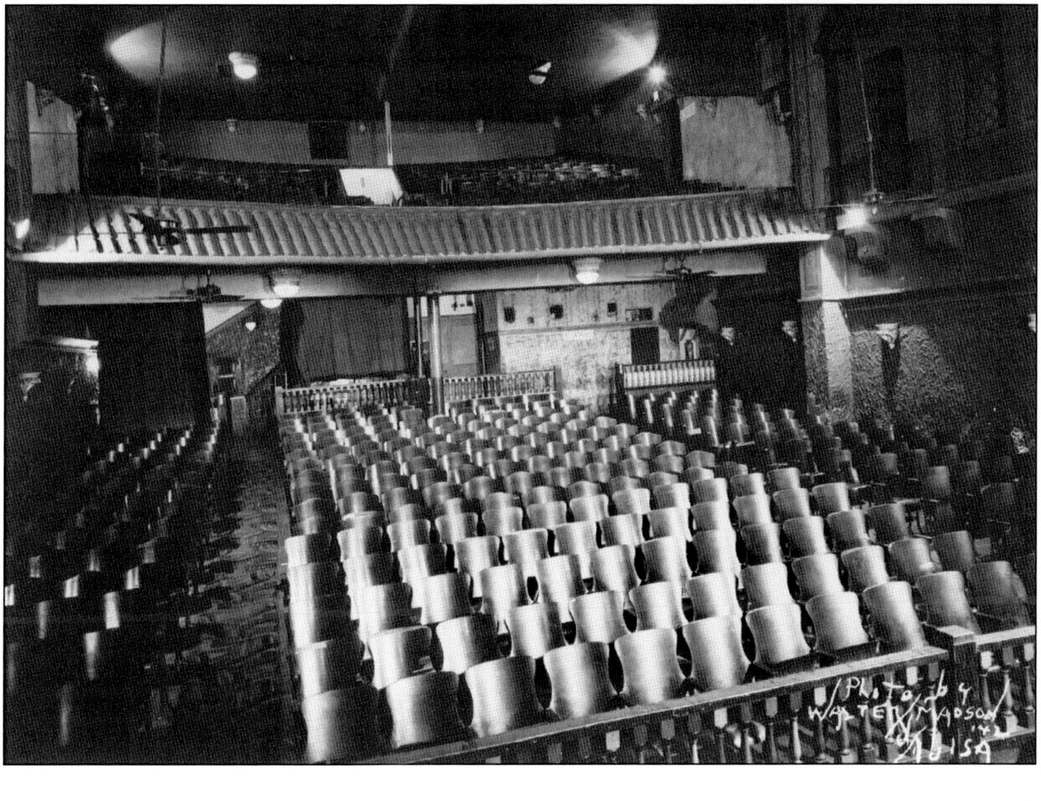

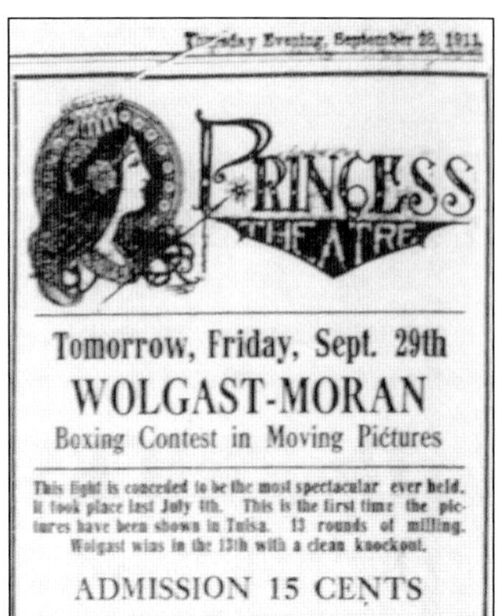

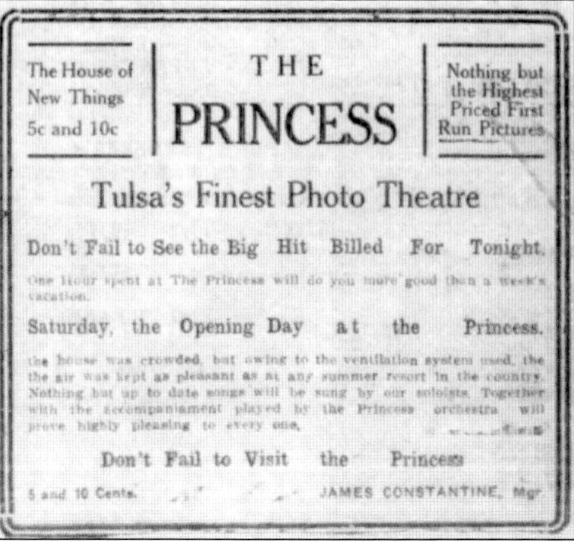

These images offer a nice snapshot of the movies in Tulsa in 1911. Above, a pair of advertisements for the Princess Theatre in the *Tulsa Democrat* promote a boxing match and the theater's opening day (August 27). Note that the advertisement on the left gives away how the fight ends! Below is a pair of 1911 *Tulsa World* advertisements for the Garden Theatre's bill of vaudeville and moving pictures. The Garden, at 402 South Main Street, predated the Majestic at that location. Although there are no known images of the Garden Theatre, there are numerous advertisements for it. (Above, courtesy of *Tulsa Democrat*; below, courtesy of *Tulsa World*.)

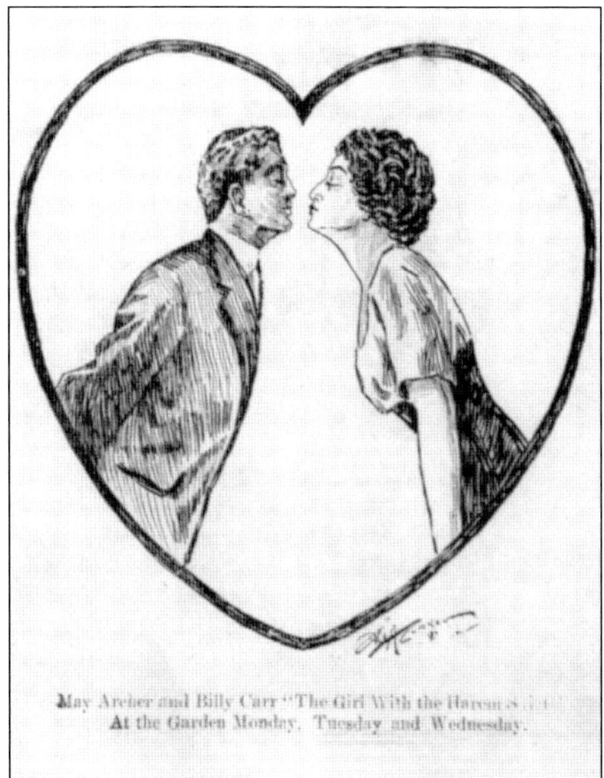

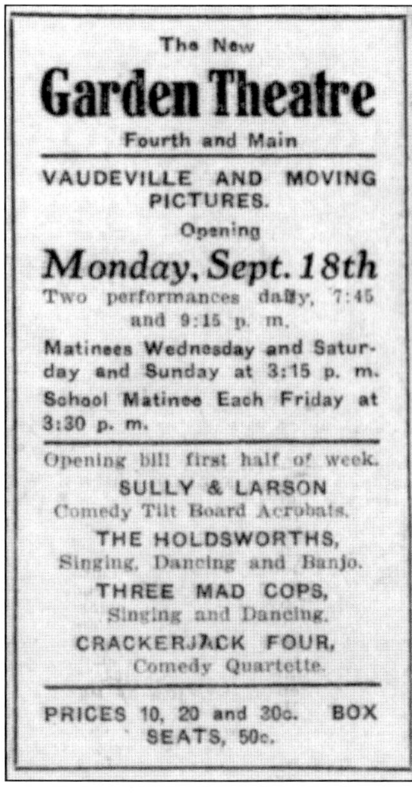

This photograph shows one of Tulsa's earliest storefront theaters, the Palace Theater, at 219 South Main Street as it appeared in 1919. The Palace opened in 1910 with live vaudeville shows, and the 1915 Civil War film *Birth of a Nation* played here. This version of the Palace closed in 1924. The Wonderland, located one block north, became the Palace in 1929. Below, an advertisement from the December 26, 1911, *Tulsa Democrat* advertises films, including the holiday feature *The Kiddies' Xmas*, from three different studios. The number of reels of the feature is mentioned in the advertisement. (Below, courtesy of *Tulsa Democrat*.)

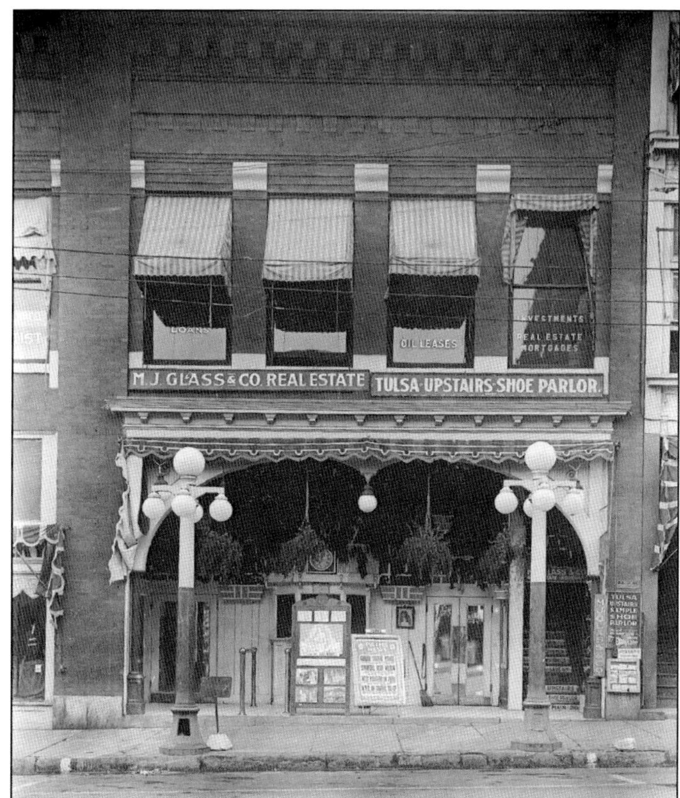

Palace Theater—Today

First Run Lubin in Two Reels

"THE KIDDIES' XMAS"

Shown again today by request, in addition to regular program

First run Kalem, "DAN, THE LIGHT HOUSE KEEPER," an interesting story of life on the seacoast.

First run Edison, "HOW SIR ANDREW LOST HIS VOTE." A unique and very clever comedy.

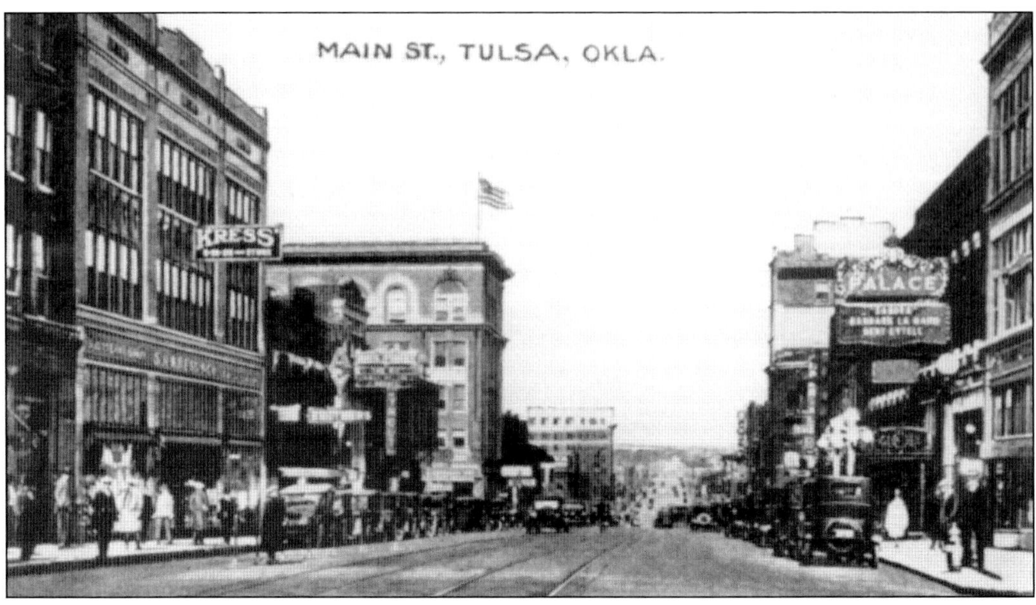

In this northward-facing view of Main Street from 1924, one can see how Tulsa's downtown buildings continued to get bigger and taller as the city developed. The Palace Theater is on the right. A sign for Kress, a five-and-dime store, is visible at left.

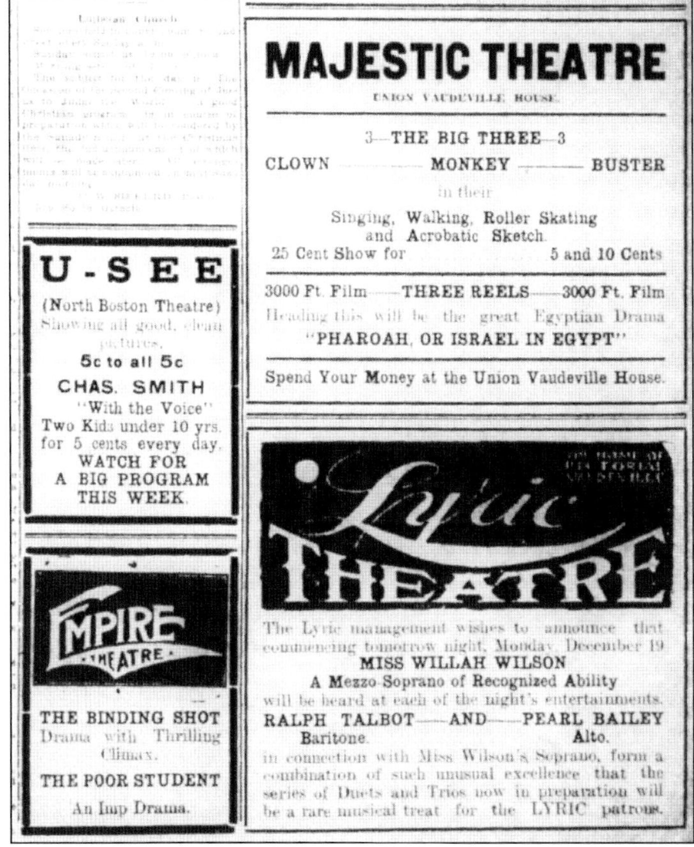

MAJESTIC THEATRE

UNION VAUDEVILLE HOUSE

3—THE BIG THREE—3

CLOWN ——— MONKEY ——— BUSTER

in their

Singing, Walking, Roller Skating and Acrobatic Sketch.

25 Cent Show for ——— 5 and 10 Cents

3000 Ft. Film—THREE REELS—3000 Ft. Film

Heading this will be the great Egyptian Drama

"PHAROAH, OR ISRAEL IN EGYPT"

Spend Your Money at the Union Vaudeville House.

U-SEE

(North Boston Theatre)

Showing all good, clean pictures.

5c to all 5c

CHAS. SMITH

"With the Voice"

Two Kids under 10 yrs. for 5 cents every day.

WATCH FOR A BIG PROGRAM THIS WEEK.

Lyric THEATRE

The Lyric management wishes to announce that commencing tomorrow night, Monday, December 19

MISS WILLAH WILSON

A Mezzo-Soprano of Recognized Ability

will be heard at each of the night's entertainments.

RALPH TALBOT—AND—PEARL BAILEY

Baritone. Alto.

in connection with Miss Wilson's Soprano, form a combination of such unusual excellence that the series of Duets and Trios now in preparation will be a rare musical treat for the LYRIC patrons.

EMPIRE THEATRE

THE BINDING SHOT

Drama with Thrilling Climax.

THE POOR STUDENT

An Imp Drama.

These advertisements in the December 18, 1910, *Tulsa World* provide a window into early theater in Tulsa. They list a variety of vaudeville acts and films playing at the U-See, Empire, Majestic, and Lyric theaters. The Lyric Theatre's advertisement lists "Ralph Talbot baritone" as a performer; Talbot would eventually own Tulsa's "Big Four" theaters—the Majestic, Rialto, Ritz, and Orpheum. (Courtesy of *Tulsa World*.)

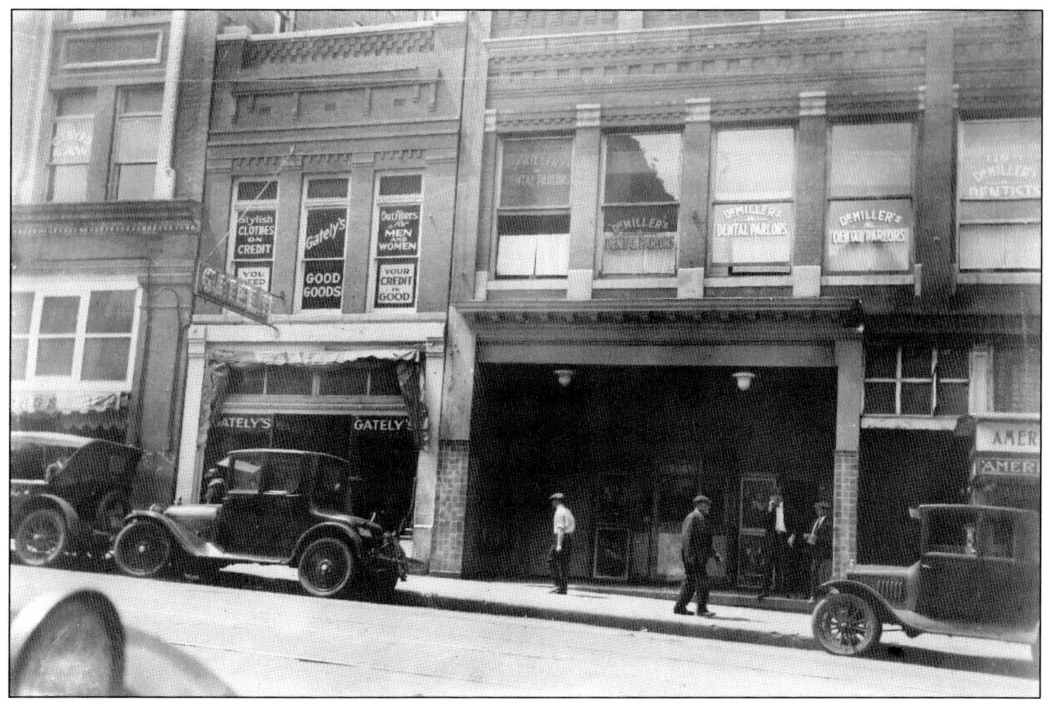

Wonderland, located at 118 South Main Street, was built by Dr. C.W. McCarty in 1911 as a nickelodeon. This 1923 photograph shows several automobiles from the era. During its 40-year history, the theater operated under three different names. Renamed the Palace in 1929, the theater underwent an Art Deco remodel in 1935 before becoming the State Theatre. It closed in 1955. This block, the location of some of Tulsa's oldest buildings, was razed for an urban renewal project to build the Williams Center Tower in the 1970s.

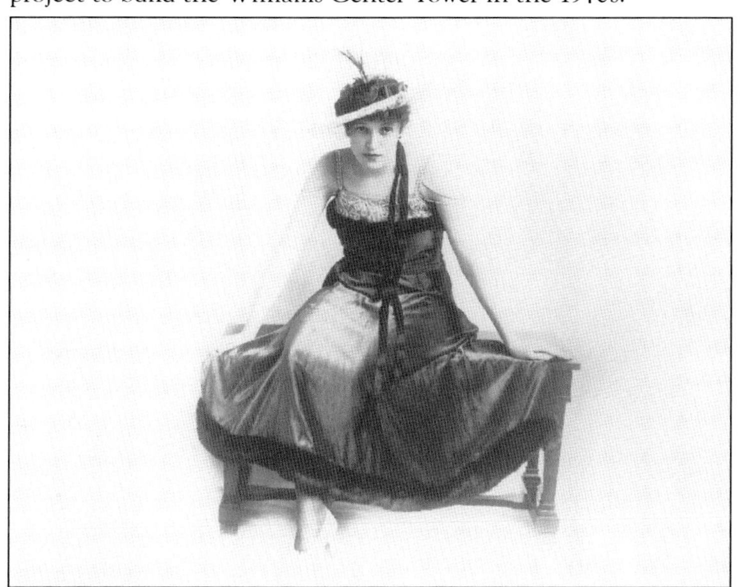

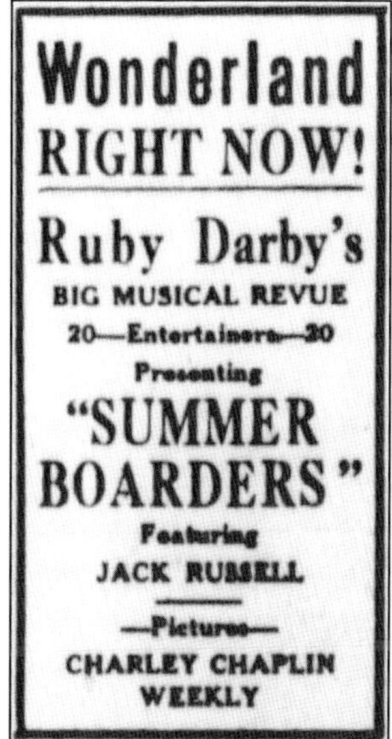

Along with its films, the Wonderland hosted some of Tulsa's first vaudeville shows. Performer Ruby Darby is pictured along with an advertisement for her musical revue, *Summer Boarders*. The weekly "Charley" [*sic*] Chaplin pictures are also mentioned. (Above right, courtesy of *Tulsa World*.)

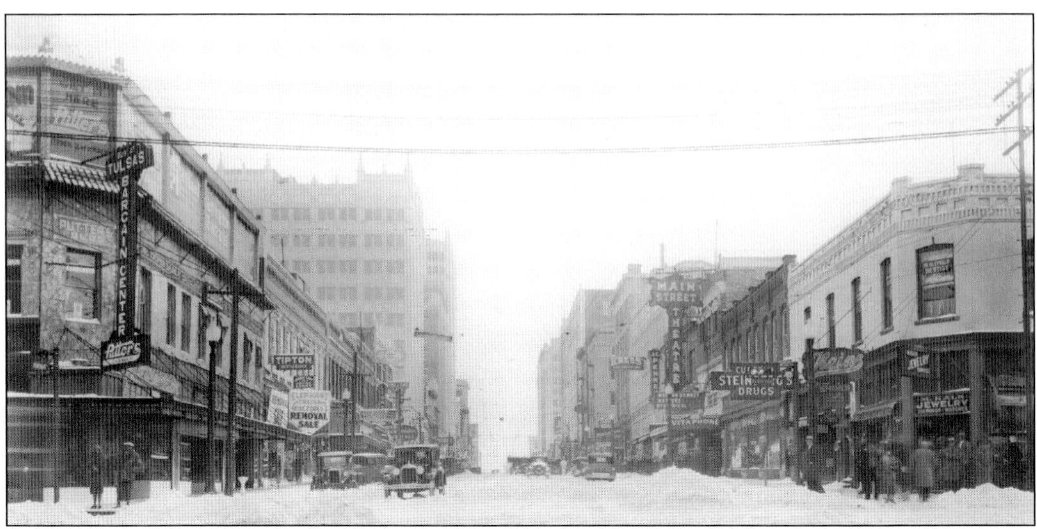

The January 1930 photograph above looks south from Second and Main Streets and was taken after a 14-inch snowfall. The Main Street Theatre, located at 210 South Main Street, opened in 1923 and is visible at right. Other businesses in that block included Hein's Shoes, M. Kalk Jewelry, and J.C. Penney. Tulsa's Bargain Center is across the street on the corner. Below, Main Street Theatre is shown around 1934 after a remodel. Posters and photographs displayed out front promote *Blonde Bombshell* starring Jean Harlow. There are also posters for the shorts that accompanied the film, including *Dora's Dunking Doughnuts*, a 1933 short featuring Shirley Temple. (Below, courtesy of Oklahoma Historical Society.)

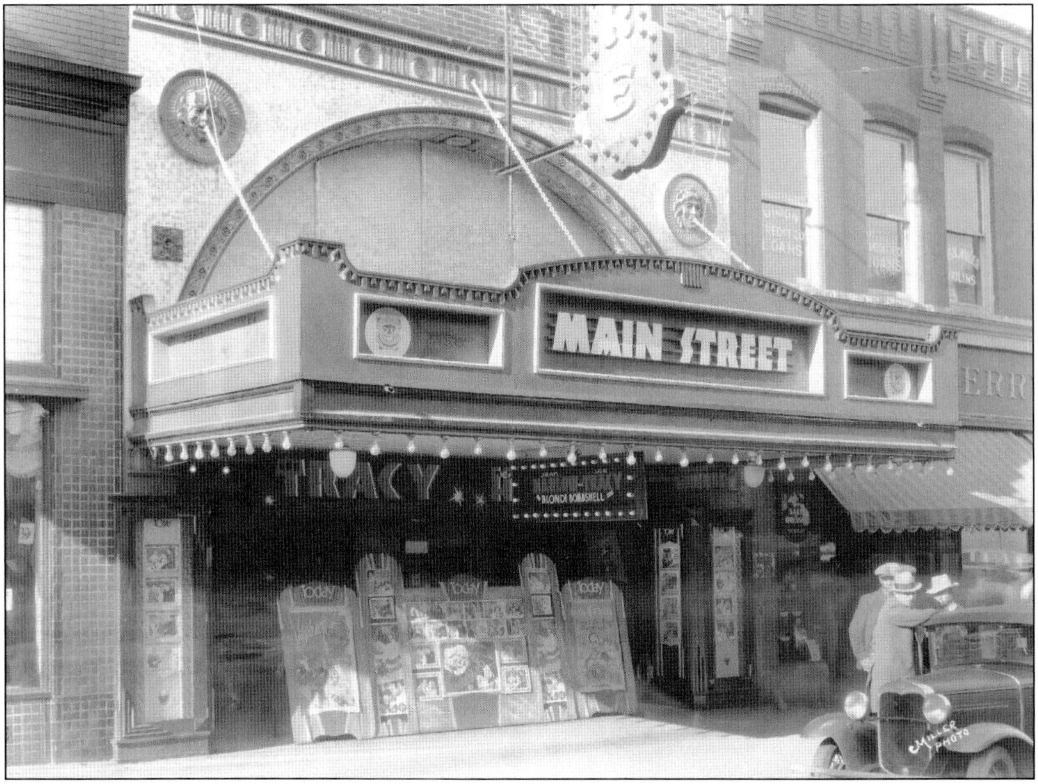

The Strand Theatre, located at 117 South Main Street, was playing *Mad Love*, starring actress Pola Negri, when this photograph was taken in 1923. Tulsa's first female theater owner-manager, Hazel McCoy, operated the Strand from 1915 to 1947. This block was home to some of Tulsa's earliest buildings and was razed to make way for the Williams Center Tower project in the early 1970s.

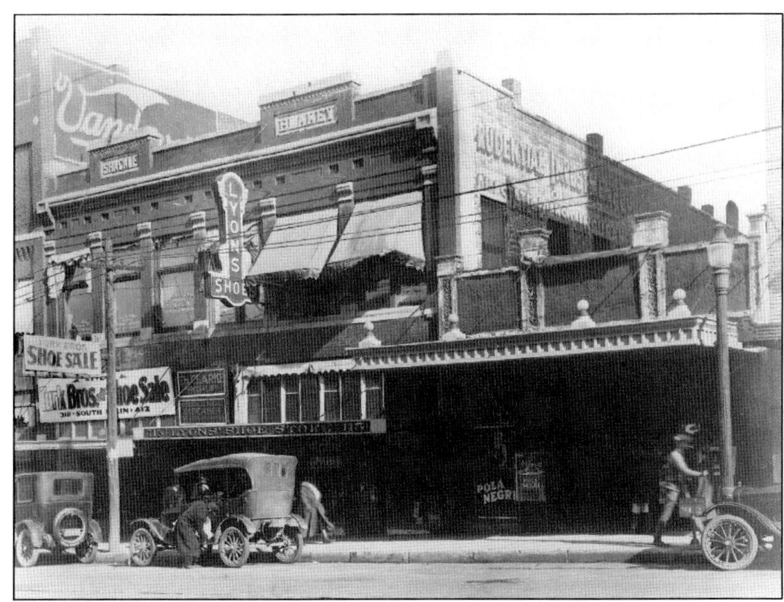

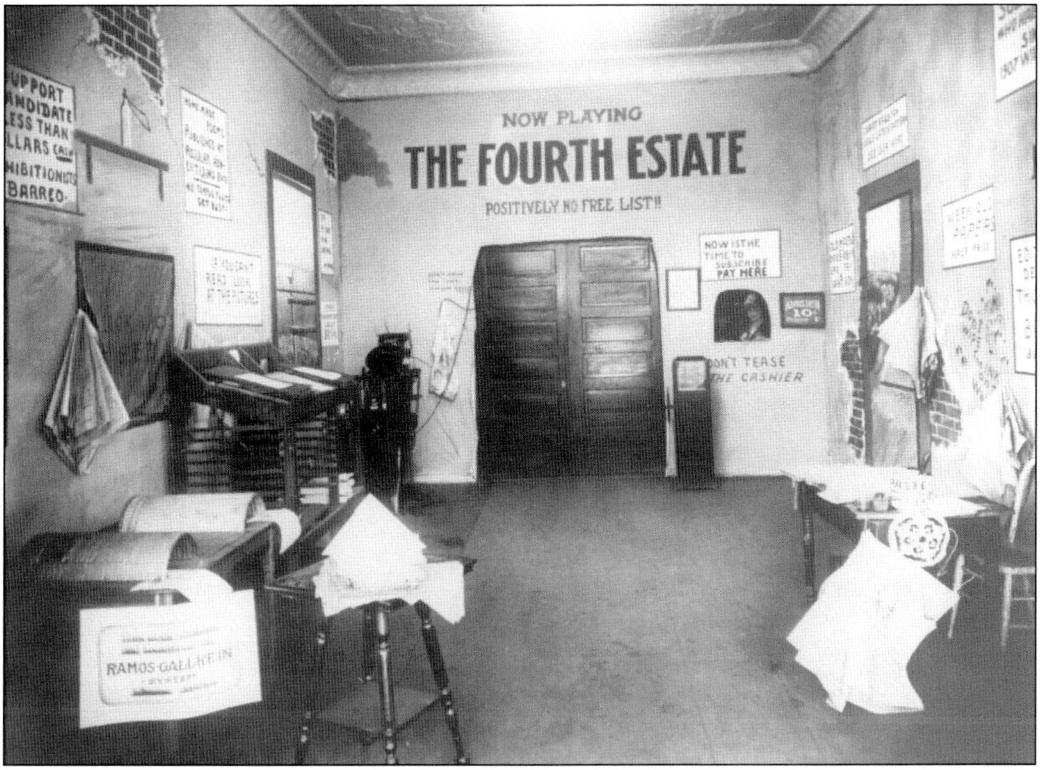

The Liberty Theater, located at 402 South Main Street, took over a space that was previously the Majestic when that theater built a new structure next door. In this 1919 image, the lobby is decorated like a newspaper office for the film *The Fourth Estate*. The room is covered with interesting tongue-in-cheek newspaper signage, including "don't tease the cashier."

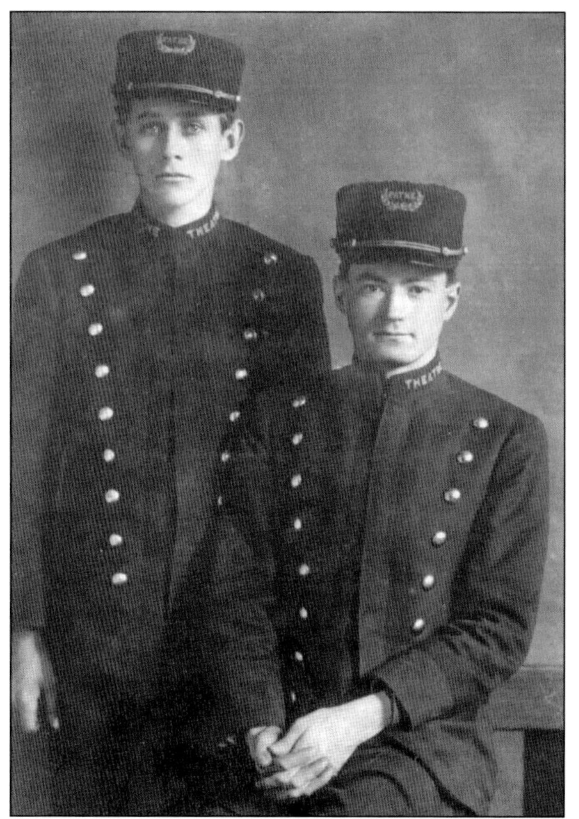

The usher was a big part of the moviegoing experience, especially in early theaters with tight seating. These uniformed employees were responsible for crowd control. Ushers patrolled the theater with flashlights during the movie, making sure everyone adhered to the house rules, such as keeping feet off the seats and not disturbing other patrons. This c. 1910 portrait shows two unidentified ushers from the Pathé Theater in their military-style uniforms.

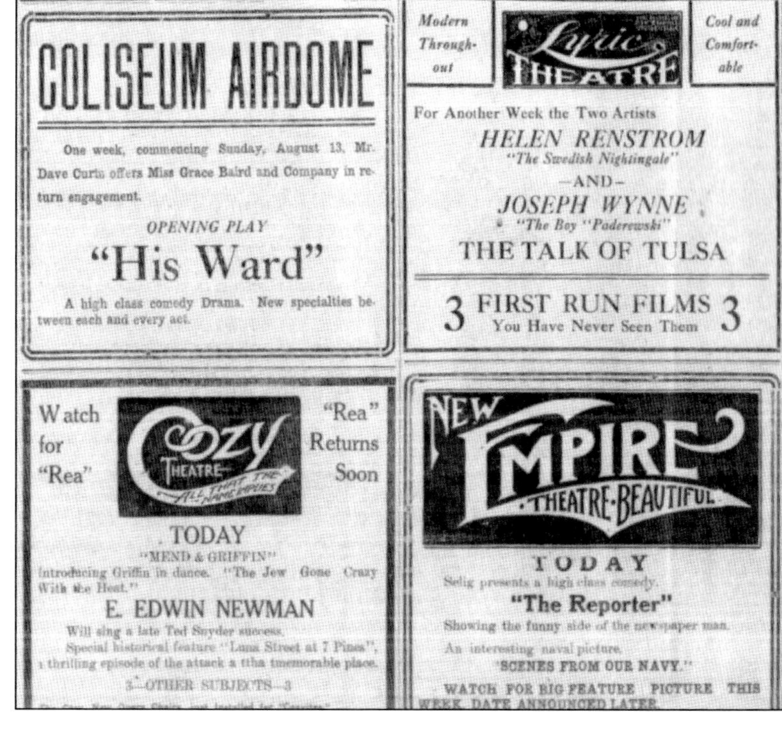

COLISEUM AIRDOME

One week, commencing Sunday, August 13, Mr. Dave Curtis offers Miss Grace Baird and Company in return engagement.

OPENING PLAY

"His Ward"

A high class comedy Drama. New specialties between each and every act.

Modern Throughout

Lyric Theatre

Cool and Comfortable

For Another Week the Two Artists

HELEN RENSTROM

"The Swedish Nightingale"

—AND—

JOSEPH WYNNE

"The Boy "Paderewski"

THE TALK OF TULSA

3 FIRST RUN FILMS 3

You Have Never Seen Them

Watch for "Rea"

Cozy Theatre

"Rea" Returns Soon

TODAY

"MEND & GRIFFIN"

Introducing Griffin in dance. "The Jew Gone Crazy With the Heat."

E. EDWIN NEWMAN

Will sing a late Ted Snyder success.

Special historical feature "Luna Street at 7 Pines", a thrilling episode of the attack a ttha memorable place.

3—OTHER SUBJECTS—3

NEW EMPIRE

THEATRE-BEAUTIFUL

TODAY

Selig presents a high class comedy.

"The Reporter"

Showing the funny side of the newspaper man.

An interesting naval picture.

"SCENES FROM OUR NAVY."

WATCH FOR BIG FEATURE PICTURE THIS WEEK. DATE ANNOUNCED LATER.

This cluster of advertisements from the August 13, 1911, *Tulsa Democrat* demonstrates how early theaters—and theater names—came and went. The Coliseum Airdome and New Empire Theatre-Beautiful were both short-lived. The Empire's space at 117 South Main Street became the Yale in 1912 and the Strand in 1915. (Courtesy of *Tulsa Democrat*.)

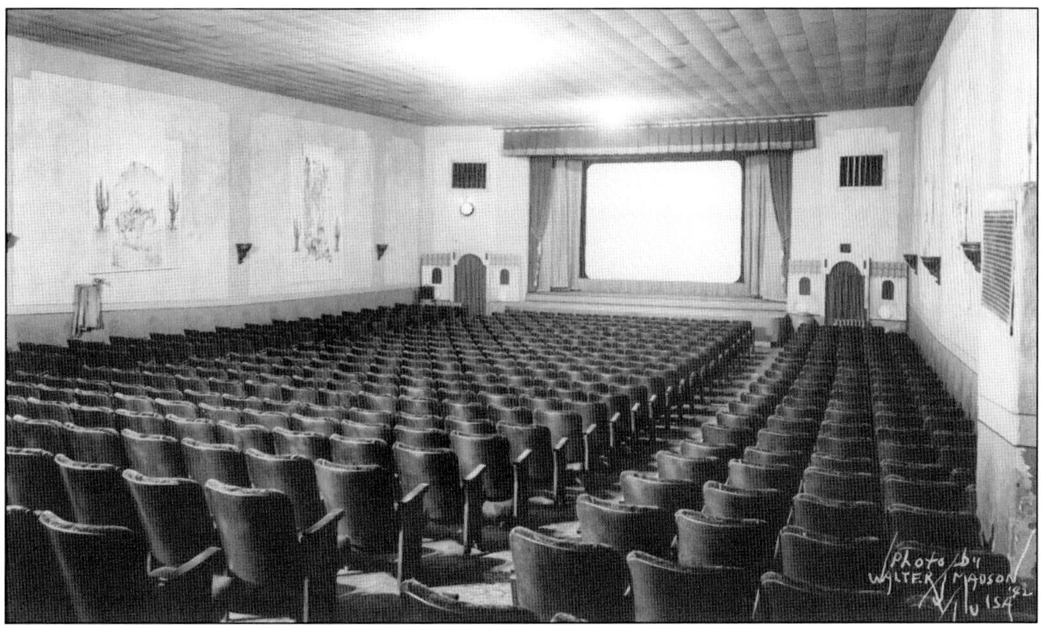

This 1942 view inside the Cozy Theatre, which was located on the viaduct at 8 North Main Street, shows a Southwestern motif with desert images, stucco, and terra-cotta tile. Moviegoers likely remember the steep slope of the seating area and the railroad tracks that ran below the building. (Courtesy of Oklahoma Historical Society.)

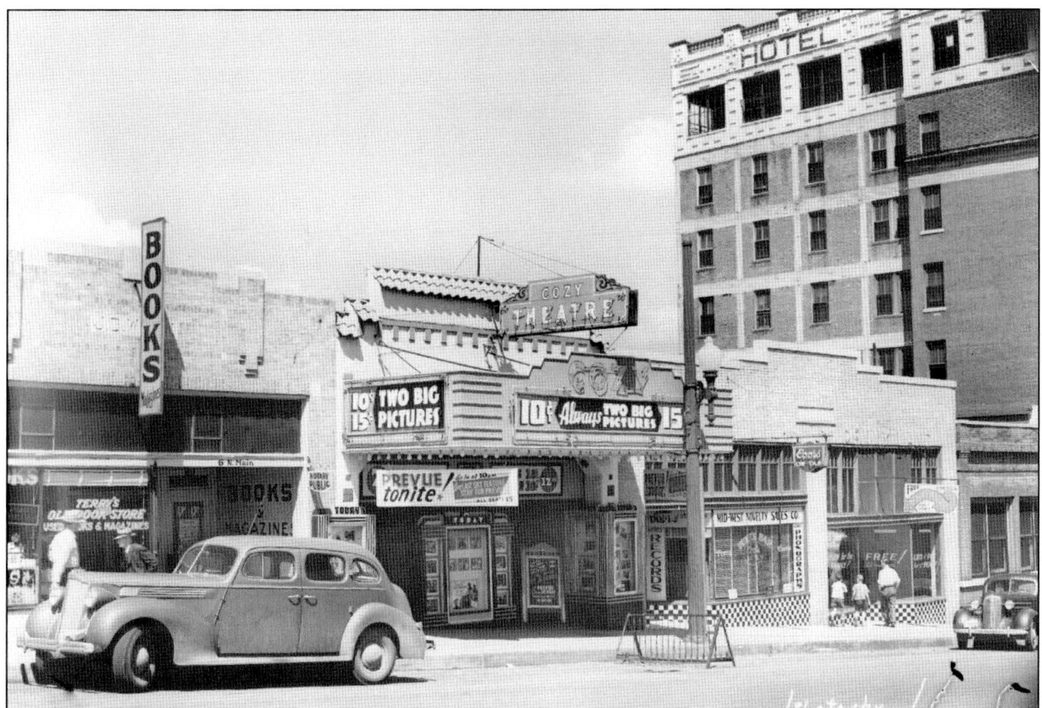

The Cozy Theatre and its next-door neighbor, Terry's Old Book Store, were both longtime fixtures on the viaduct on North Main Street. The Cozy, which operated until 1960, was known for showing B movies and double features. (Courtesy of Oklahoma Historical Society.)

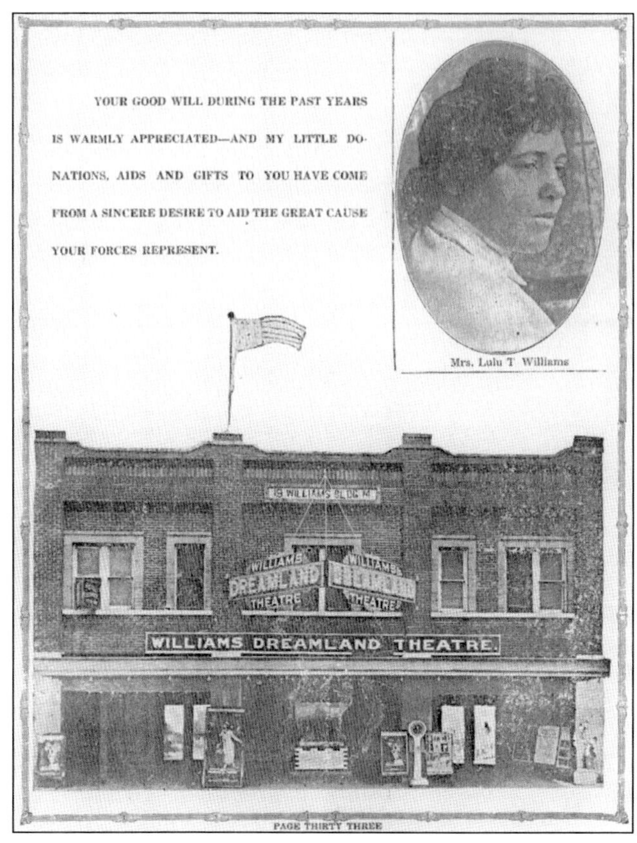

YOUR GOOD WILL DURING THE PAST YEARS IS WARMLY APPRECIATED—AND MY LITTLE DONATIONS, AIDS AND GIFTS TO YOU HAVE COME FROM A SINCERE DESIRE TO AID THE GREAT CAUSE YOUR FORCES REPRESENT.

Mrs. Lulu T. Williams

PAGE THIRTY THREE

Tulsa's Greenwood neighborhood, also known as Black Wall Street, was one of the most prosperous African American communities in the country during the early 20th century. The area was filled with successful businesses and highly educated residents. Greenwood boasted multiple movie theaters, including the Williams Dreamland Theatre, which opened in 1914. To keep the theater as modern as possible, it was renovated just a few years later—in 1918—at a cost of $10,000. John and Loula Williams owned the Williams Dreamland Theatre in addition to several other businesses along Greenwood Avenue. The Williams family is pictured below in the early 1910s.

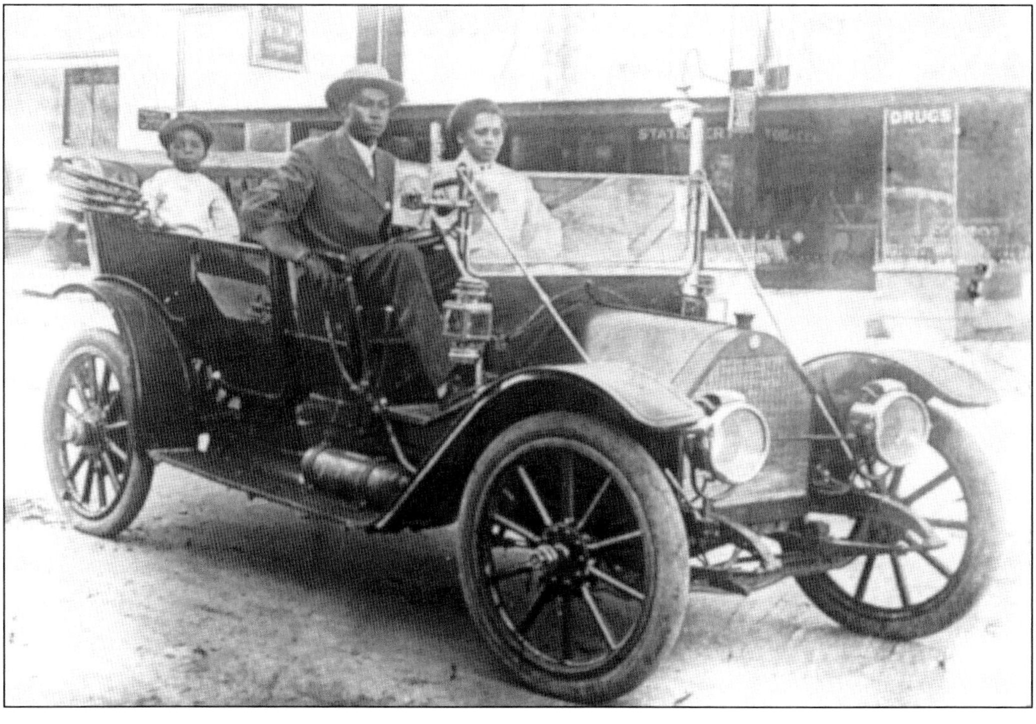

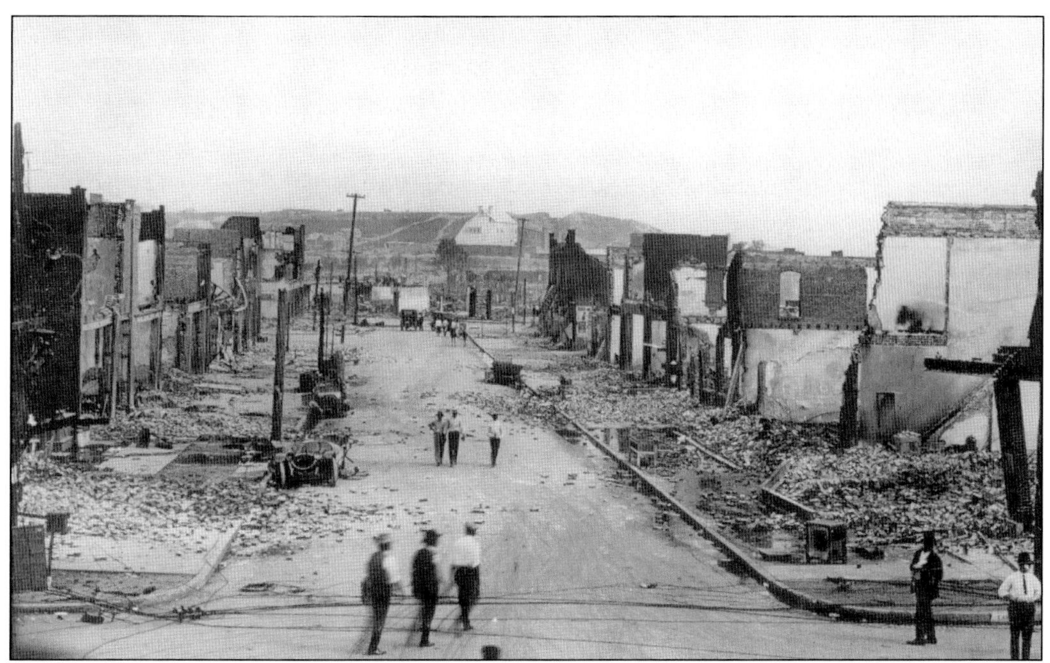

In June 1921, the Greenwood community was left in ruins following the Tulsa Race Massacre. During the two-day event, mobs of white citizens attacked, destroyed, and looted businesses and homes and killed many Greenwood residents. The above photograph is looking north on Greenwood Avenue from Archer Street and shows part of the devastated commercial district. This block was home to the Williams Dreamland Theatre and the Dixie Theatre. Below is a view of part of the same block from the other end of the street. Near the center of the image are the remains of the Dixie Theatre with its name visible on the side of the building.

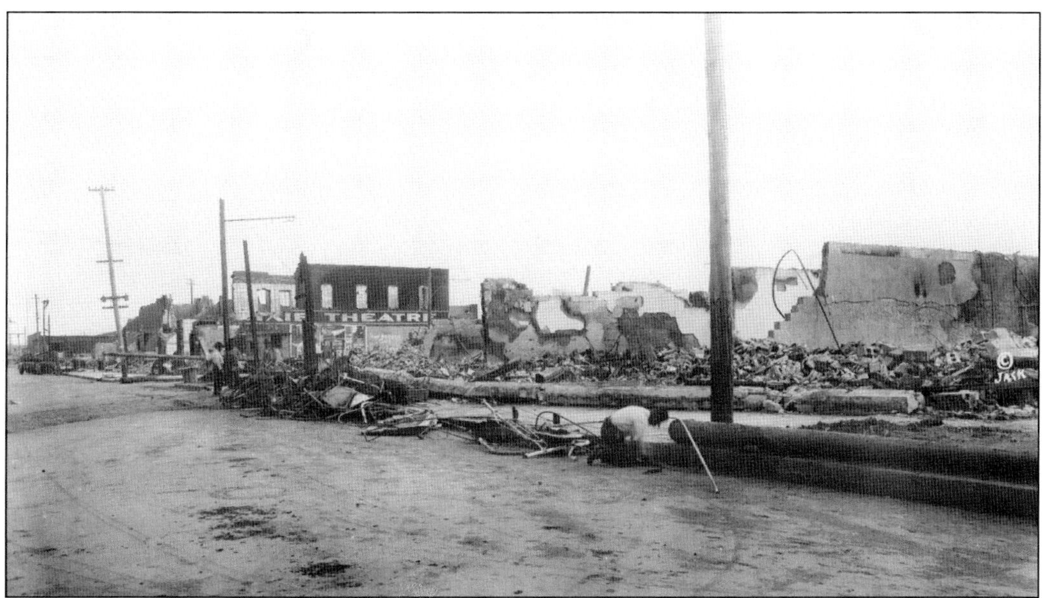

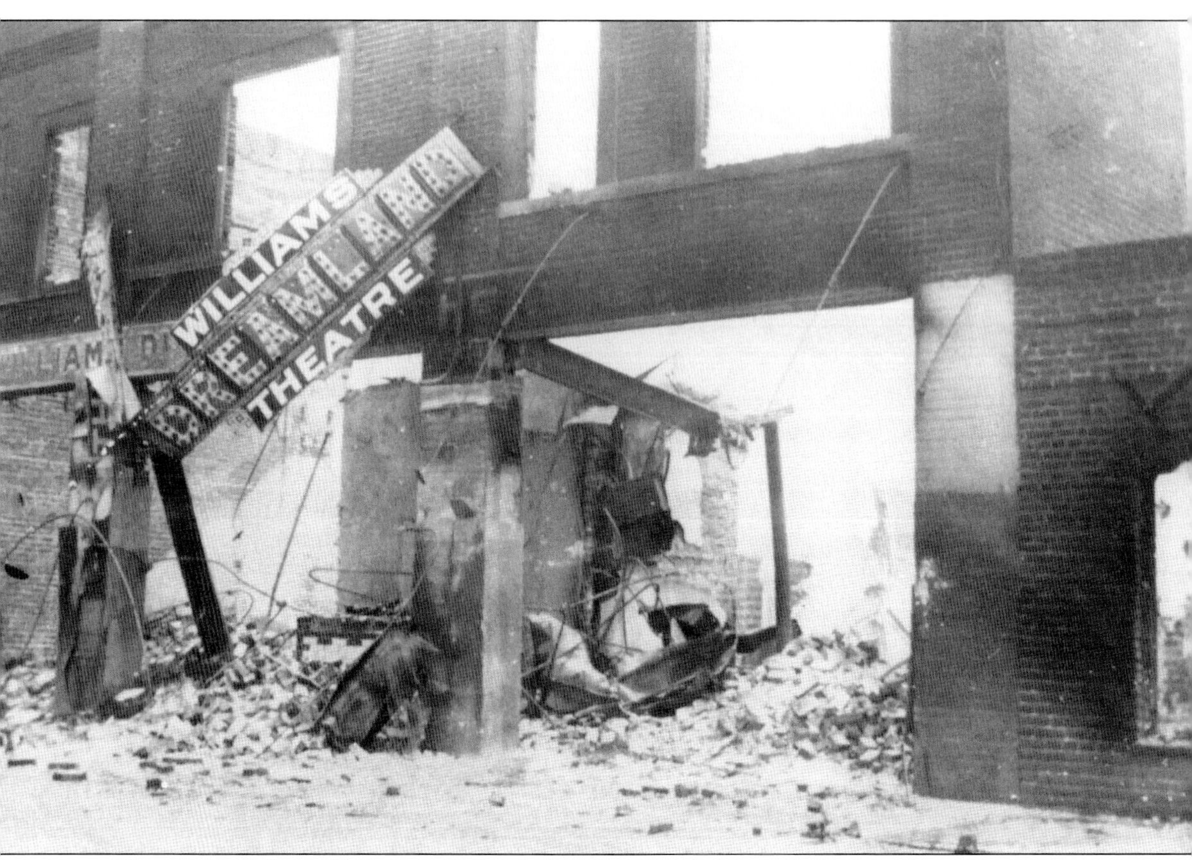

This image of the Williams Dreamland Theatre after the 1921 Tulsa Race Massacre has become iconic as representing the destruction of the event. The photograph has been referenced in art, culture, and history since 1921. The Williams Dreamland Theatre was also featured in the HBO series *Watchmen*.

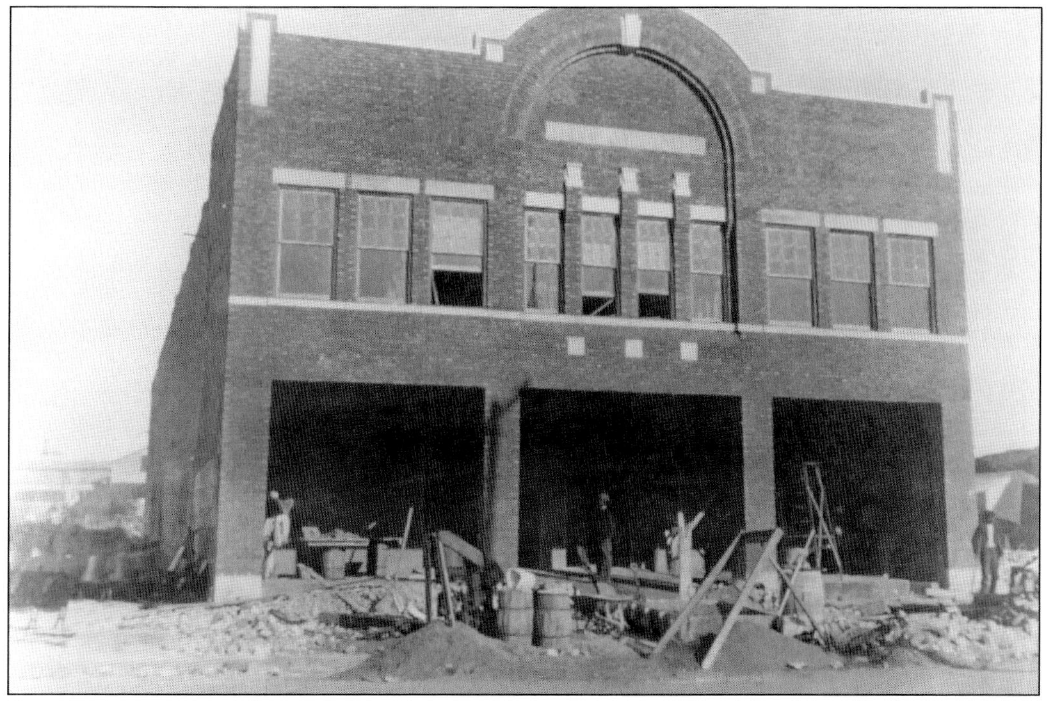

Despite the immense destruction and minimal assistance from outside of the Black community, Greenwood began to rebuild almost immediately after the Tulsa Race Massacre. By the mid-1920s, the community had regained much of its previous success. This image shows the new Dreamland Theatre under construction in 1921. Although there is not a specific date for this image, a series of photographs taken 60 days after the massacre show a number of commercial structures in a similar state of being rebuilt. (Courtesy of Greenwood Cultural Center.)

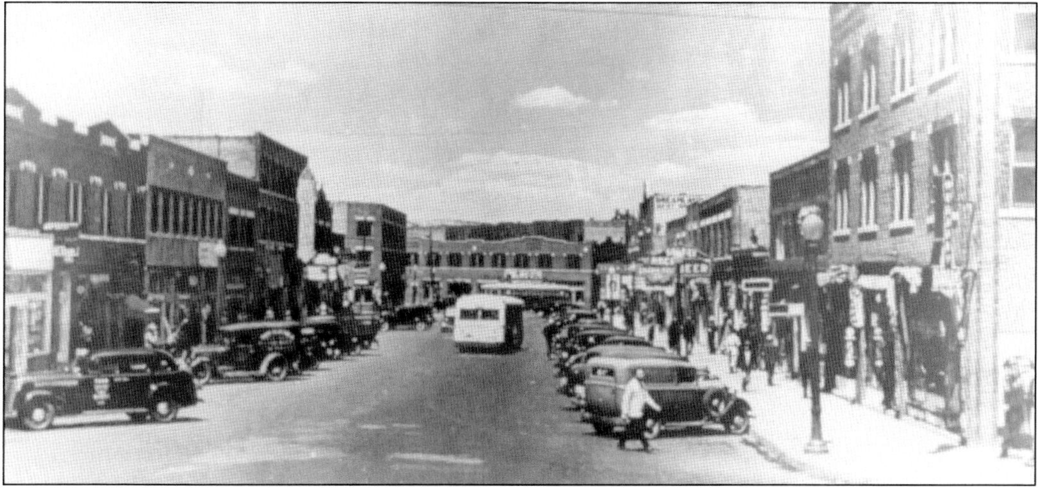

By 1930, there were nearly twice as many residents of Greenwood as there had been a decade earlier. Many homes and businesses were rebuilt at the same locations where their predecessors were destroyed in 1921. This image from 1938 shows a thriving business district, including the Dixie and Dreamland Theatres in nearly the same spots where they were previously located. Other theaters came and went over the years, including the Rex and Regal. In the early 1940s, the directory for Greenwood included more than 400 businesses.

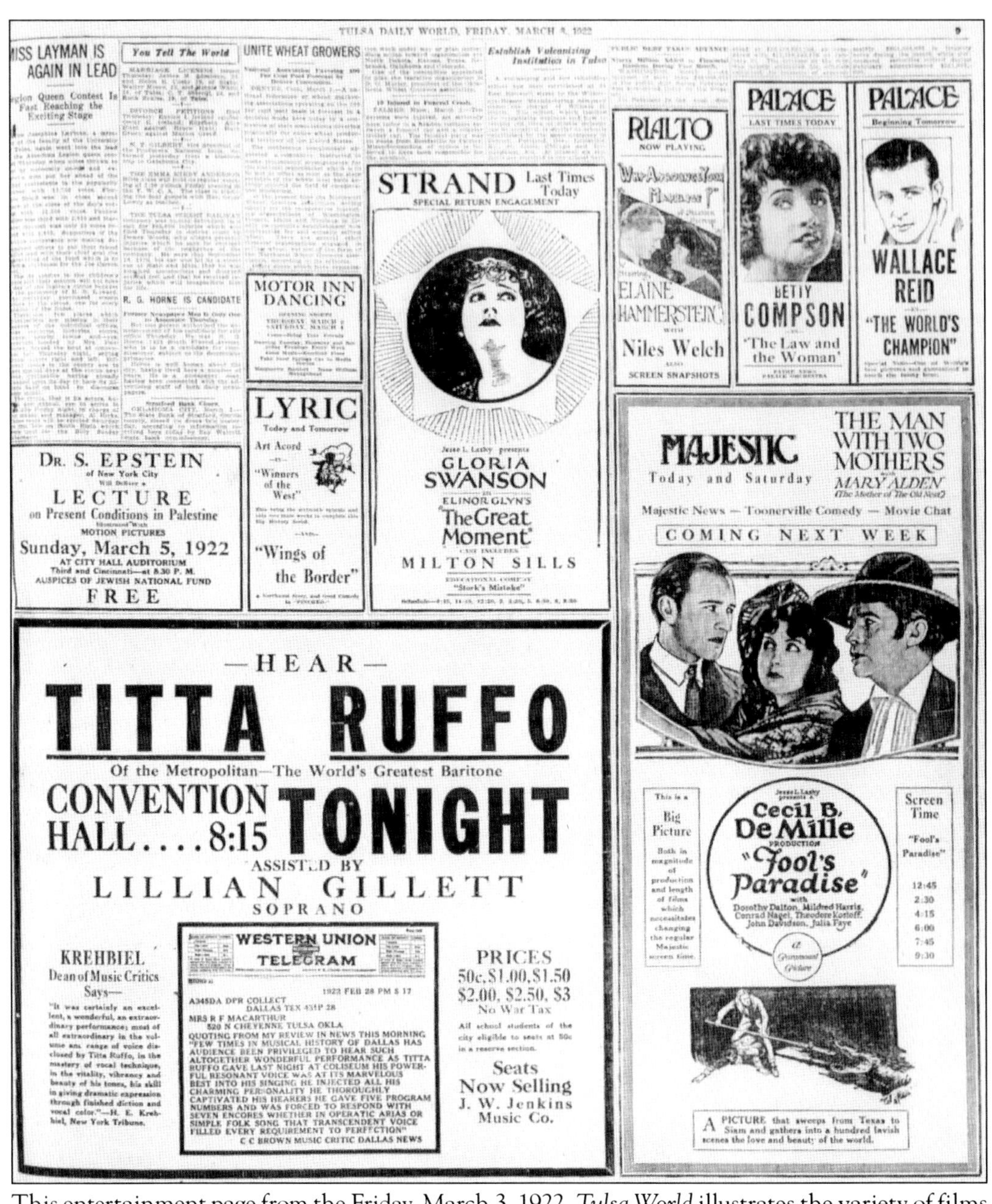

TULSA DAILY WORLD, FRIDAY, MARCH 3, 1922

MISS LAYMAN IS AGAIN IN LEAD

You Tell The World

UNITE WHEAT GROWERS

R. G. HORNE IS CANDIDATE

DR. S. EPSTEIN
of New York City
LECTURE
on Present Conditions in Palestine
MOTION PICTURES
Sunday, March 5, 1922
AT CITY HALL AUDITORIUM
Third and Cincinnati—at 8:30 P. M.
AUSPICES OF JEWISH NATIONAL FUND
FREE

MOTOR INN DANCING

LYRIC
Today and Tomorrow
Art Acord
"Winners of the West"
"Wings of the Border"

STRAND Last Times Today
SPECIAL RETURN ENGAGEMENT
Jesse L. Lasky presents
GLORIA SWANSON
in
ELINOR GLYN'S
The Great Moment
MILTON SILLS

RIALTO
NOW PLAYING
ELAINE HAMMERSTEIN
Niles Welch
SCREEN SNAPSHOTS

PALACE
LAST TIMES TODAY
BETTY COMPSON
"The Law and the Woman"

PALACE
Beginning Tomorrow
WALLACE REID
in
"THE WORLD'S CHAMPION"

MAJESTIC
Today and Saturday
THE MAN WITH TWO MOTHERS
with
MARY ALDEN
(The Mother of The Old Nest)
Majestic News — Toonerville Comedy — Movie Chat
COMING NEXT WEEK

This is a Big Picture
Both in magnitude of production and length of films which necessitates changing the regular Majestic screen time.

Jesse L. Lasky presents a
Cecil B. De Mille PRODUCTION
"Fool's Paradise"
with
Dorothy Dalton, Mildred Harris, Conrad Nagel, Theodore Kosloff, John Davidson, Julia Faye
a Paramount Picture

Screen Time
"Fool's Paradise"
12:45
2:30
4:15
6:00
7:45
9:30

A PICTURE that sweeps from Texas to Siam and gathers into a hundred lavish scenes the love and beauty of the world.

—HEAR—
TITTA RUFFO
Of the Metropolitan—The World's Greatest Baritone
CONVENTION HALL....8:15
TONIGHT
ASSISTED BY
LILLIAN GILLETT
SOPRANO

KREHBIEL
Dean of Music Critics
Says—
"It was certainly an excellent, a wonderful, an extraordinary performance; most of all extraordinary in the volume and range of voice disclosed by Titta Ruffo, in the mastery of vocal technique, in the vitality, vibrancy and beauty of his tones, his skill in giving dramatic expression through finished diction and vocal color."—H. E. Krehbiel, New York Tribune.

WESTERN UNION
TELEGRAM
1922 FEB 28 PM 5 17
A345DA DPR COLLECT
DALLAS TEX 431P 28
MRS R F MACARTHUR
520 N CHEYENNE TULSA OKLA
QUOTING FROM MY REVIEW IN NEWS THIS MORNING "FEW TIMES IN MUSICAL HISTORY OF DALLAS HAS AUDIENCE BEEN PRIVILEGED TO HEAR SUCH ALTOGETHER WONDERFUL PERFORMANCE AS TITTA RUFFO GAVE LAST NIGHT AT COLISEUM HIS POWERFUL RESONANT VOICE WAS AT ITS MARVELOUS BEST INTO HIS SINGING HE INJECTED ALL HIS CHARMING PERSONALITY HE THOROUGHLY CAPTIVATED HIS HEARERS HE GAVE FIVE PROGRAM NUMBERS AND WAS FORCED TO RESPOND WITH SEVEN ENCORES WHETHER IN OPERATIC ARIAS OR SIMPLE FOLK SONG THAT TRANSCENDENT VOICE FILLED EVERY REQUIREMENT TO PERFECTION"
C C BROWN MUSIC CRITIC DALLAS NEWS

PRICES
50c, $1.00, $1.50
$2.00, $2.50, $3
No War Tax
All school students of the city eligible to seats at 50c in a reserve section.
Seats Now Selling
J. W. Jenkins Music Co.

This entertainment page from the Friday, March 3, 1922, *Tulsa World* illustrates the variety of films being shown in Tulsa at the peak of the silent-film era, from Gloria Swanson's *The Great Moment* at the Strand to Betty Compson's *The Law and the Woman* at the Palace. Swanson and Compson both made the transition to talkies, and Compson later became the first actress to portray Belle Starr on film in 1928's *Court-Martial.* There is an advertisement for acclaimed director Cecil B. DeMille's *Fool's Paradise* at the Majestic as well as one for Wallace Reid in *The World's Champion*. Reid, a silent film star who earned the moniker "the screen's most perfect lover," has been largely forgotten, and many of his films are considered to be "lost." (Courtesy of *Tulsa World*.)

Two

Big Four

Tulsa's Downtown Movie Palaces

By the 1920s, film had become a well-established part of American life, and most new theaters were designed to present both vaudeville shows and motion pictures. Feature-length movies introduced in the 1910s increased revenues, allowing theater owners to build more elaborate movie houses that were steeped in glamour, luxury, and comfort. In Tulsa, these movie palaces were represented by the "Big Four"—the Ritz, Orpheum, Majestic, and Rialto.

The Majestic opened in 1910 at 4 East Third Street before moving to a larger space at 402 South Main Street. In 1918, a new Majestic opened next door at 406 South Main Street, which became its home for more than 50 years. The new theater had a seating capacity of 1,000. When it was built, the Majestic had the largest marquee in the state. It was also the first theater in Tulsa to show a sound film (in 1927) and the first 3D movie (in 1952).

In 1918, the Rialto opened at 7 West Third Street. The next year, the Orpheum began operating next door at 15 West Third Street, where it would remain until a brand-new theater was constructed in 1924. When the Orpheum vacated its space, the Rialto took over at 15 West Third Street by simply moving its signs. The Rialto was the first theater in Tulsa to be air-conditioned and held the state premiere for the movie *Oklahoma!*.

After initially opening on West Third Street, the Orpheum built a grand new structure at 12 East Fourth Street in 1924. Inside, the decor included reproductions of Greek and Roman statues overlooking 1,600 seats. In 1926, future Miss America Norma Smallwood was crowned Miss Tulsa on the Orpheum stage.

The grandest of the downtown movie palaces, the Ritz, opened in May 1926 at 18 West Fourth Street. The building was filled with elegant artwork, marble, mirrors, light fixtures, statues, and olive trees. But it was the theater ceiling that was most noteworthy. Above the audience was a blue plaster ceiling with suspended stars that twinkled. A special projector created the illusion of clouds moving overhead to produce the feeling of being outdoors.

The decline of downtown in favor of suburban shopping areas with more parking affected the theaters. All four closed and were demolished within a short time frame during an era of urban renewal. Although it was built last, the Ritz was the first to close, shutting its doors in 1960. The Orpheum lasted until 1970. That same year, the Majestic became an adult theater, and it closed for good in 1973. The Rialto was demolished in 1973.

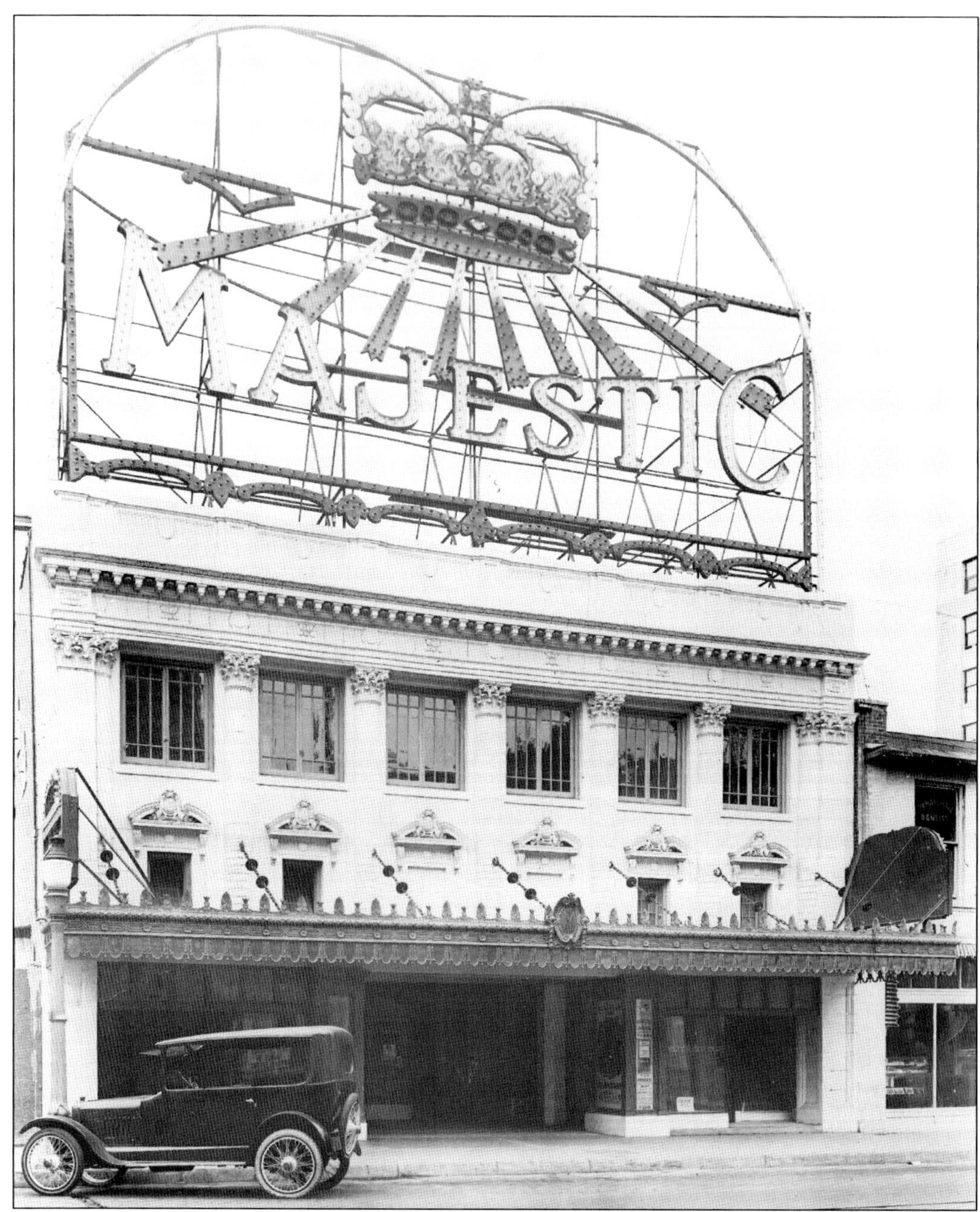

On June 27, 1918, a new Majestic opened at 406 South Main Street, next door to its previous location. Built by Dr. C.W. McCarty and E.R. Perry, the new theater had 1,000 seats, making it one of the biggest theaters in town. At the time, the Majestic had the largest electric marquee in the state and was the first Tulsa movie house with a real theater organ. Shortly after the theater opened, a crowd gathered outside to listen to updates on the World Series. Journalist Glenn Condon shouted updates he received on the newspaper wire out the windows to the crowd. This picture of the Majestic was taken shortly after it opened and shows the earliest version of the structure at 406 South Main Street.

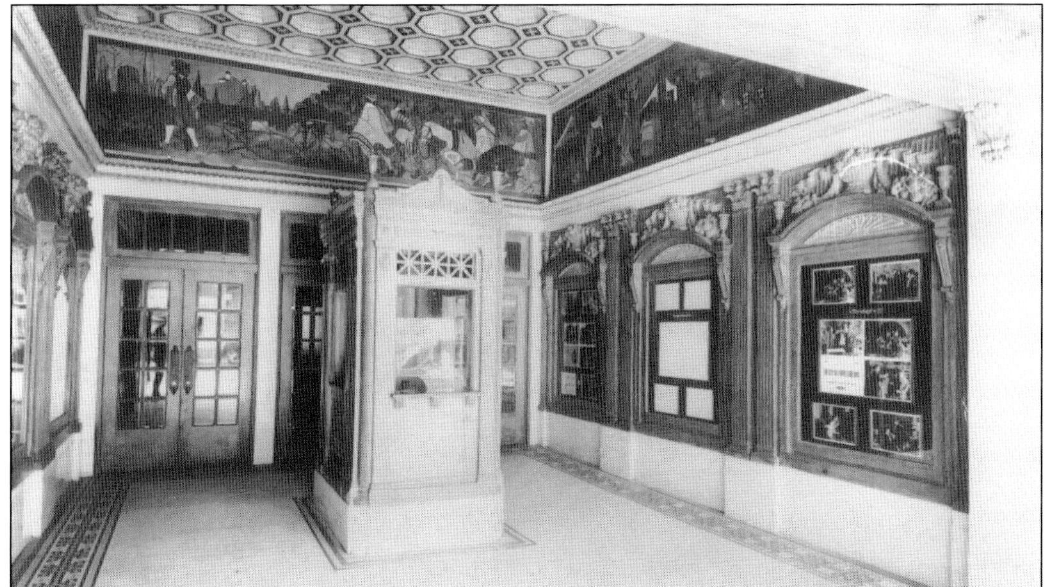

An ornate entrance welcomed moviegoers to the new Majestic when it opened in 1918. The theater cost $150,000 to build and included a specially made $25,000 pipe organ. Newspapers reported that there were only two other similar organs in the entire country. As the new Majestic's earliest patrons stepped into the entryway, they were greeted by posters and publicity photographs for *She Loved Him Plenty* and *City of Purple Dreams*.

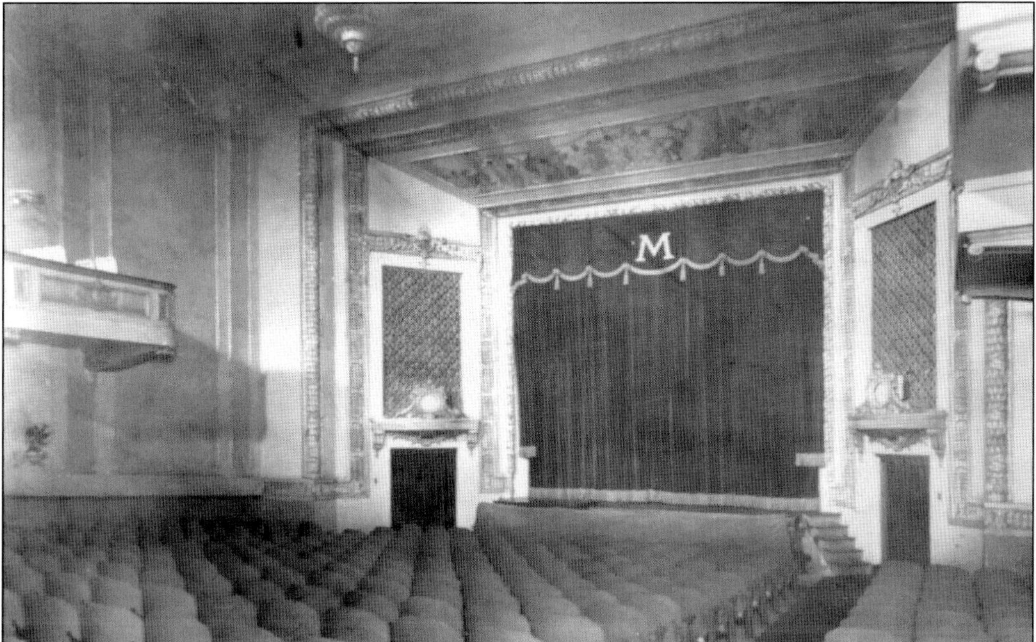

The Majestic's large auditorium featured a decorative M centered on the stage curtains. Just above the stage was a mural of *The Feast of Bacchus* by artist William Stein. The theater provided an air-cooling system in addition to ceiling fans to keep the audience comfortable in their cushioned chairs. It was in these seats that Tulsans saw the first film with sound, *The Jazz Singer*, in 1927—the Majestic was the first theater in Oklahoma to show it.

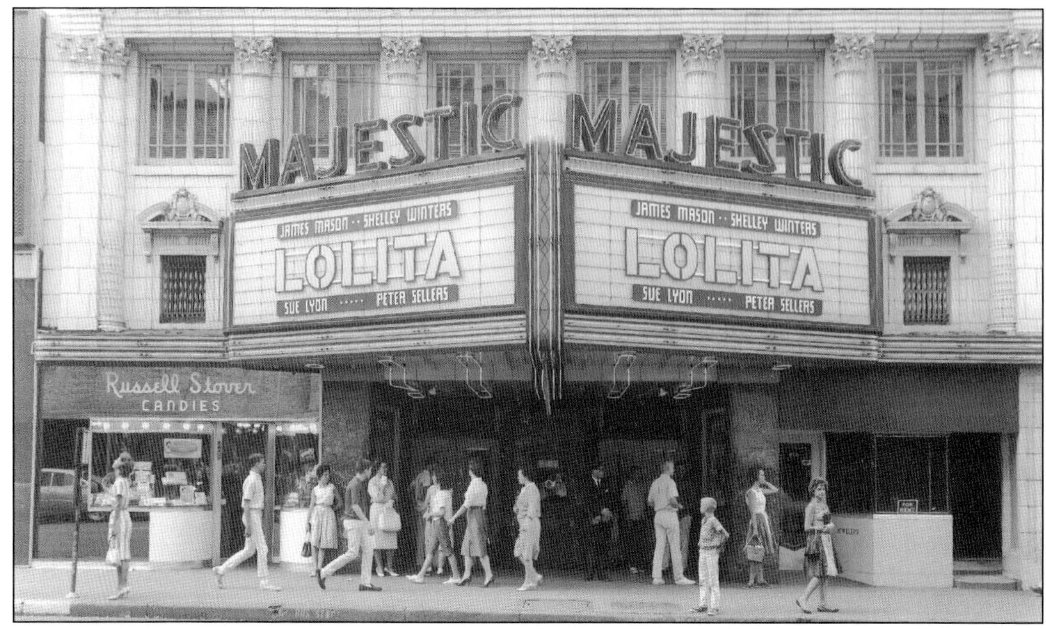

The exterior of the Majestic changed dramatically with a new marquee. By the 1950s, the theater began losing out on first-run films but was still the venue for Tulsa's first 3D film, *Bwana Devil*, in 1952. This 1962 photograph advertises *Lolita* on the marquee. A few years later, the Majestic became an adult theater, and it closed for good in 1973. The building was razed that year, and a parking garage now stands in its place.

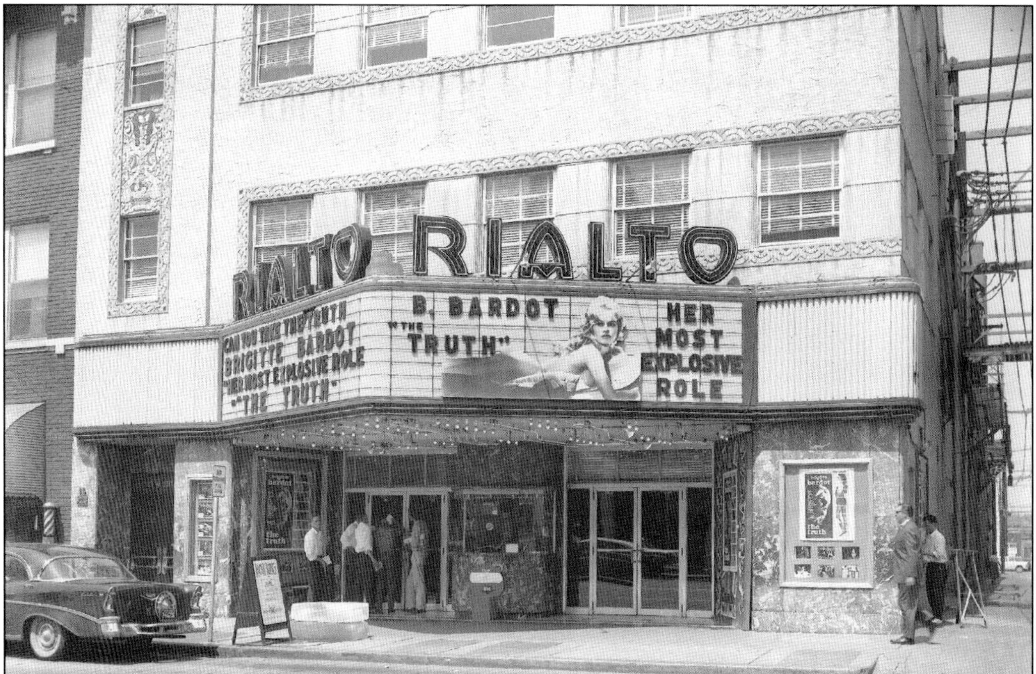

The Rialto operated in three different locations, but it was the structure at 15 West Third Street that is best remembered. This address was originally home to the Orpheum, with the Rialto next door. When a new Orpheum was built in 1924, the Rialto moved into its vacated spot.

The Rialto was the first theater to include air-conditioning and the first venue in the state to show the movie *Oklahoma!* In 1955, in order to earn the right to host the *Oklahoma!* event, the owners paid $56,000 for a state-of-the-art Todd-AO screen and sound system. *Oklahoma!* played at the Rialto for months, which was highly unusual at the time. The Rialto is pictured at night on September 21, 1961.

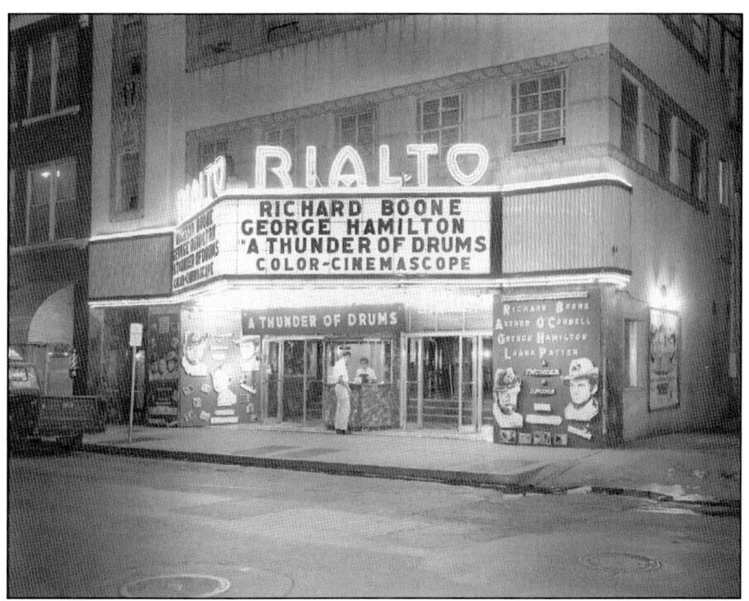

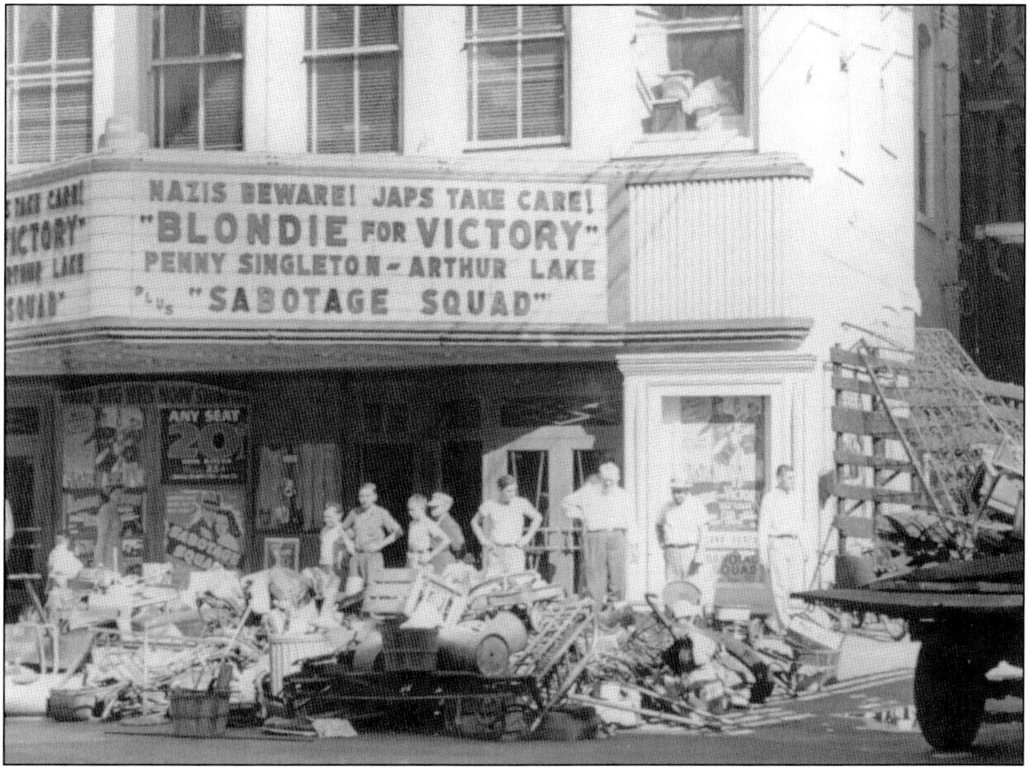

Theaters frequently hosted special events, and the Rialto was no exception. As shown in this photograph taken during World War II, the Rialto hosted a scrap drive for the community. Citizens were asked to contribute items that would prove useful in the war effort, including products made out of rubber, most types of metal, kitchen fat, newspapers, rags, and other materials. This particular scrap drive in 1942 was in conjunction with the film *Blondie for Victory*, a patriotic film encouraging women to contribute to activities on the home front.

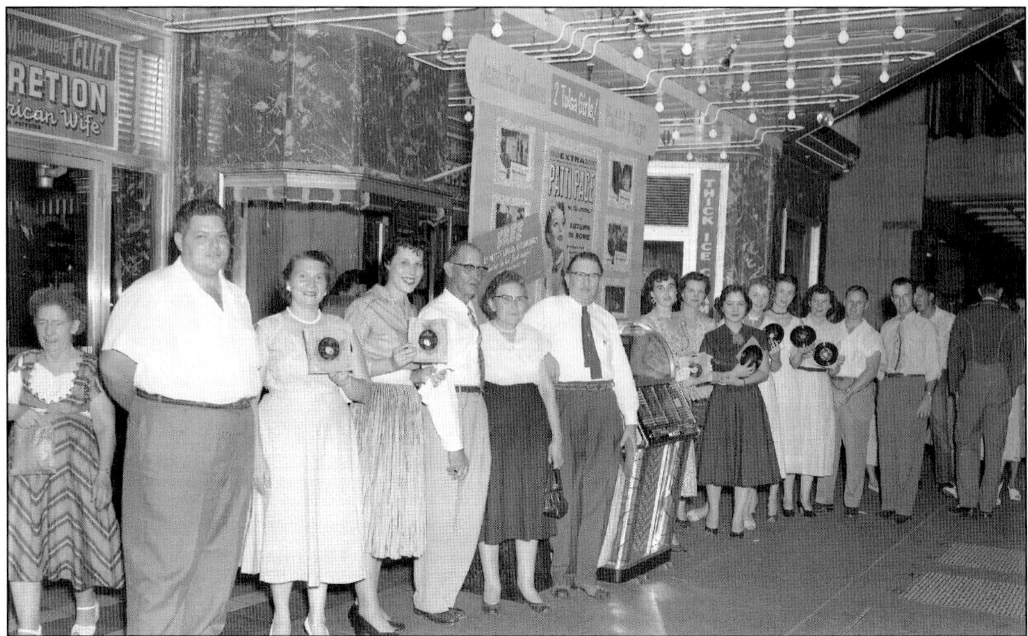

This photograph, taken in front of the Rialto, features a group participating in a promotion for the film *Indiscretion of an American Wife*. The top sign reads, "Jennifer Jones / Two Tulsa Girls! / Patti Page." Jones starred in the movie, while Page, who first achieved fame singing live over Tulsa's KVOO radio, contributed two songs to the soundtrack. Several members of the group are holding 45-rpm vinyl records of Page's songs.

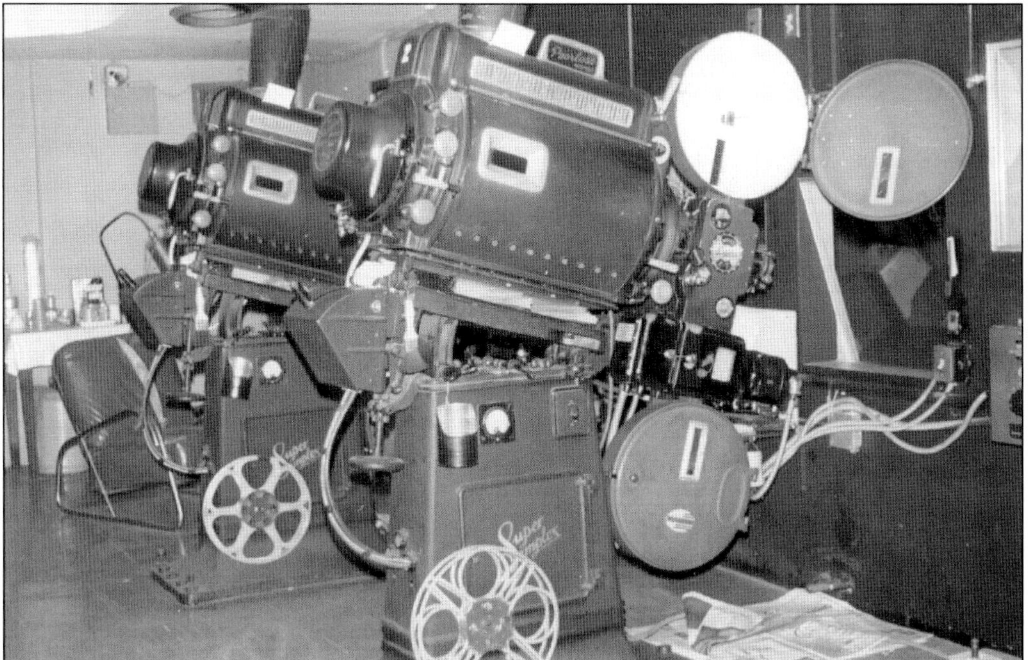

Getting a glimpse inside a theater's projection room is a rare treat that allows the audience to see the mechanics behind the magic. Shortly before the Rialto closed and was demolished in 1973, someone snapped this picture of the Super Simplex machines that brought films to life.

The new Orpheum opened in 1924 at 12 East Fourth Street after previously operating on West Third Street. The theater's original marquee emphasized the Orpheum's focus on live vaudeville entertainment. In fact, the name Orpheum was given to theaters across the country that were part of the Orpheum vaudeville circuit. This view looks west on Fourth Street toward Main Street.

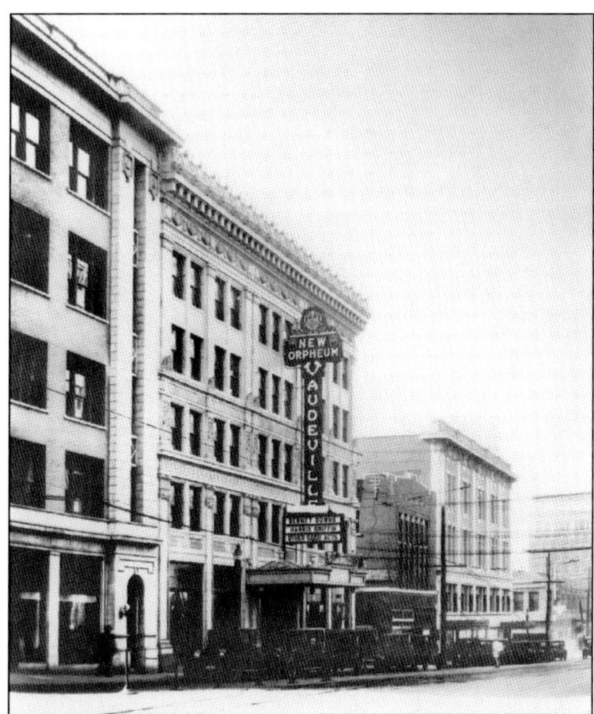

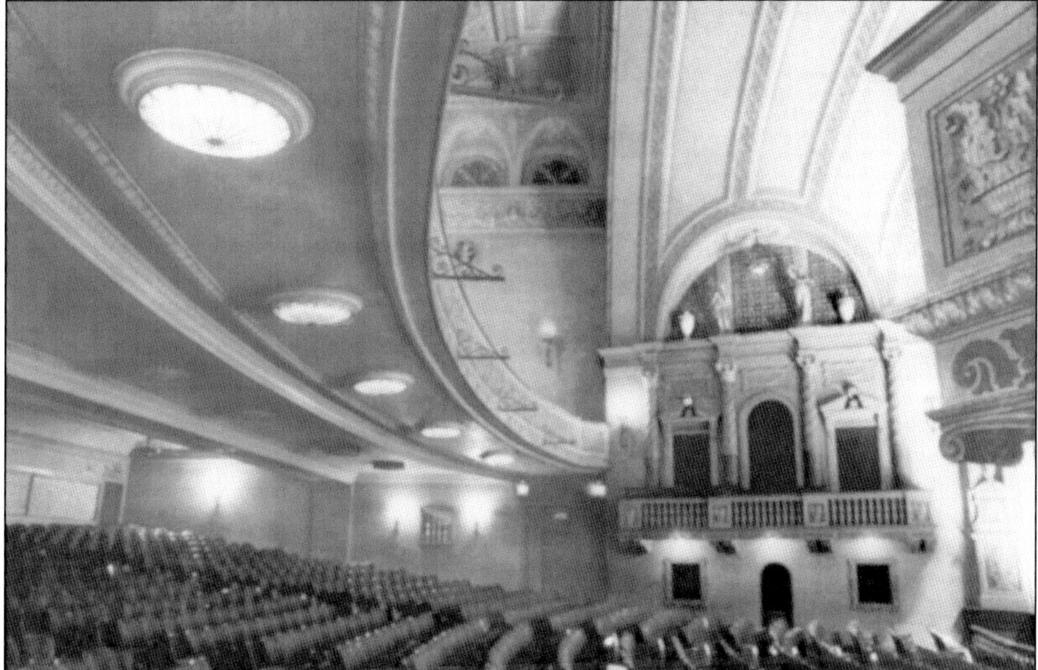

The Orpheum contained Greek and Roman statue reproductions, which, along with its elegant lighting fixtures, gave it the appearance of a European palace. The owners employed a pit orchestra for the vaudeville acts, so they saw no need for a large pipe organ. The Orpheum's Wurlitzer, with a two-manual console, was the smallest of the organs at the four downtown theaters. (Courtesy of Nancy Schallner.)

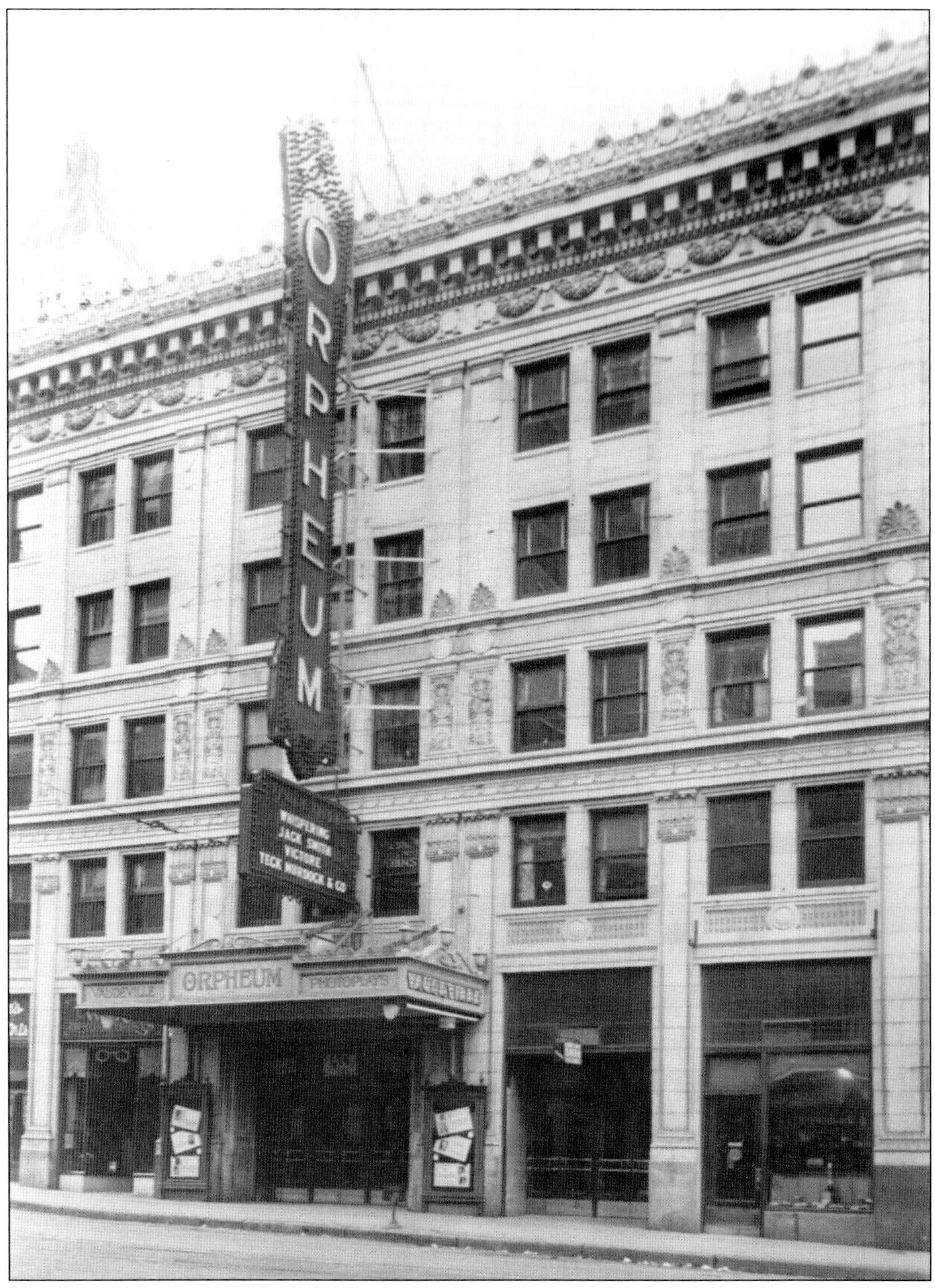

This late-1920s photograph of the Orpheum shows many of the theater's architectural details. Designed by architect John Eberson in a Renaissance Revival style, the building was five stories tall and faced with terra-cotta. The marquee shown here replaced the original one when the Orpheum began showing movies as its primary business in 1929. First-run films came two years later.

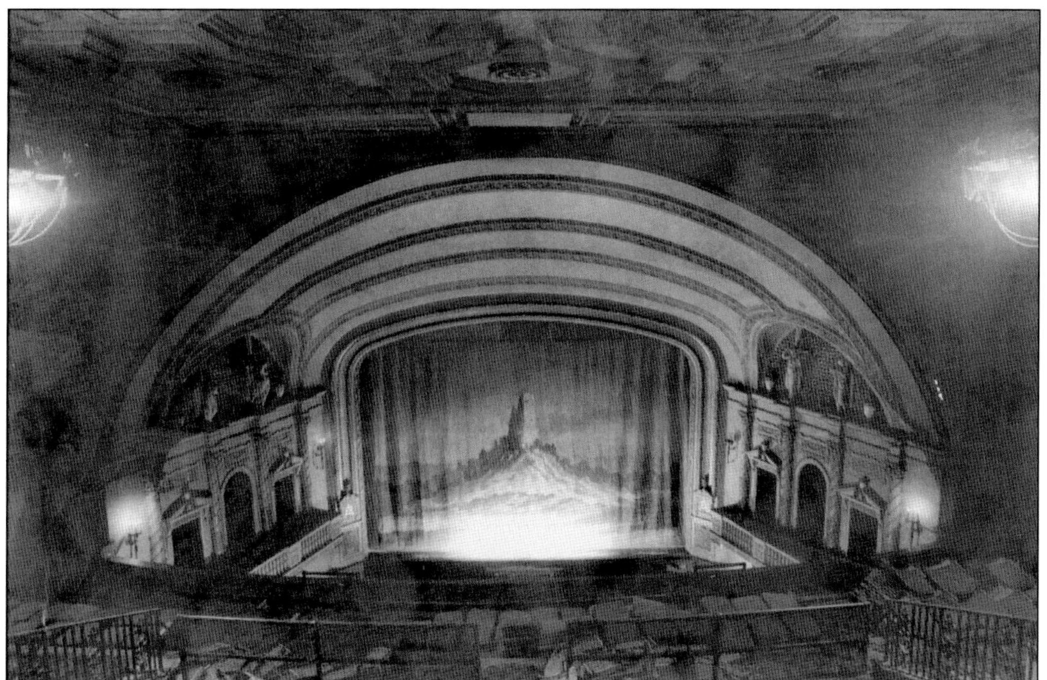

The elegant interior of the Orpheum reflected the exterior architectural style and cemented its role as a movie palace. Wall treatments and light fixtures made the audience feel surrounded by luxury while they viewed famous performers on stage and screen. Many other events were held at the Orpheum. In 1926, Norma Smallwood was crowned Miss Tulsa on the theater's stage before later becoming Miss America. Other audiences watched Tulsan Jennifer Jones on stage for the premiere of *The Song of Bernadette*, and later, Susan Hayward and Robert Preston introduced their movie *Tulsa*. (Both, courtesy of Beryl Ford Collection/Rotary Club of Tulsa.)

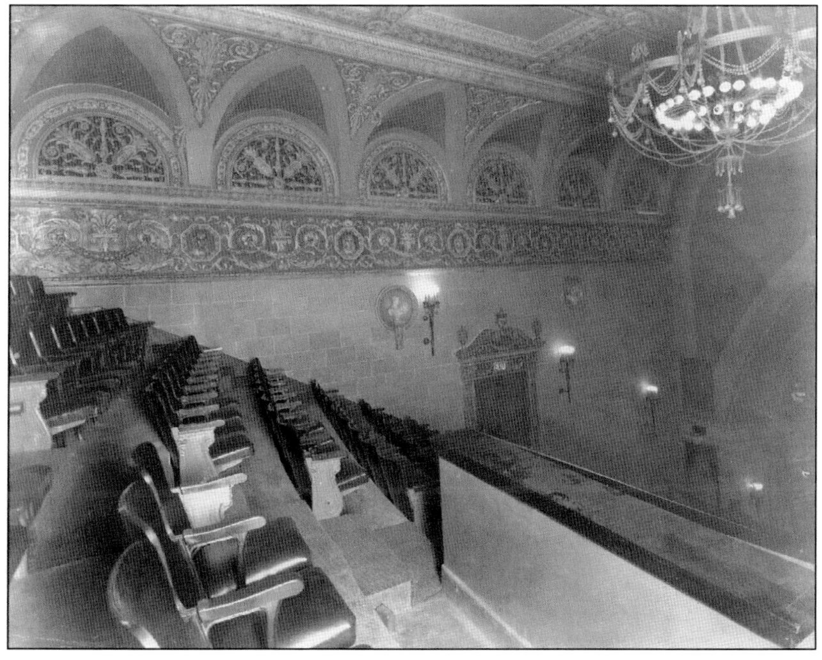

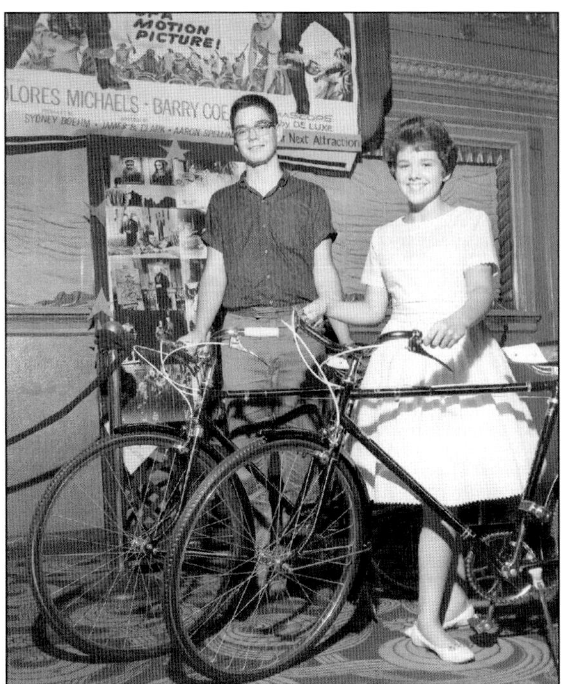

Tulsa theaters held a lot of contests and giveaways through the years. In the 1960s, there were many promotions for children, including yo-yo, essay-writing, and coloring contests. Some theaters gave away dishes with ticket admission or had drawings for door prizes, including groceries. This image shows the winners of a bicycle contest at the Orpheum around 1960.

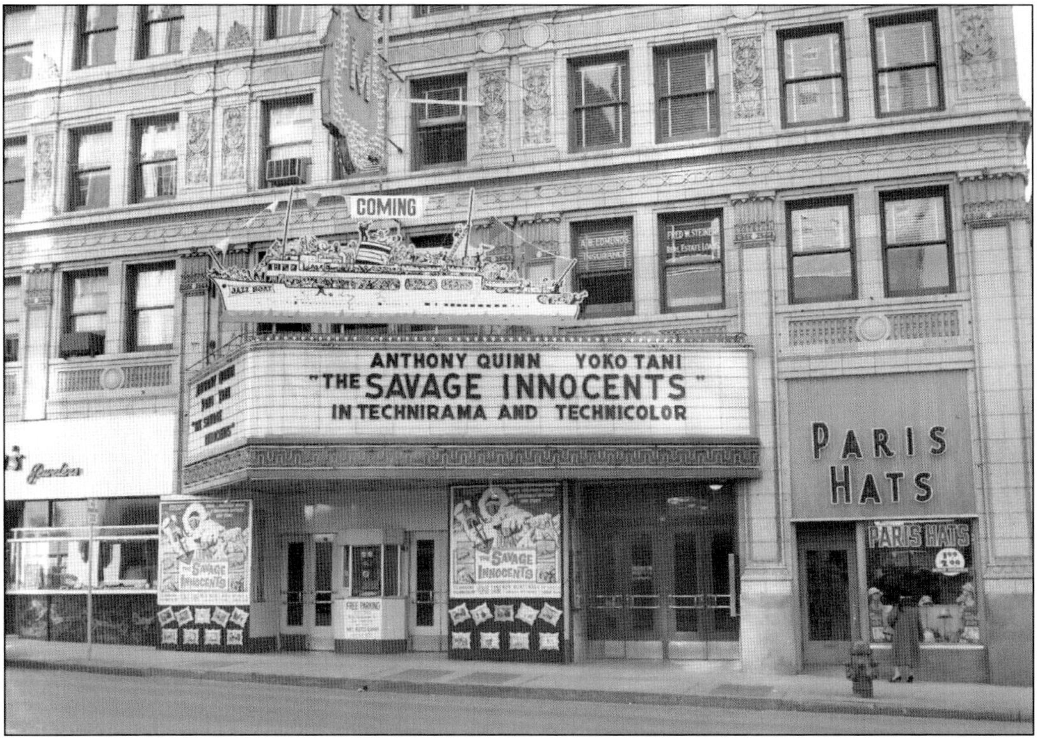

At the dawn of its last decade of operation in 1960, the Orpheum showed *The Savage Innocents*, an adventure crime drama starring Anthony Quinn. The glory days of the downtown theaters were gone by this time. Parking was a persistent problem, and by the middle part of the 1960s, there was a mass exodus to the suburbs and their new shopping malls.

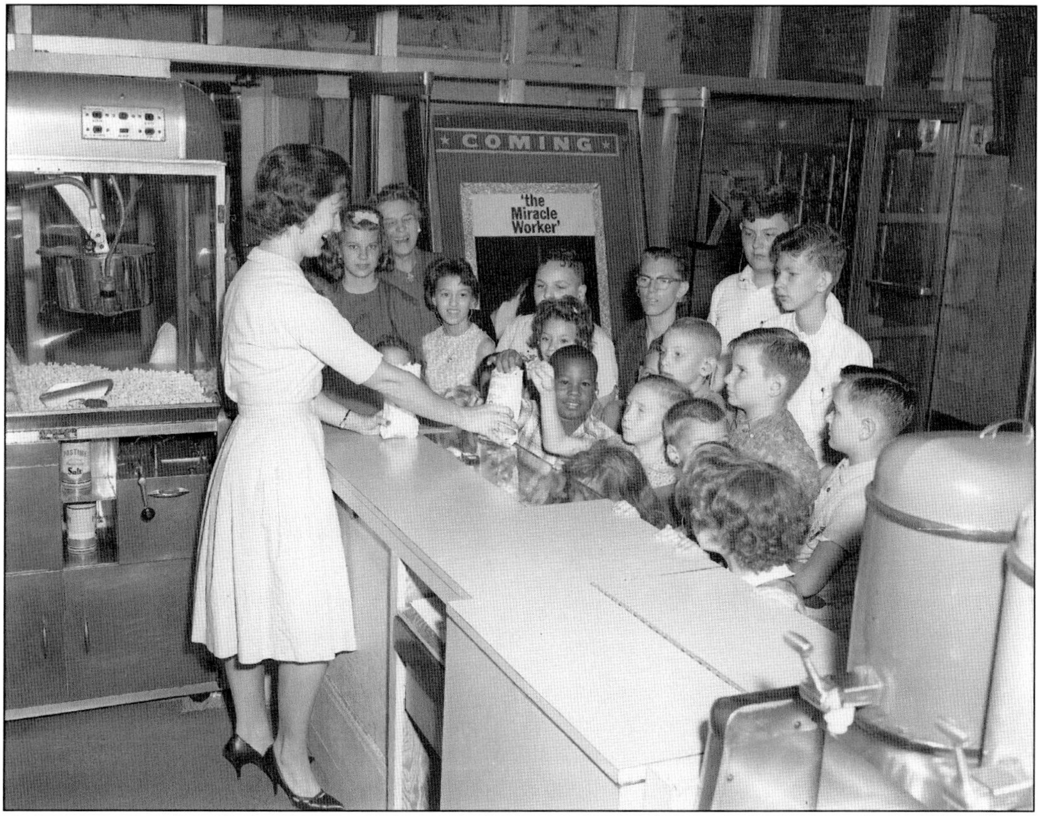

Baby boomers who grew up in Tulsa often got discount tickets through various promotions. Some Tulsans recall coupons in the newspaper for discount admission. One promotion involved a contest offering free admission with certain combinations of bottle caps. In the 1960s, kids searched for pop bottles they could return for a nickel to make movie money. Above, kids crowd around the Orpheum's concession stand around 1962. In an unscientific survey in 2020, popcorn and Coke or Pepsi were voted the favorite treats enjoyed by people who attended movies in Tulsa. Other concession treats included a drink concocted with a little bit of each flavor of soda, Payday or Butterfinger candy bars, or a pickle for a nickel. At right, a line of children loops around the sidewalk for the 1960 sci-fi adventure *The Lost World*.

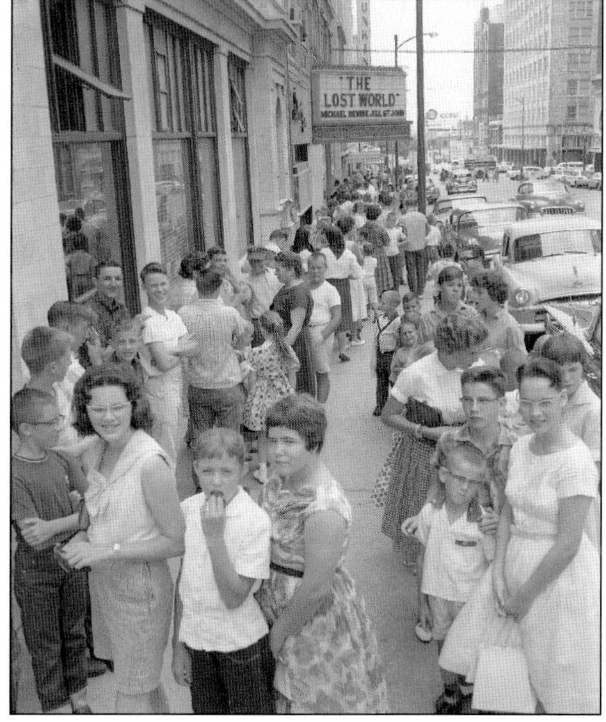

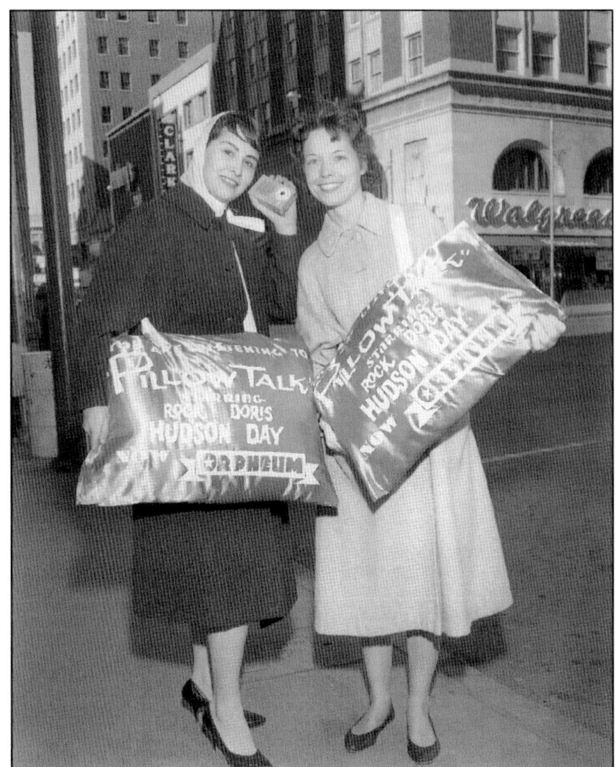

This publicity photograph for the 1959 film *Pillow Talk*, starring Rock Hudson and Doris Day, was taken in downtown Tulsa. These two women are promoting the movie by holding pillows with the Orpheum logo on the pillowcases. The woman on the left is holding a transistor radio to her ear; it was new technology at the time.

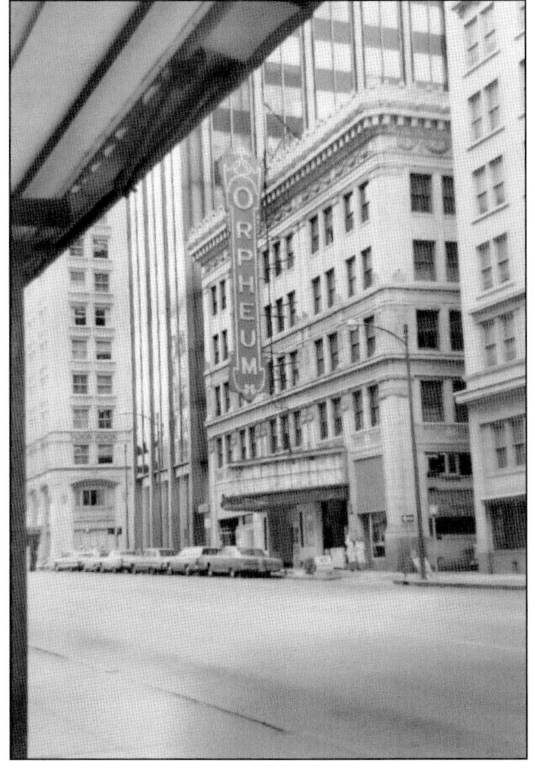

While attending college, Dennis Scott worked at the Orpheum and played the theater's Wurlitzer organ whenever he could. In 1970, before the theater's closing, Scott returned from lunch to find two men loading the organ onto a truck. They had purchased it, and Scott was heartbroken. Thirty-three years later, as president of the Chicago Theater Organ Society, Scott saw an online post from a Texas man looking for a good home for an organ from a Tulsa theater. It was the same organ, and it now resides in Scott's home. (Courtesy of Kent Schnetzler.)

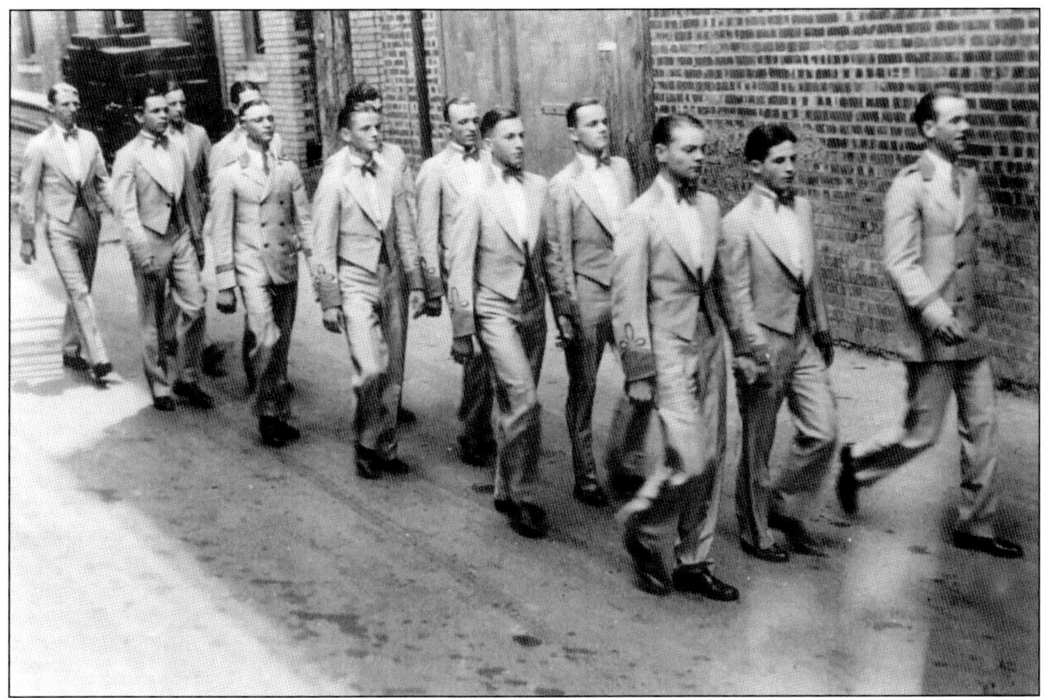

During the movie palace era, it was an honor to work as an usher at one of the Big Four theaters. Ushers went through extensive training that could resemble military marching. In this mid-1930s photograph, a group of ushers participates in training exercises in the alley adjacent to the Orpheum. The ushers pictured include Kirby Malone, William Hewett, Dewey Wilson, Edwin Wilson, Ed Disler, Dick Poulton, and head usher Jack Neece (leading the group).

Despite their formal training, many ushers were young people and liked to have fun with their friends. This image, from a series of photographs belonging to Clyde C. Wilson, shows ushers from the Orpheum and Rialto posing on the roof of one of the theaters. The picture is captioned "Orpheum Usher Force." Wilson worked at both the Orpheum and Rialto and was head usher around 1930; he is likely the person kneeling in the center. (Courtesy of Pati Wilson.)

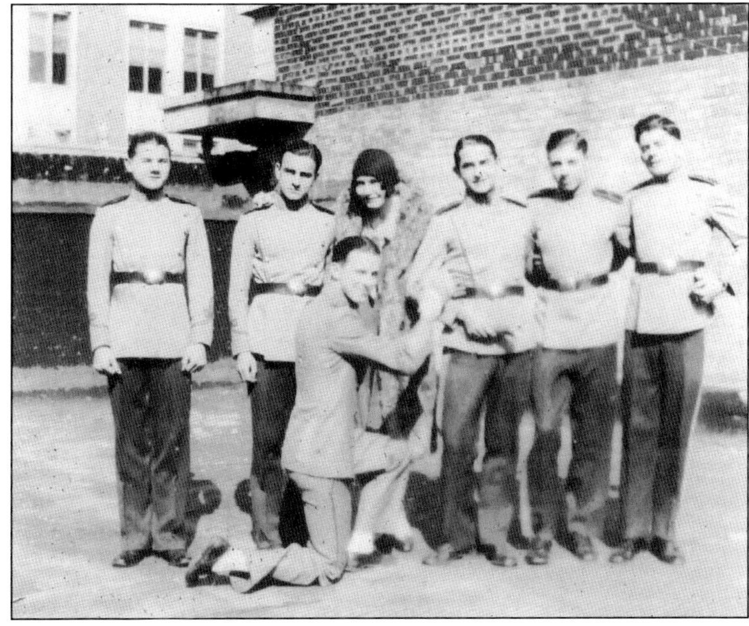

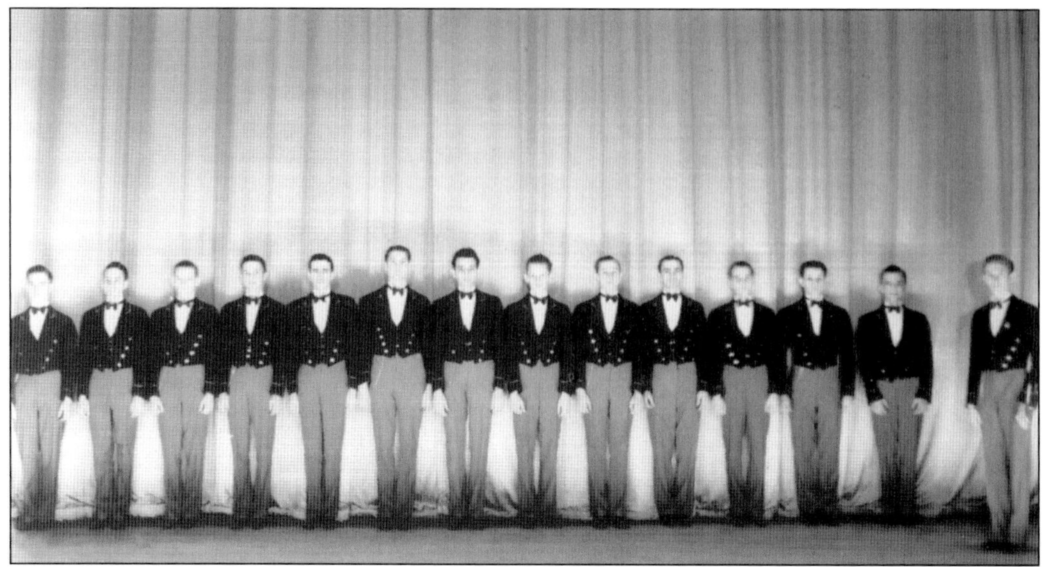

The Ritz was Tulsa's premier movie palace, and as such, it seems appropriate that the ushers there donned the most formal uniforms. As with other theaters, the ushers used elaborate hand signals for crowd control as they guided guests to their seats and shined their flashlights on anyone behaving badly. Ushers in this photograph include Jeff Polk, ? Kirpatrick, ? Shirtleff, ? Hendrix, Jack Flannigan, ? Reynolds, A.V. Lynn, Warren Patton, Claude Keith, Don Hathaway, ? Griffin, Dick Smith, and chief usher Ralph Drewry.

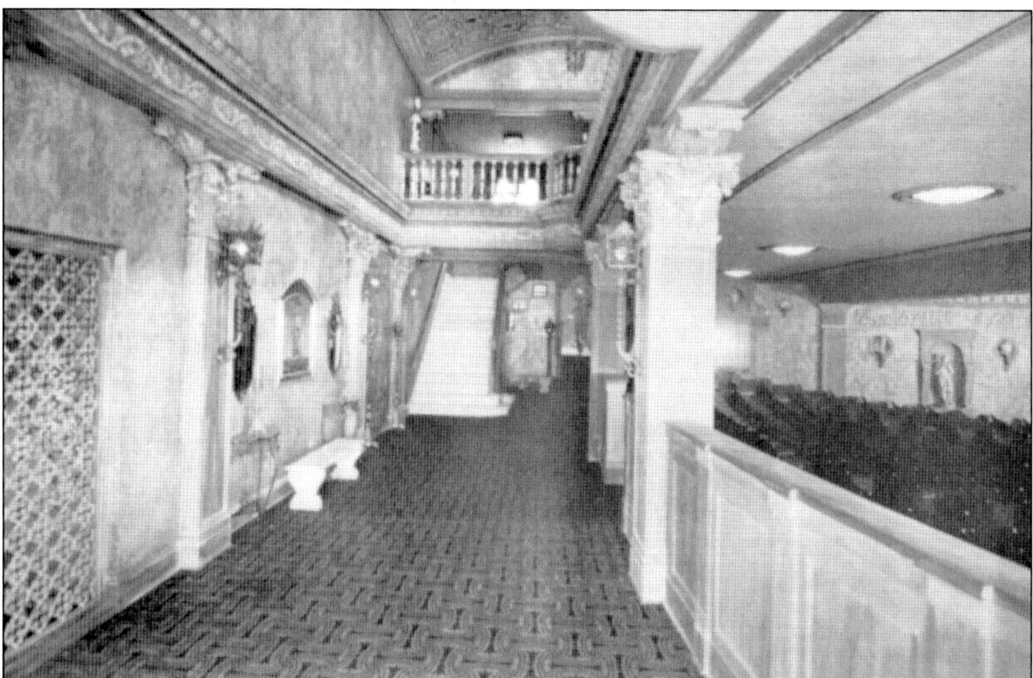

The grandeur of the Ritz is apparent even in this foyer at the back of the theater with its ornate columns and white marble bench. Over 50 years after working there, a former usher recalled sitting on this bench and relayed what a huge honor it was to be an usher at the Ritz. (Courtesy of Beryl Ford Collection/Rotary Club of Tulsa.)

Tulsa's grandest movie palace, the Ritz, opened on May 11, 1926, and cost $400,000 to build. Located at 18 West Fourth Street, it was only a block away from the Orpheum, though the two theaters were rarely photographed together. The Ritz marquee took three months to build in Chicago and cost $15,000; the colorful lights would brighten downtown for 35 years.

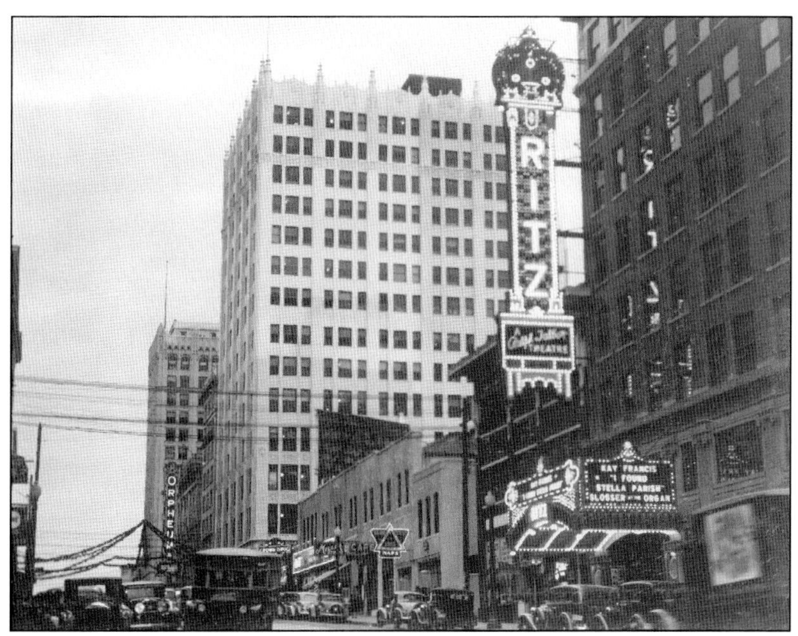

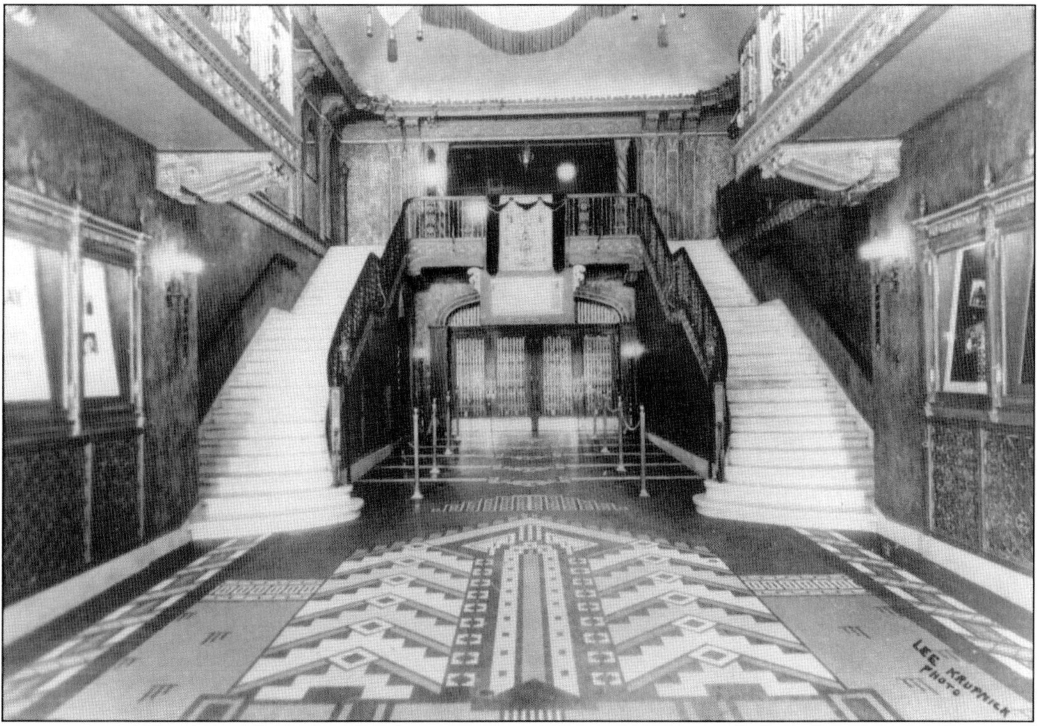

The Ritz was one of owner Ralph Talbot's first-run theaters. When planning the building, Talbot reportedly asked architect John Eberson to design the finest movie house in the Southwest. The lobby, shown here, featured marble and mirrors to welcome moviegoers and Art Deco patterns incorporated into the floor.

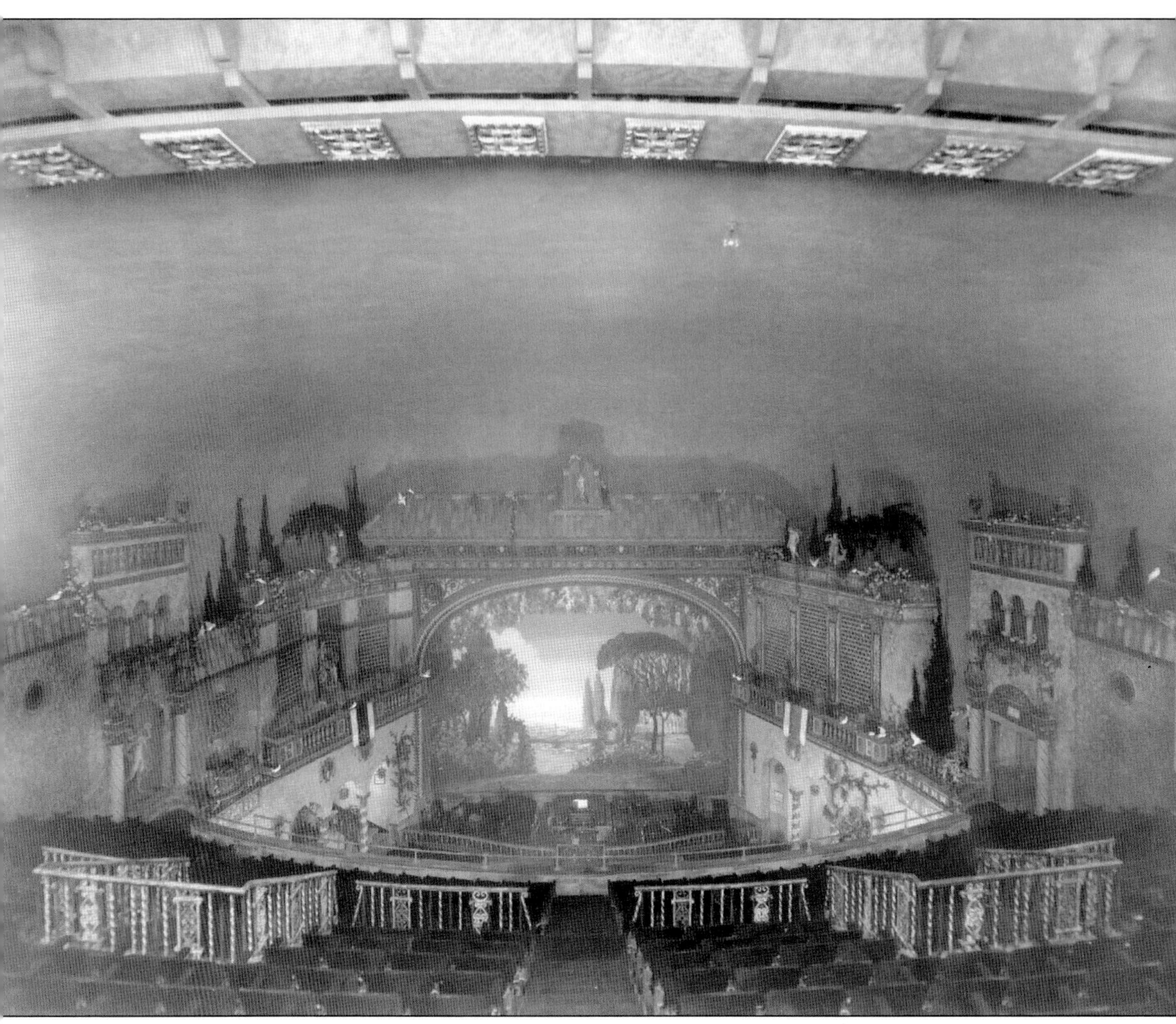

The interior of the Ritz was designed in Atmospheric/Italian Renaissance style by famed theater architect John Eberson. The sides of the auditorium included columns, statues, and olive trees to resemble an Italian villa. The ceiling simulated being outdoors under a night sky with electric twinkling stars in a deep blue sky and rolling clouds. The clouds were projected above 1,500 seats by a Brenograph machine. The effect was so real that when the Ritz first opened, a patron asked, "What do you do when it rains?" The theater also featured the largest pipe organ in Tulsa. It was designed by Wade Hamilton, who played it as house organist for the first few years of the theater's existence. Despite being engineered to be a movie palace, the Ritz's interior still included an enormous stage and all the necessary equipment for live productions.

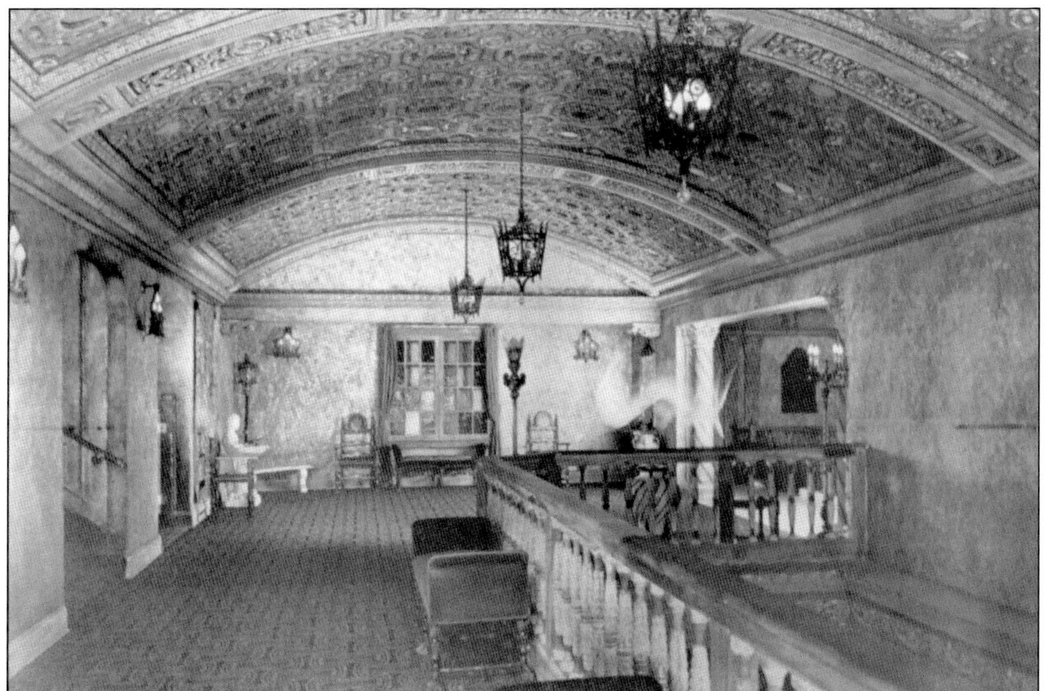

The Ritz was opulent and luxurious. In this view of the theater's mezzanine shortly after opening, every surface is elaborately decorated. Stairs leading up to the next level are visible at left. (Courtesy Beryl Ford Collection/Rotary Club of Tulsa.)

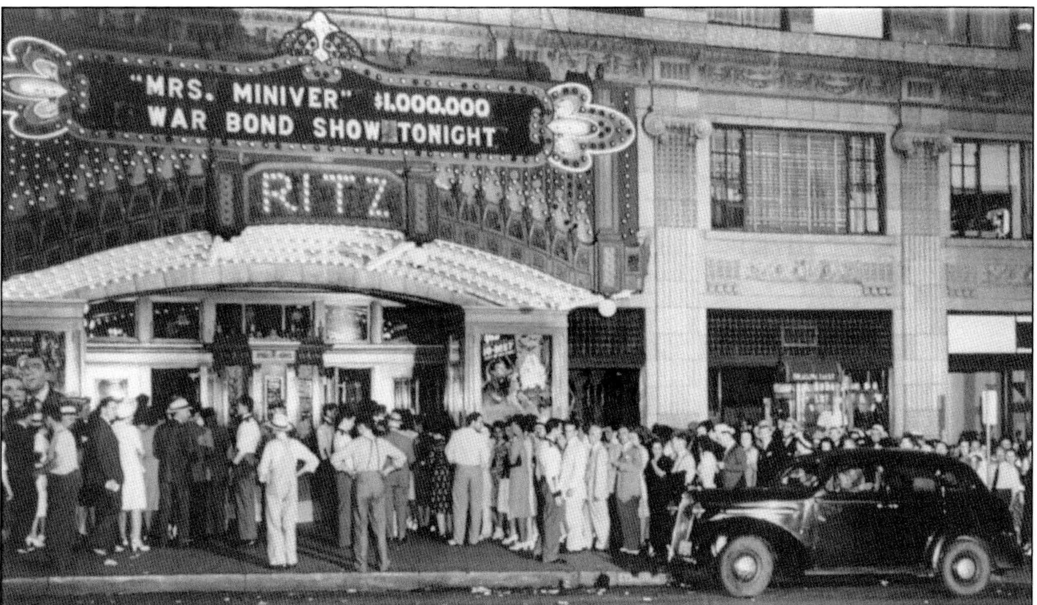

In this 1942 image, the Ritz was hosting a war bond fundraiser. War bonds were issued by the government to help finance military operations during the war. The constant reminders to buy bonds generated capital for the government and helped civilians feel more involved in the war effort. Events at theaters, such as this one featuring *Mrs. Miniver*, often revolved around a film with a military or patriotic theme. (Courtesy Beryl Ford Collection/Rotary Club of Tulsa.)

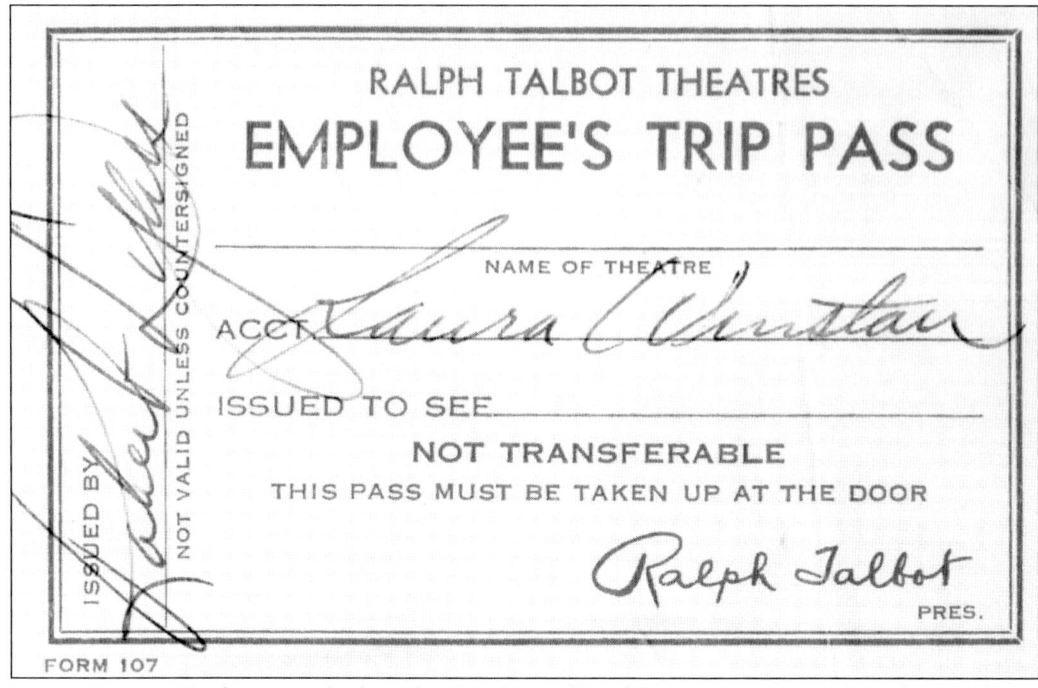
RALPH TALBOT THEATRES

EMPLOYEE'S TRIP PASS

NAME OF THEATRE

ACCT. Laura Winstan

ISSUED TO SEE

NOT TRANSFERABLE

THIS PASS MUST BE TAKEN UP AT THE DOOR

Ralph Talbot

PRES.

ISSUED BY

NOT VALID UNLESS COUNTERSIGNED

FORM 107

Laura Winston Birdsong worked in the Ritz box office from 1943 to 1949. One day, Birdsong learned that a con man had cheated the Orpheum ticket girl out of $5 while asking for change. When the man shoved a $20 into the Ritz ticket booth seeking change, Birdsong kept it! The man threatened to summon the police. Birdsong said, "Go ahead! I bet they would love to hear about what you did at the Orpheum." The man left. Birdsong's supervisor said, "Don't ever do that again! Your life is worth more than twenty dollars!" (Courtesy of Laura Winston Birdsong.)

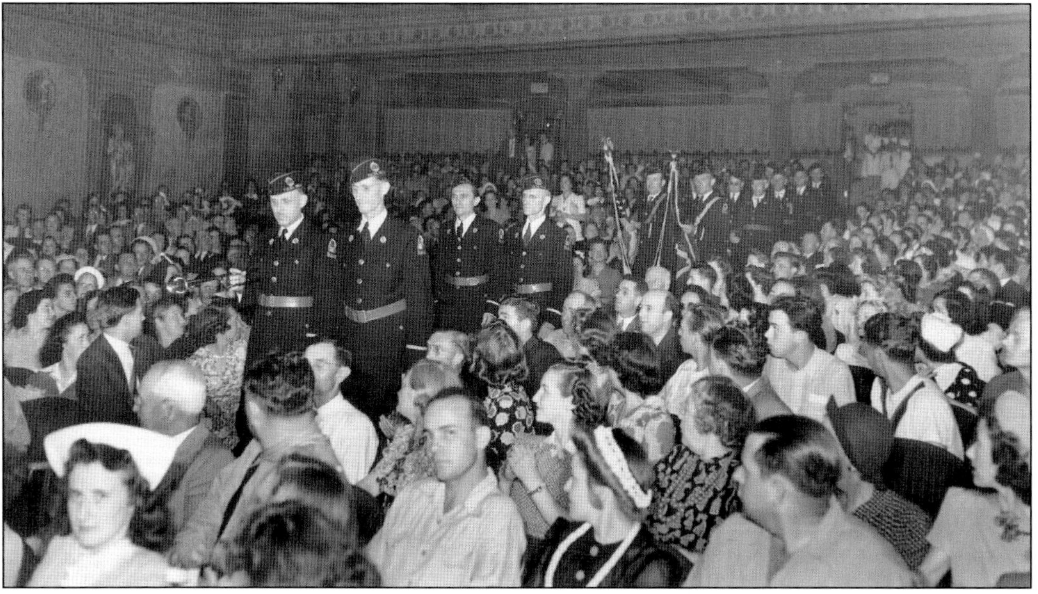

Many different types of events were held at the Ritz because of its large capacity, including town hall meetings and fashion shows. During this event in the early 1940s, the crowd is watching the presentation of colors. (Courtesy Beryl Ford Collection/Rotary Club of Tulsa.)

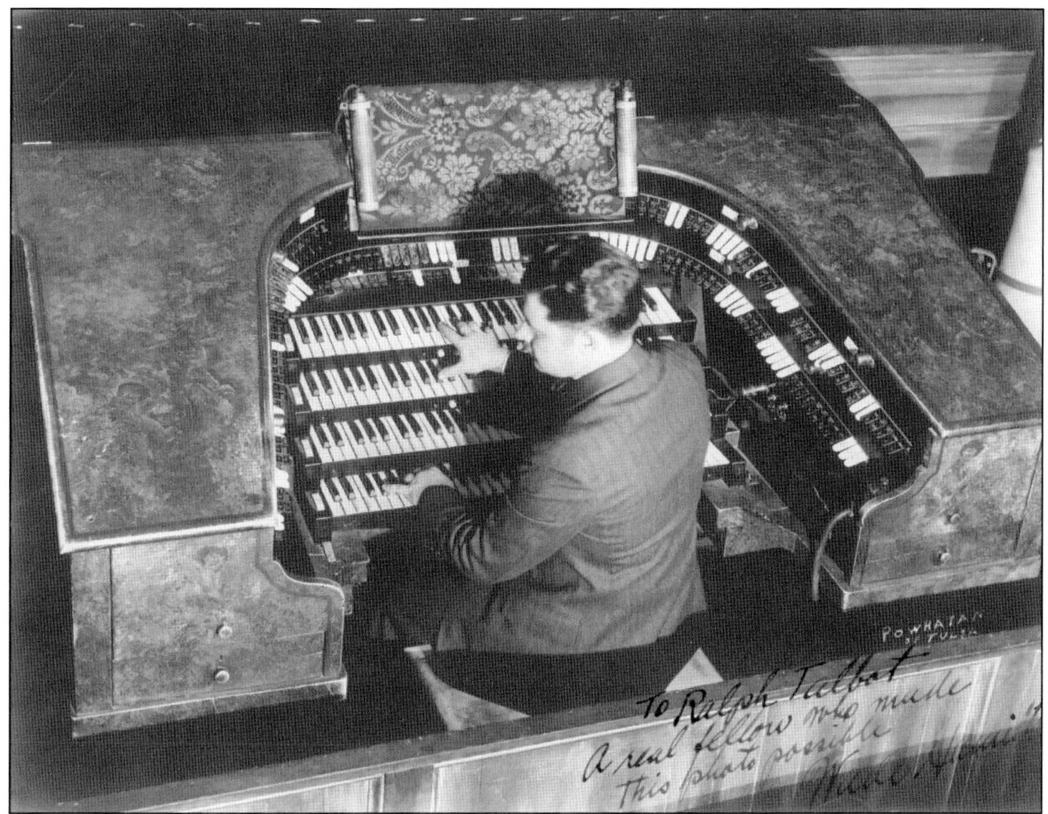

The Ritz organist played a vital role in the theater's unique between-movies entertainment. The music started, and slowly, the organ would rise from the orchestra pit with Milton Slosser or Wade Hamilton (pictured) bathed in a spotlight. The organist played and also led audience sing-alongs with lyrics projected onto the screen. The message on this photograph signed by Hamilton reads, "To Ralph Talbot, a real fellow who made this photo possible."

238 GENERAL ADMISSION

BALCONY

CECIL B. DeMILLE'S
PRODUCTION
"THE TEN COMMANDMENTS"

APRIL 4 1957

THU. 8:00 P.M.

EST. PRICE 1.343
FED. TAX .13
STATE TAX .027
$1.50

RITZ THEATRE
TULSA, OKLA.

Southwest Globe Ticket Co. - Dallas

THU. 8:00 P.M.
APRIL 4 1957
Good Only

BALCONY $1.50

GOOD THIS DATE and TIME ONLY

GENERAL ADMISSION 238

This ticket to see Cecil B. DeMille's *The Ten Commandments* on Thursday, April 4, 1957, at the Ritz would have created a memorable night—and a long one! With a running time of three hours and forty minutes (plus intermission), this showing of the epic Bible story starring Charlton Heston, Yul Brynner, and Anne Baxter would have ended around midnight. (Courtesy of Steve Clem.)

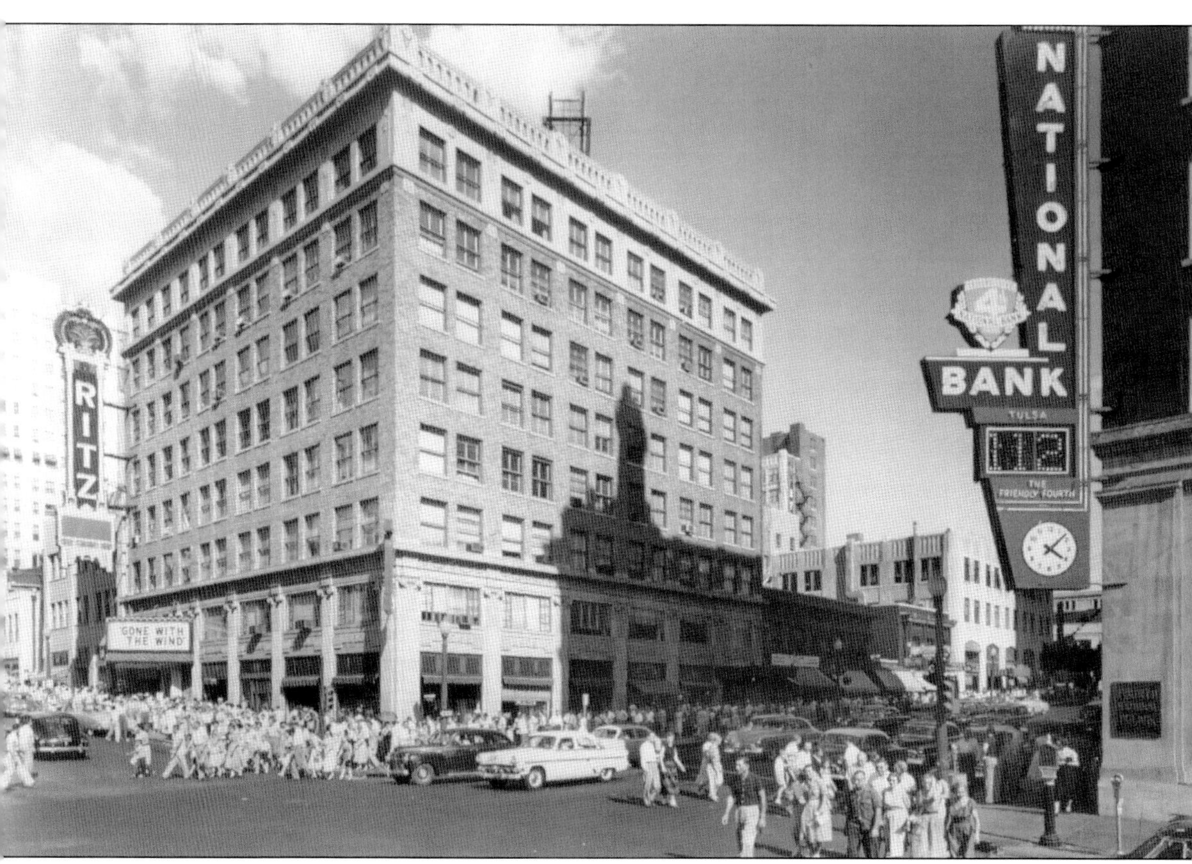

During a 1960 newspaper interview, Ralph Talbot, who owned the Big Four theaters for many years, described his favorite memories. The most exciting was when *Gone with the Wind* was released in 1939. He described the scene: "We had two shows a day with reserved seats only, and the line would stretch from the Ritz box office down Third Street to Boulder Avenue, down Boulder to Fourth, and along Fourth to the Western Union office." It seems that not much changed when the film was rereleased in the mid-1950s—crowds still lined up around the block, as shown in this image. One of the noteworthy details in this photograph is that the Fourth National Bank thermometer in the foreground reads 112 degrees. On this particular day, was the crowd there for the film or the air-conditioning? The image also provides a good view of the entire Ritz Building at Fourth Street and Boulder Avenue.

Three

Other Downtown Movie Houses

Cozy Spots in the City Center

In the mid-20th century, the Big Four downtown theaters were Tulsa's home for first-run pictures. If people wanted to see a movie when it was released, they went to the Majestic, Rialto, Orpheum, or Ritz. However, if one was willing to wait a few weeks and see a film at a discounted price, there were a variety of other downtown movie houses.

The State Theatre, located at 118 South Main Street, originally opened as the Wonderland, one of Tulsa's earliest theaters, in 1911. It later became the Palace, and after a 1935 Art Deco remodel by Tulsa architect Joseph R. Koberling, it reopened as the State.

The Tulsa Theatre, located at 215 South Main Street, had a stylish Streamline design by Dallas-based Corgan & Moore, the architects who also designed the Will Rogers and Pines theaters. The 900-seat Tulsa operated from 1941 to 1970.

In 1930, the Tower Theatre opened near Eleventh Street and Denver Avenue on Tulsa's busy Route 66. It closed in 1955.

The Uptown Theater, located near the corner of Archer and Main Streets, was another early theater that remained open into the 1960s. The Uptown, which had previously been known as the Gayety and Paris theaters, had a smaller 300-seat auditorium.

In the 1960s and 1970s, Tulsa's downtown theaters began to disappear. Many were demolished during that era as part of urban renewal projects. Urban renewal encouraged new development of distressed areas. One of those projects, for the Williams Center Tower (later the BOK Tower), leveled several city blocks, including a few theaters. Tulsa's oldest buildings were lost during that project; some of them had housed the first storefront theaters from the silent-film era.

However, the Williams Center Tower project did actually add one theater. The Williams Center Forum included shops, an ice rink, and a theater—Williams Center Cinema. Remembered for its long mural that featured early movie stars, the theater operated from 1978 to 1995. It showed mainly foreign and specialty films such as *Polyester* and *Chan is Missing*. The premiere of the movie *The Outsiders* was held there in 1983.

When the Williams Center Cinema closed in 1995, it left downtown Tulsa empty of movie theaters.

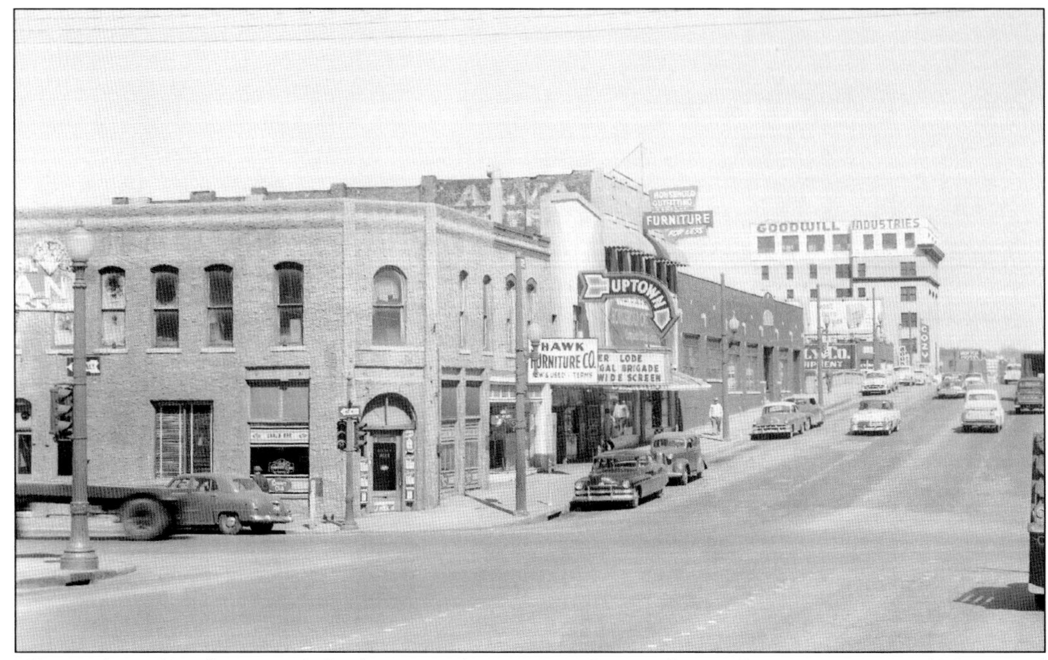

This early-1950s photograph looking north on Main Street shows the intersection of Main and First Streets. The Uptown Theater is visible at 18 South Main Street. The 300-seat theater had a nearly 40-year history, operating at different times as the Paris and Gayety theaters. (Courtesy of Beryl Ford Collection/Rotary Club of Tulsa.)

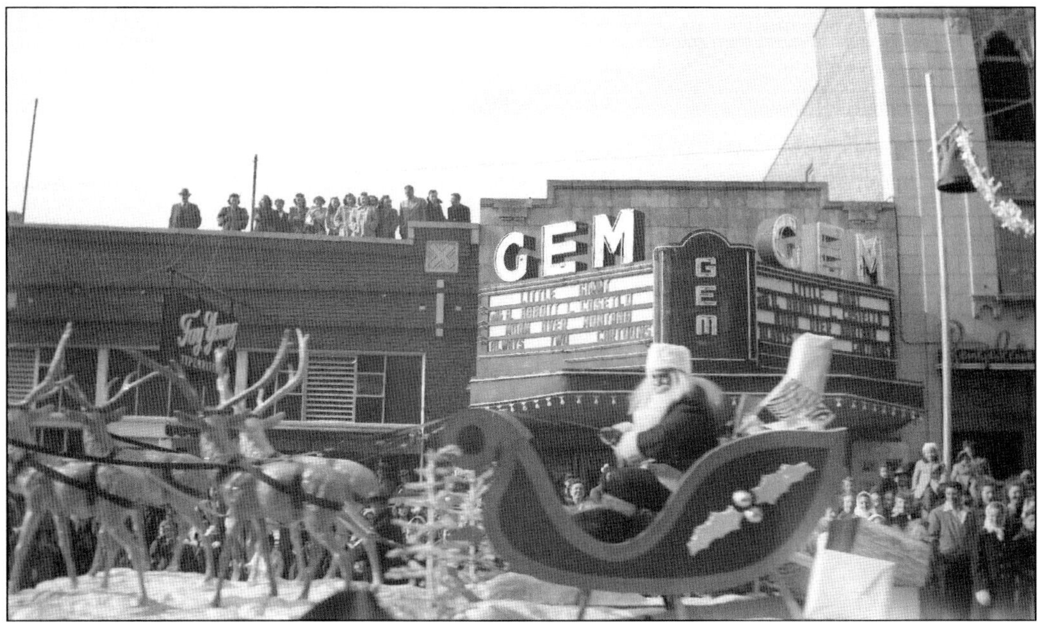

The Gem Theater, located at 618 South Main Street, was just south of the Zigzag Art Deco–style Public Service Company of Oklahoma building. The 411-seat Gem operated from 1934 to 1951 showing second-run movies. This c. 1946 image captures Santa and his sleigh passing by the theater during the annual Tulsa Christmas Parade as a crowd watches from the roof. (Courtesy of Murrel Wilmoth.)

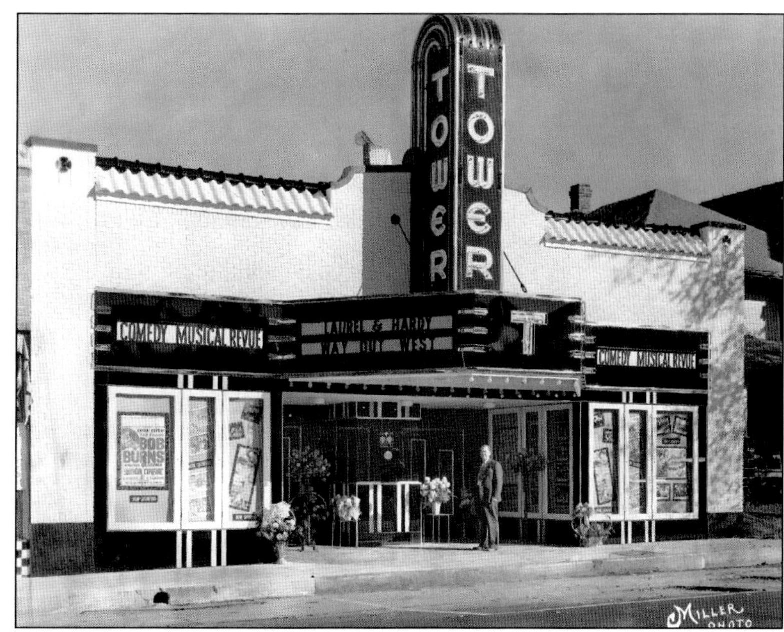

The Tower Theatre had a Deco design created by Southwest movie theater designer W. Scott Dunne. It sat near the corner of Eleventh Street and Denver Avenue. The Tower was one of six theaters motorists encountered while passing through Tulsa on Route 66, a.k.a. America's Main Street. (Courtesy of Oklahoma Historical Society.)

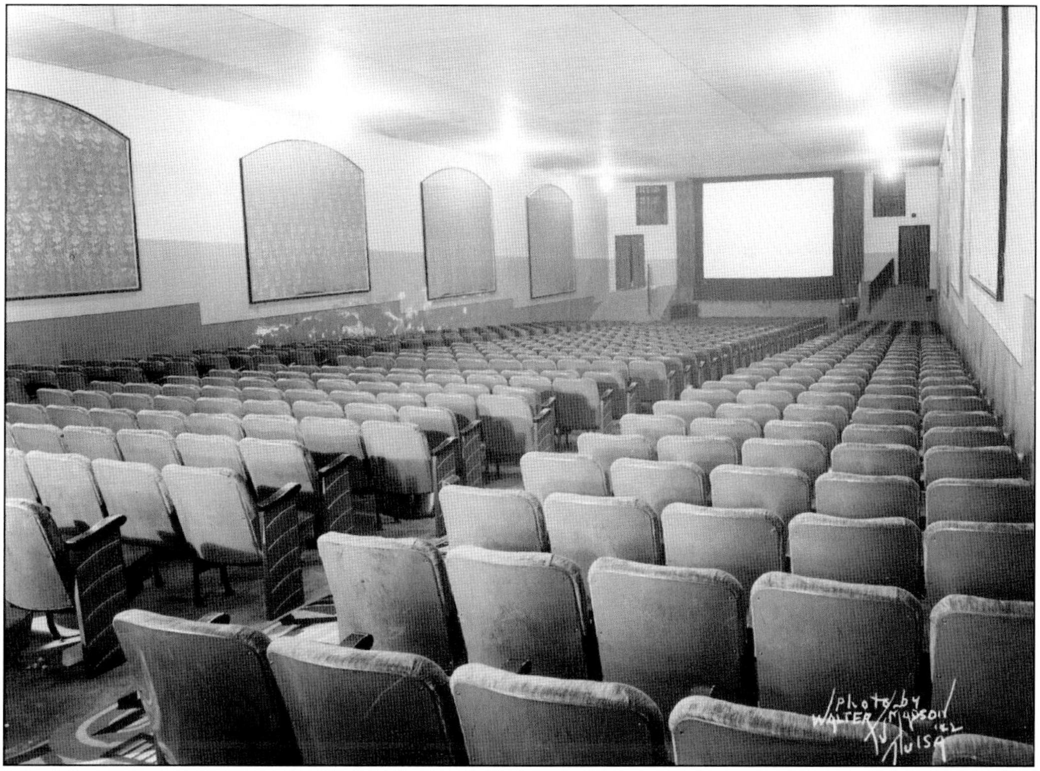

The Tower's auditorium held 600 patrons. After closing in 1955, it became the Fondalite Club, a live performance venue where a young country fiddler named Charlie Daniels, playing with his band the Jaguars, met Hazel Alexander. They got married in Tulsa and were together for over 50 years (until Charlie passed away in June 2020). The building was razed to make way for a parking lot in the 1980s. (Courtesy of Oklahoma Historical Society.)

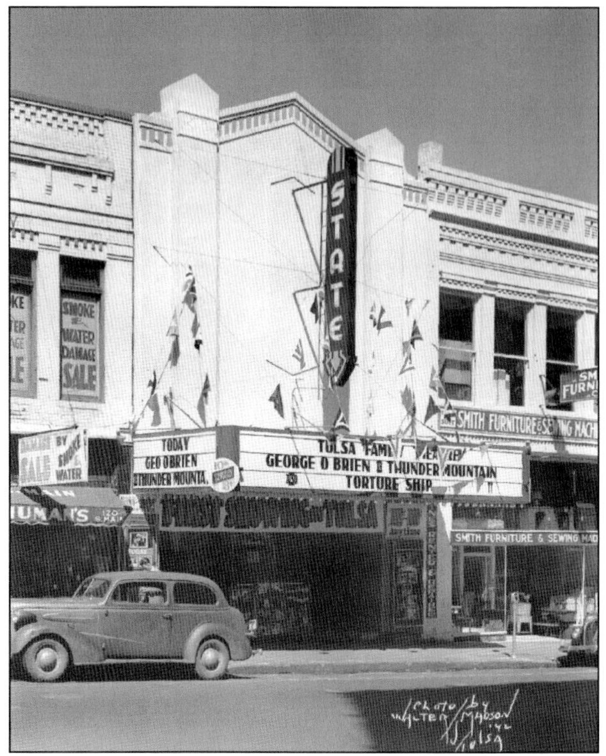

The building at 118 South Main Street was home to many theaters. After opening as the Wonderland nickelodeon in 1911, it later became the Palace Theatre. In 1935, as part of an effort to modernize the oldest part of Tulsa's business district, the theater received an Art Deco remodel designed by Tulsa architect Joseph R. Koberling and reopened as the State Theatre. These 1942 photographs show the interior and exterior of the State. It closed in 1955 and was demolished in 1973. (Both, courtesy of Oklahoma Historical Society.)

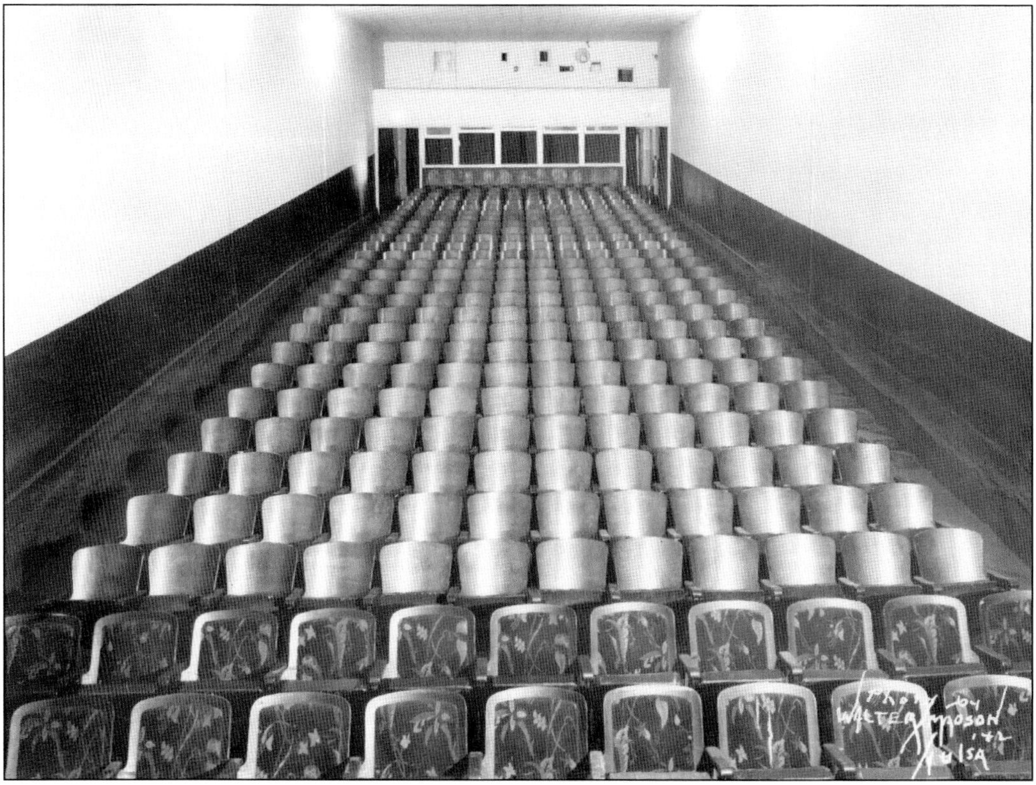

The Tulsa Theatre, located at 215 South Main Street, is pictured around the time it opened in 1941. It had a Streamline Deco design created by Corgan & Moore, who also designed the Will Rogers Theatre. The movie on the marquee is *The Mortal Storm*, a drama starring Margaret Sullavan and James Stewart. (Courtesy of Oklahoma Historical Society.)

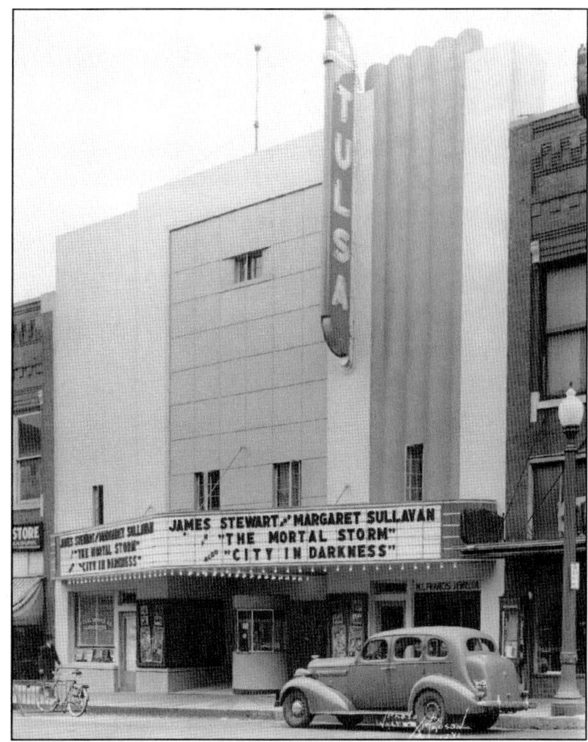

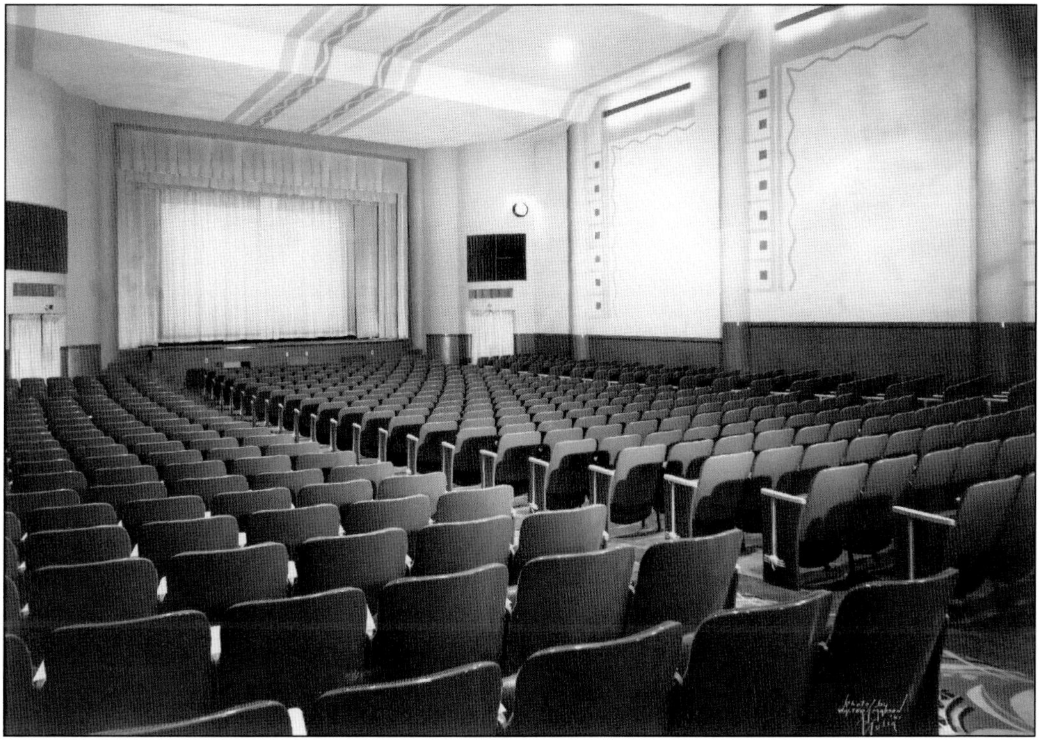

This is a 1942 photograph of the Tulsa Theatre's reverse layout auditorium. The stylish theater seated 1,000 people. (Courtesy of Oklahoma Historical Society.)

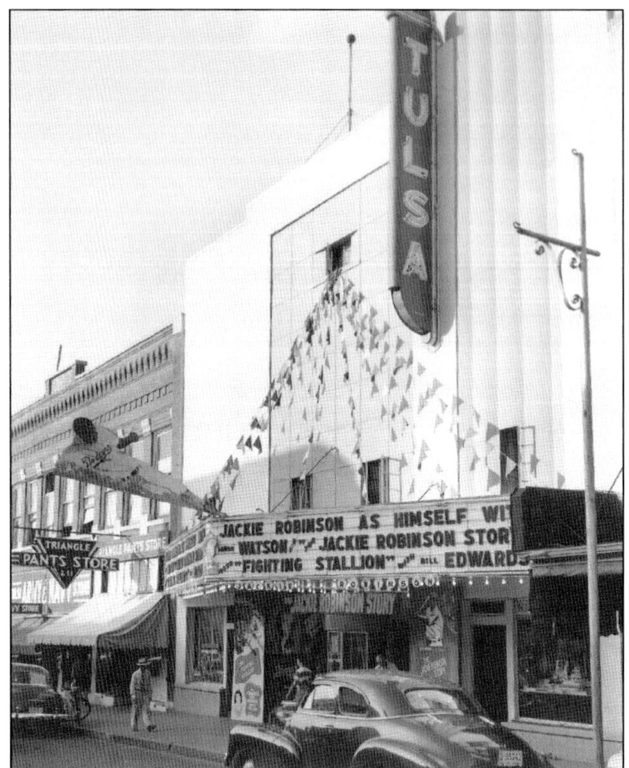

This c. 1950 photograph shows the Tulsa Theatre featuring *The Jackie Robinson Story*, starring Jackie Robinson as himself. The film illustrates Robinson's struggle to overcome bigotry on his way to becoming the first Black player in Major League Baseball. (Courtesy of Oklahoma Historical Society.)

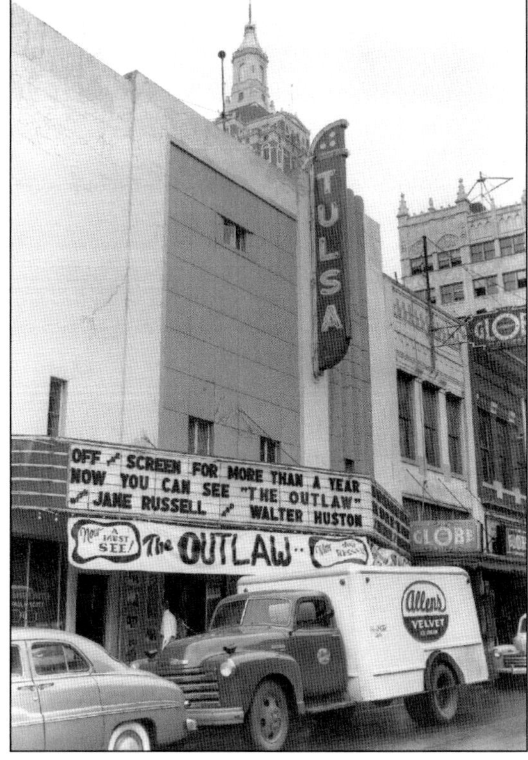

Although the film *The Outlaw*, starring Jane Russell, was ready for release in 1941, it did not appear in theaters until two years later due to censorship problems. After some cuts were made, the film appeared in 1943, but it was withheld from wide release until 1946. Controversy and curiosity made *The Outlaw* a hit at the Tulsa Theatre and other movie houses that exhibited it.

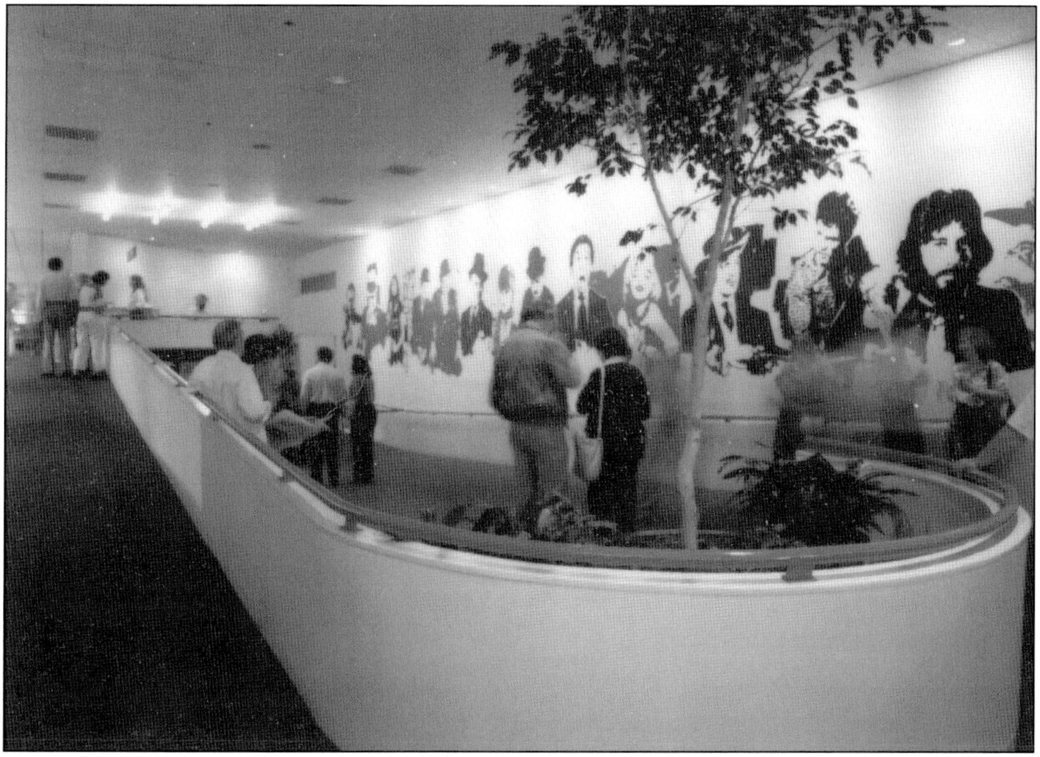

Urban renewal projects in the 1960s and 1970s led to the demolition of many of Tulsa's historic theaters. One project—the Williams Center Tower (later the BOK Tower)—took out several historic theaters, but it also gave one back. When the Williams Center Forum opened, it included retail shops, an ice rink, and a movie theater. The Williams Center Cinema operated from 1978 to 1995. The theater's lobby featured a long mural (above) featuring movie stars past and present. Below, skaters enjoy Tulsa's only indoor ice rink. (Both, courtesy of David Kimball.)

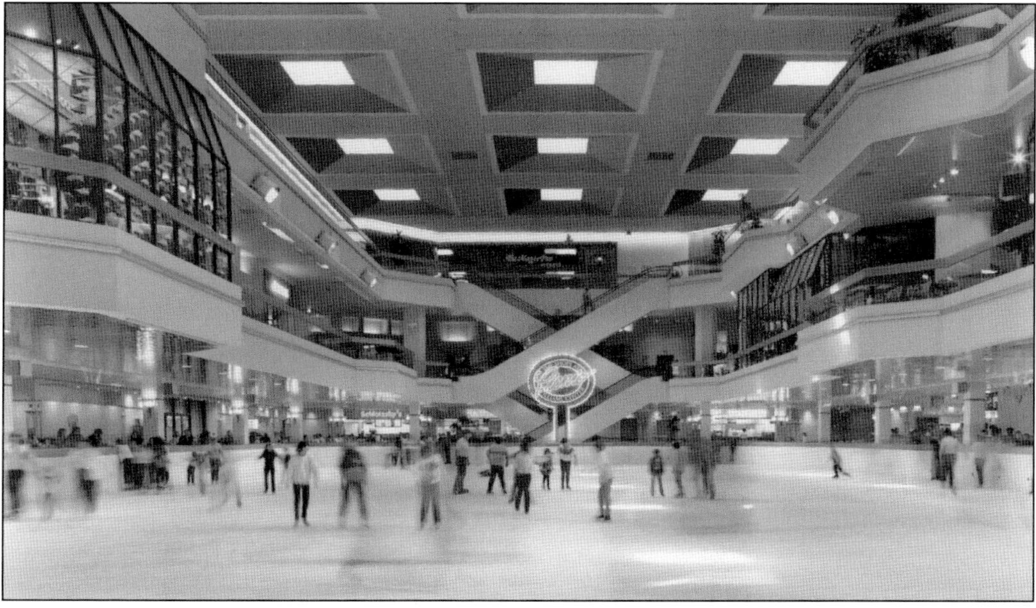

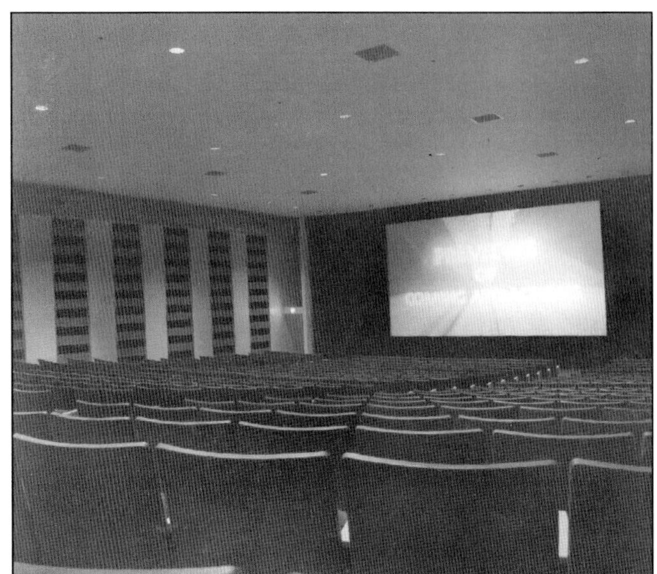

This 1985 photograph shows the inside of the Williams Center Cinema auditorium. Robin Redding, who managed the theater from 1982 to 1984, says one of the theater's biggest films was *Polyester*, starring Divine and Tab Hunter. *Polyester*, directed by John Waters, was released in "Odorama"—moviegoers received a scratch-and-sniff card to activate at different points in the film. Redding said another popular film was Francis Ford Coppola's *One from the Heart*, which screened when Coppola was in Tulsa filming *The Outsiders* and *Rumble Fish*. (Courtesy of David Kimball.)

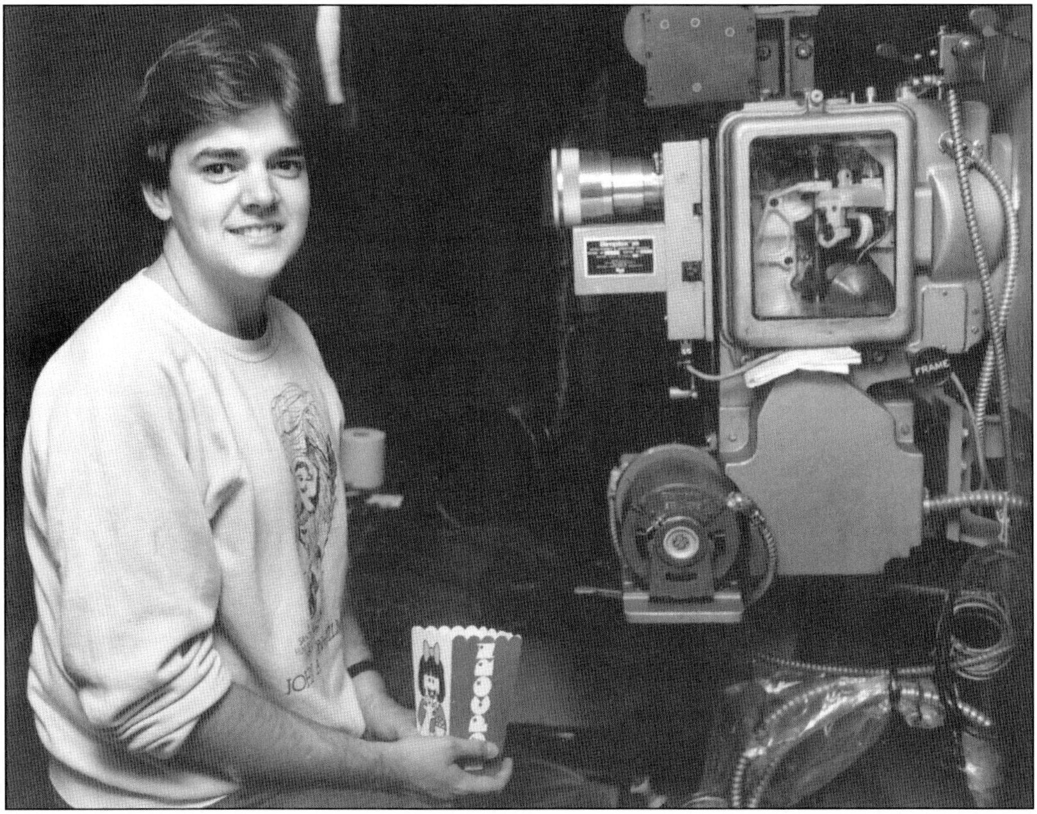

David Kimball became theater manager at Williams Center Cinema in 1984. Kimball is shown in the projection booth the following year. He later became involved in Tulsa's Circle Cinema, a theater with a similar mission as an independent art movie house. Williams Center Cinema also had the distinction of being the first theater in Tulsa to offer beer and wine at its concession stand. (Courtesy of David Kimball.)

Four

Neighborhood Cinema

Away from Downtown and Closer to Home

As Tulsa grew beyond downtown, new residential districts birthed neighborhood theaters, and movie houses appeared in the surrounding communities. These palaces had one large screen, ample auditoriums, and architectural individuality.

The first theater outside of downtown was the Alhambra, located at 1447 South Peoria Avenue. It opened in 1924 and became the Plaza in 1930. It briefly operated as the Premiere before being razed for a parking lot in 1961—this was a common fate for Tulsa theaters.

In 1928, the Circle Theatre opened as part of the city's first suburban shopping district, Kendall-Whittier. Reborn as Circle Cinema in 2004, it is Tulsa's only remaining historic theater. The marquee has been returned to its 1950s splendor.

Many neighborhood theaters were designed using a Streamline Art Deco style. The Delman opened in 1938 at Fifteenth Street and Lewis Avenue and is where local moviegoers first encountered Cruella de Vil in Disney's *101 Dalmatians* and Sean Connery as 007. Many remember the Deco Moderne–style Brook Theatre for *The Sound of Music*, which ran for over a year in 1965. The Pines, on Tulsa's north side, also utilized a Streamline style.

The Will Rogers Theatre, located on Eleventh Street near Yale Avenue, is another Streamline masterwork; it featured a marquee surrounding a giant cylindrical tower. The theater became a favorite of many Tulsans with its Western motif and oil painting of native son Will Rogers with a lasso. This is the theater where neighborhood kid Gailard Sartain dreamed his wide-screen dreams with his bicycle parked out front.

Many other theaters opened and were frequented by those living in the areas outside of downtown. In Tulsa's Greenwood neighborhood, the Williams Dreamland Theatre and Dixie Theatre both reopened after being destroyed in the 1921 Tulsa Race Massacre. They were later joined by others, including the Rex and the Regal.

Westsiders frequently reminisce on social media about theaters in their neighborhoods, including the Cameo, located near the entrance to Mid-Continent Refinery; the Red Fork; and the Rita.

Slightly farther afield, small-town theaters brought movies to residents without them having to go into Tulsa. These included Broken Arrow's Nushow and Arrow, the Star and Harmony in Sand Springs, the Ritz in Jenks, Bixby's Nushow, Sapulpa's Yale and Criterion, the Grotto in Turley, and the Mars in Dawson.

There were also shorter-lived theaters such as the Cove in Red Fork, north Tulsa's Peoria Theater, and the Royal on East Eleventh Street. Although they were only around for a few years, they are beloved by those who experienced cinematic magic within their walls.

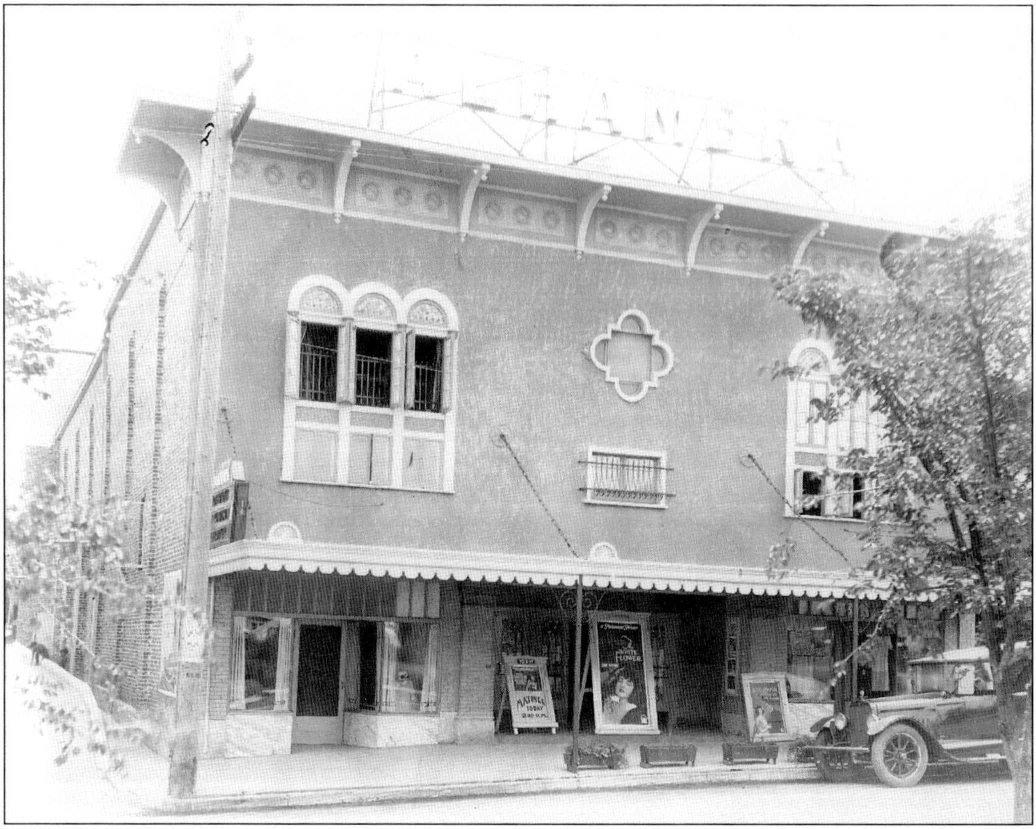

The publicity of the time said there was a new theater coming on Tulsa's south side before the Alhambra, facing west and located at 1447 South Peoria Avenue, opened in 1924. Part of the Alhambra Square complex on the northeast corner of Fifteenth Street and Peoria Avenue, the theater was designed by German-born architect O. "Otto" Kubatzky. This 700-seat theater had a Kimball organ to accompany its second-run silent films. Pictured below is the inside of Alhambra's auditorium. Like most movie houses of the silent era, it also had a stage for live performances.

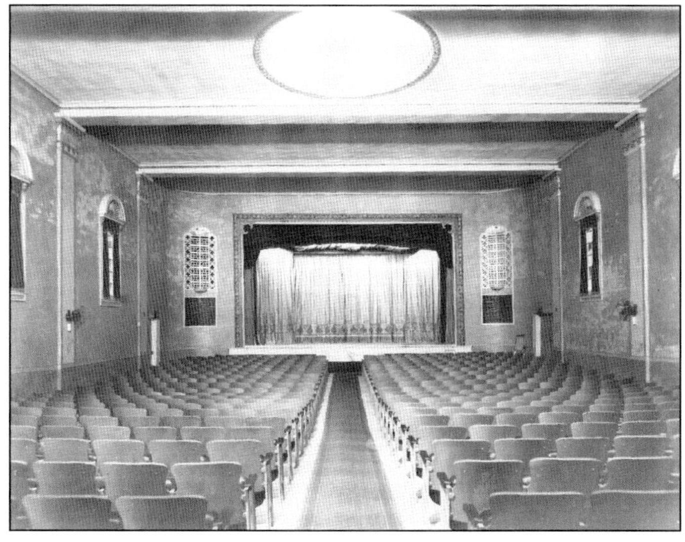

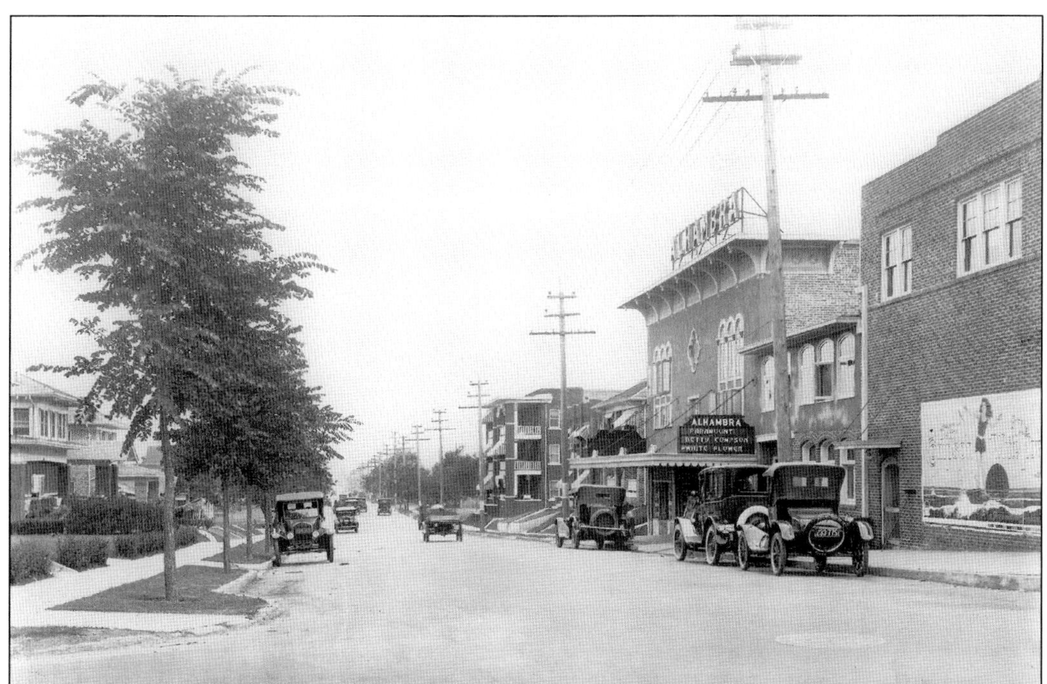

This 1920s street scene looks north on Peoria Avenue from Fifteenth Street. The Alhambra is on the right in the middle of the block. Nearly a century later, the building at far right houses the Palace Café at the west end of Cherry Street.

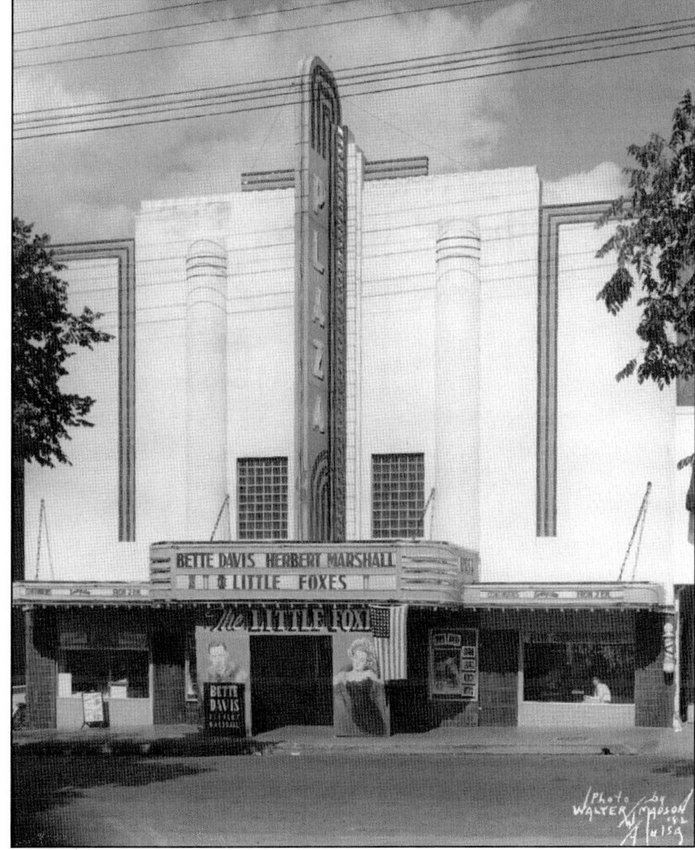

The Alhambra closed at the end of the 1920s. After a remodel to accommodate sound films, the theater reopened as the Plaza. A spectacular blaze destroyed the Plaza in 1939, and it was rebuilt. This photograph shows the new Plaza in 1942. (Courtesy of Oklahoma Historical Society.)

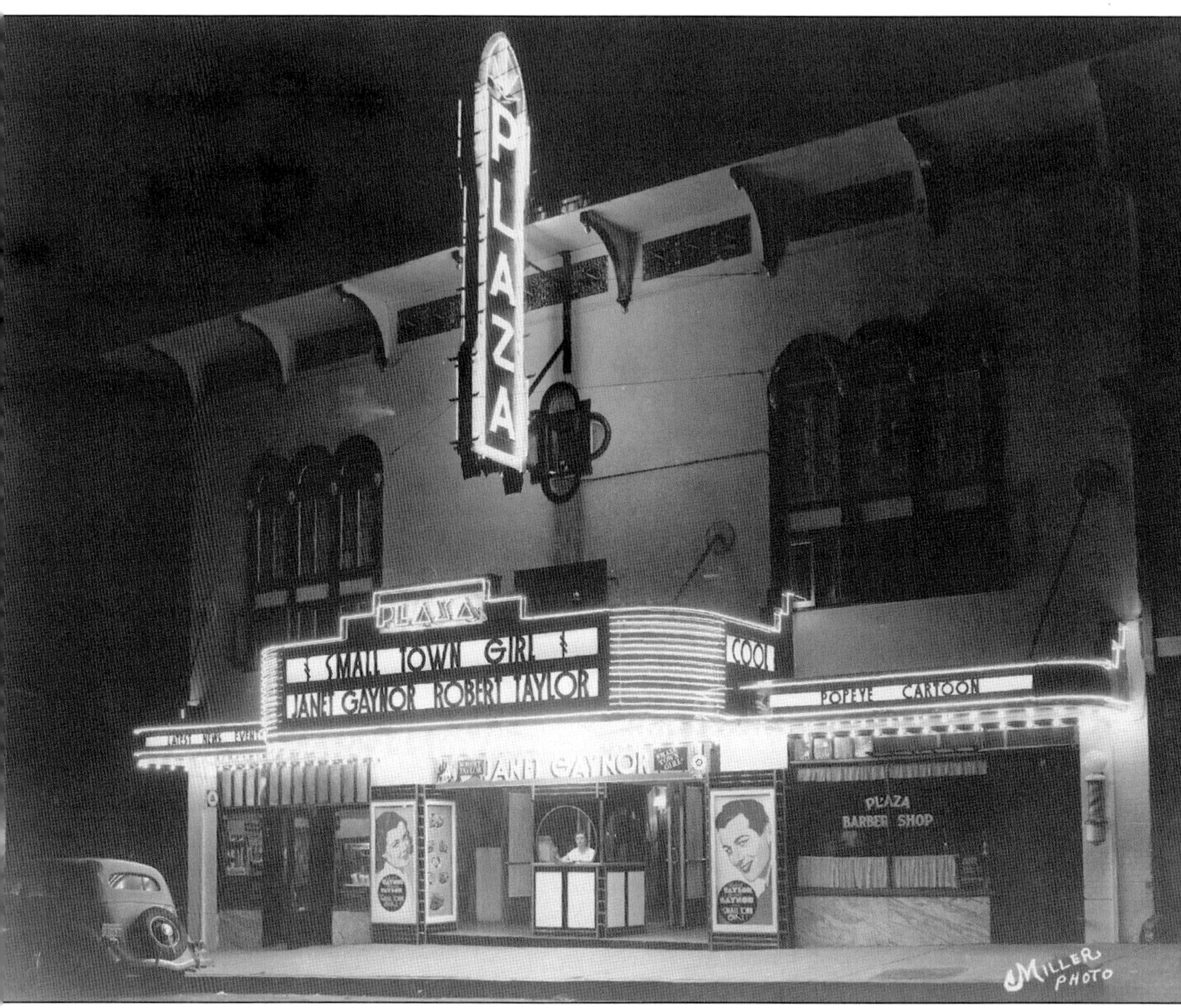

This nighttime photograph of the Plaza as it appeared in the late 1930s shows the theater's beautiful exterior, neon sign, and marquee. The film *Small Town Girl*, starring Janet Gaynor and Robert Taylor, was released in 1936. After closing as the Plaza, the theater briefly reopened as the Premiere in 1960 and specialized in roadshow releases. However, a November 1961 newspaper article announced that the theater would soon be razed for parking for Alhambra Appliances.

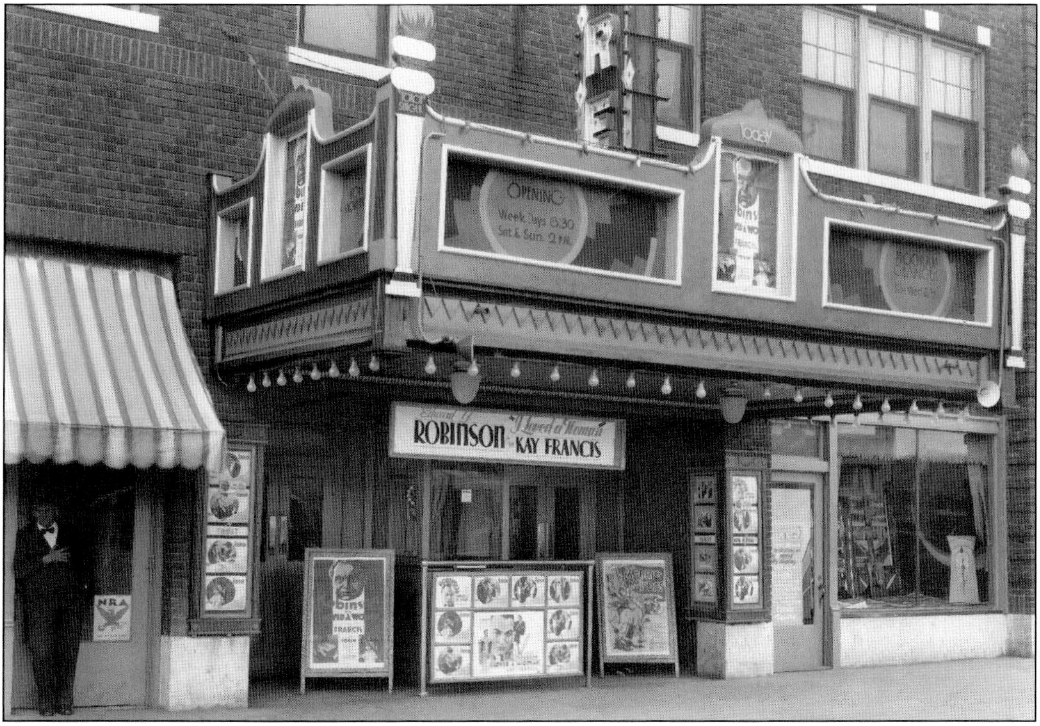

The Circle is Tulsa's only remaining historic indoor movie theater. It opened as the Circle Theatre in 1928 in the city's first suburban shopping district, Whittier Square, located at Admiral Place and South Lewis Avenue. The construction costs—$62,000—did not include the price of the Robert Morton pipe organ, which was sold to the Tulsa Scottish Rite in 1931 when the theater ceased showing silent films. (Courtesy of Oklahoma Historical Society.)

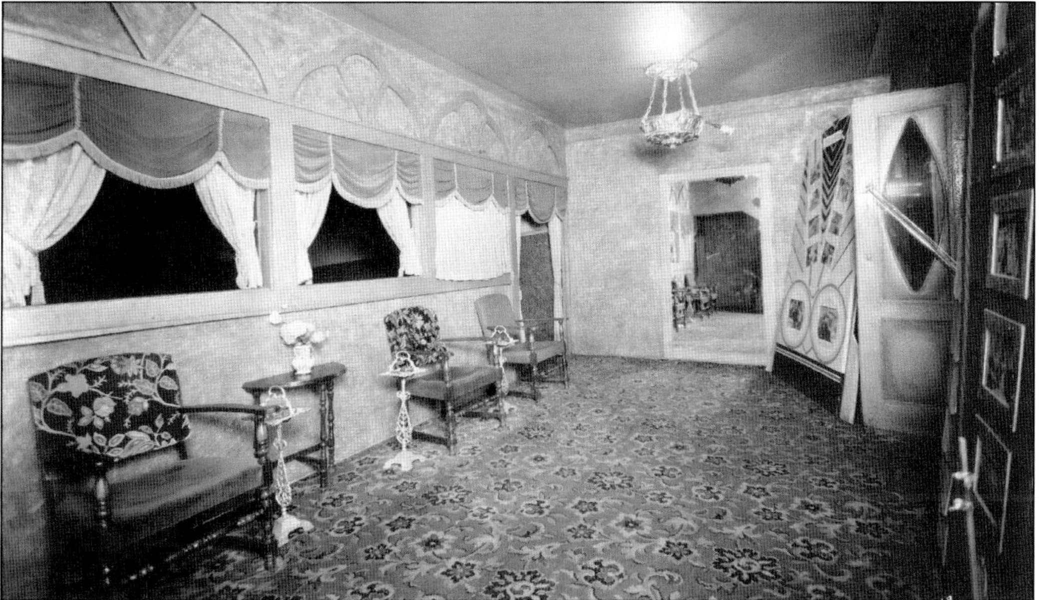

This is an interior hallway of the Circle as it appeared in 1934. The theater's lobby area was expanded into the storefront to the south in 1957. (Courtesy of Oklahoma Historical Society.)

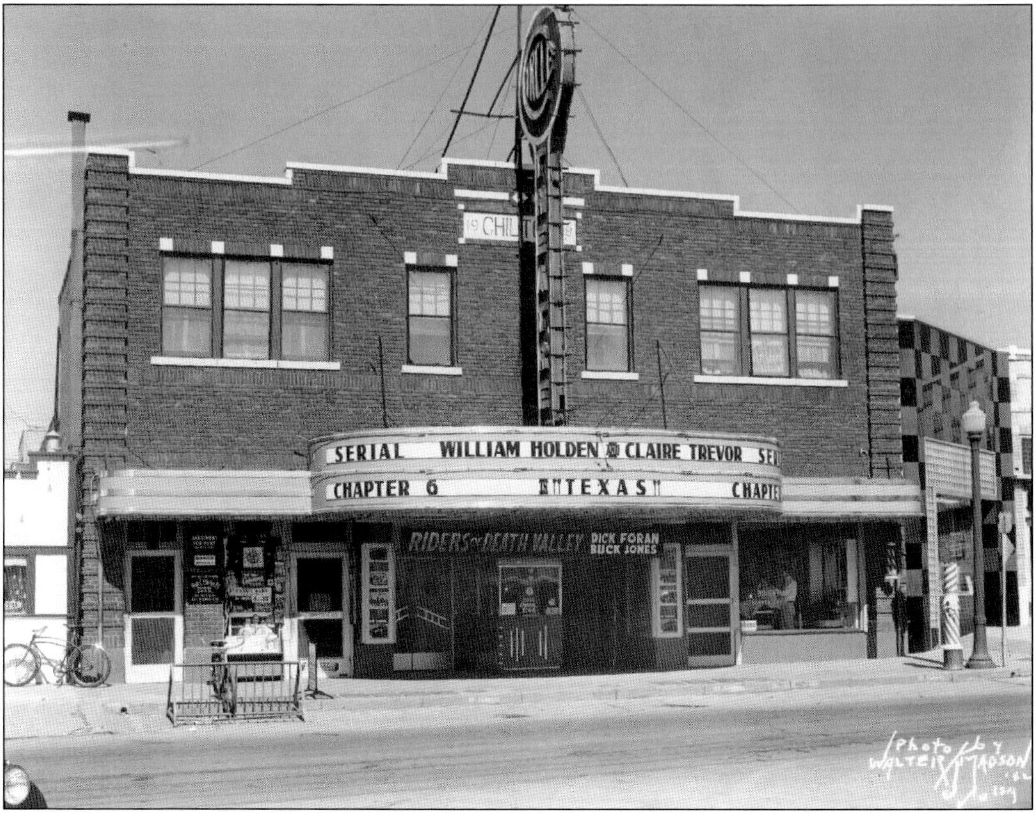

These photographs show the Circle in 1942. The movie on the marquee is *Texas*, a 1941 Western starring William Holden and Glenn Ford. As a second-run movie house, the Circle would often exhibit movies that were released the previous year. The sign was replaced in the 1950s with the one moviegoers are familiar with today. Below, the Circle's stylish auditorium is shown. (Both, courtesy of Oklahoma Historical Society.)

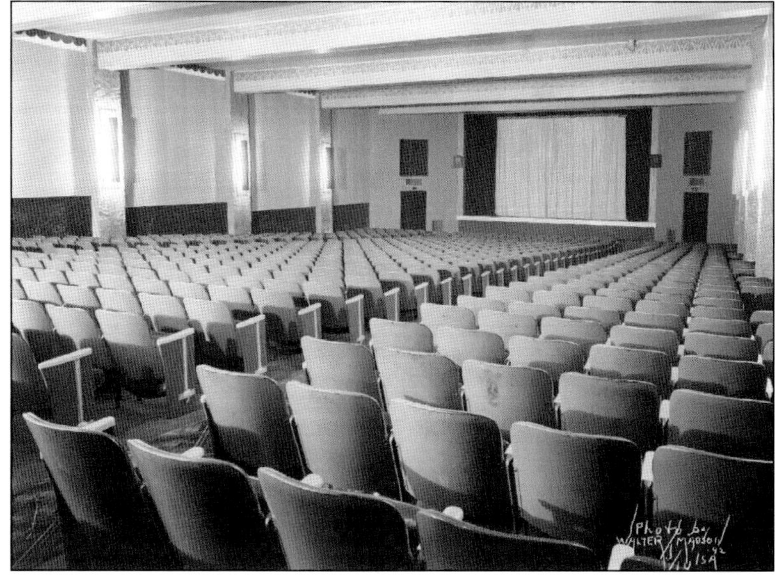

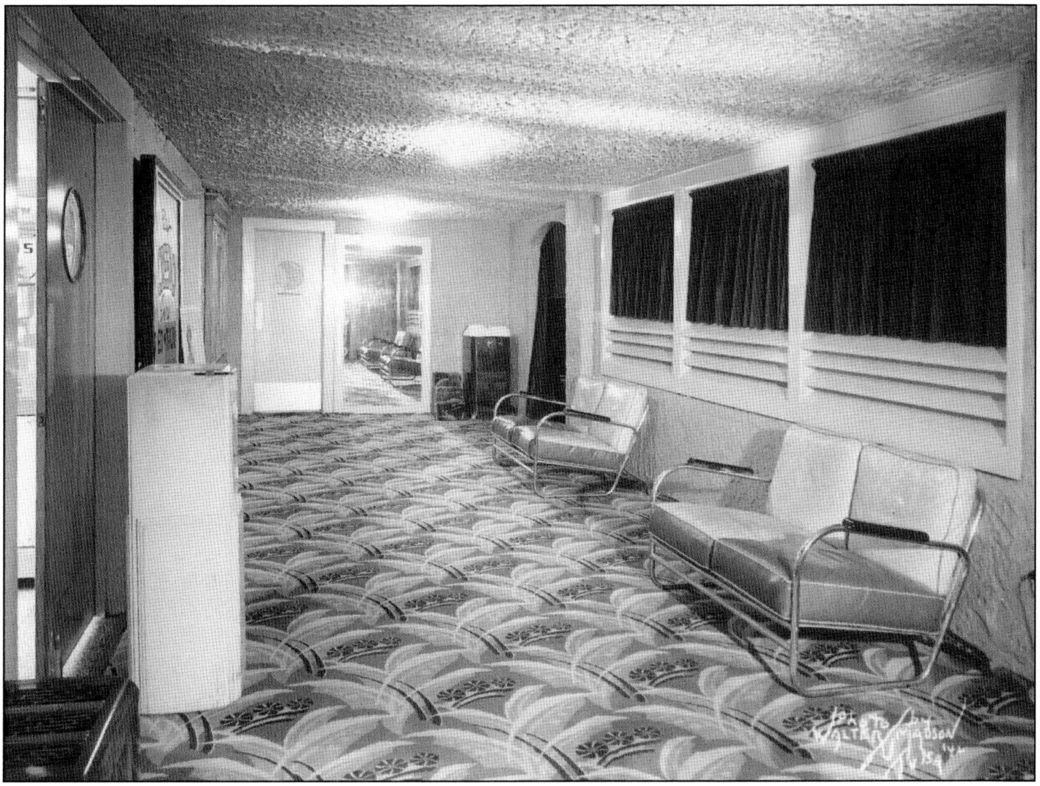

This is a view of the Circle's lobby in 1942. After many ups and downs for the theater through the decades, in 2002, the Circle Cinema Foundation began a complete transformation of the inside space, retaining the historic 1950s neon sign and marquee. The theater reopened in 2004 as Circle Cinema, Tulsa's only nonprofit independent movie house. Featuring three new auditoriums, a screening room, and a gallery, Circle Cinema is home to the Circle Theatre's original 1928 pipe organ, which was purchased by the foundation in 2004. Below is the theater's historic Simplex 35-mm movie projector, which is now displayed in the lobby. (Above, courtesy of Oklahoma Historical Society.)

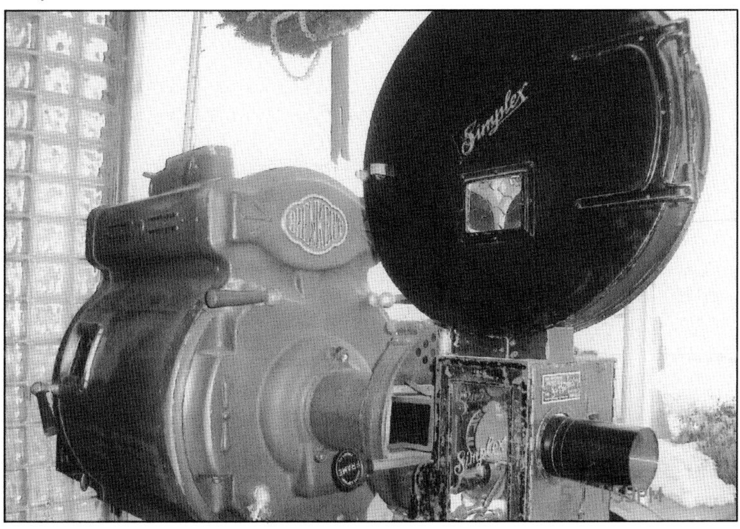

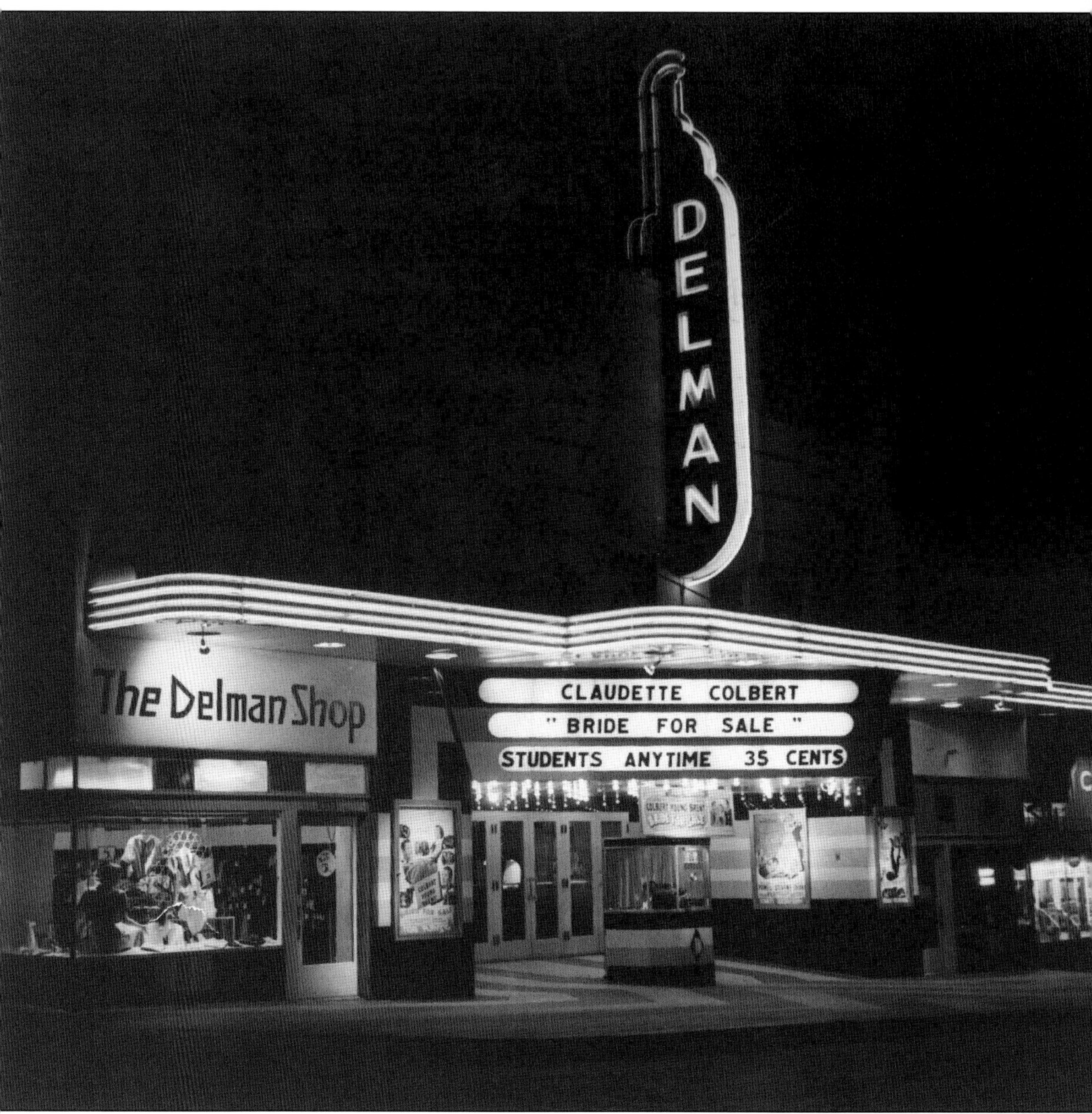

The Delman Theatre's beautiful Streamline Deco lines are accentuated in this nighttime photograph taken around 1950. The Delman, located on the northeast corner of East Fifteenth Street and South Lewis Avenue, opened in 1938. It was one of a series of Delman theaters—the others were in Houston, Dallas, and Fort Worth—built by California-based developer Isodore Adelman. He came up with the name for his movie houses by dropping the first letter of his surname. The architect, W. Scott Dunne, is known for designing more than 25 movie theaters in Texas and Oklahoma. *Bride For Sale*, a comedy starring Claudette Colbert and Robert Young, was released in late 1949. The Delman Shop (at left) and Crown Drug (at right) are also visible.

With a seating capacity of 1,186, the Delman was one of Tulsa's biggest theaters. Due to their ability to hold large crowds, theaters were important venues for getting the word out about various World War II efforts. This 1943 photograph shows a truck decorated for a parade. It has a sign that reads, "The boys at the front need your help! Turn in your salvage."

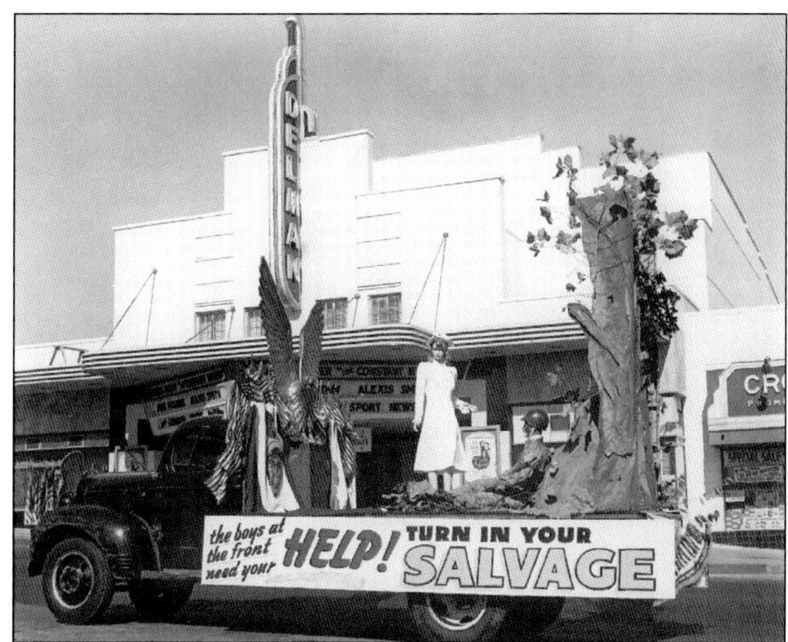

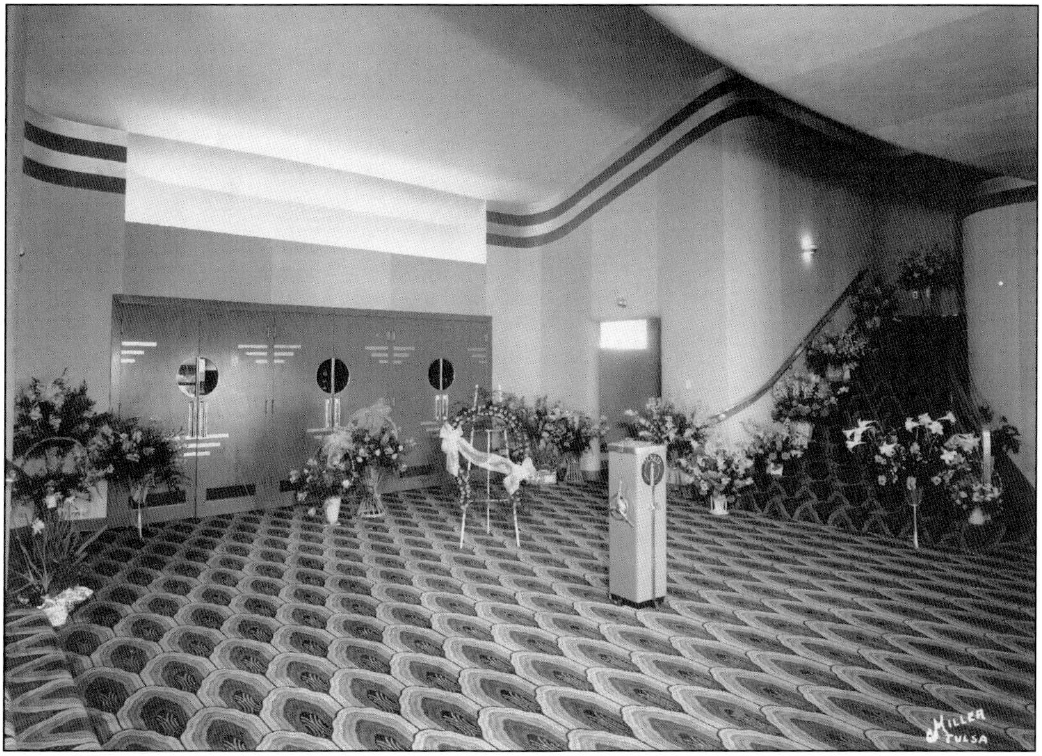

In this image, the interior of the Delman is decorated for an unknown event. The curved staircase to the balcony is visible at right. In the 1960s, the Delman was where many saw Disney films, including *101 Dalmatians* and *Jungle Book*, and the 007 films starring Sean Connery as James Bond. One moviegoer recalls seeing Alfred Hitchcock's *The Birds* at the Delman, where live parakeets were released inside the theater to heighten the effect. (Courtesy of Oklahoma Historical Society.)

Starts December 4th

DELMAN THEATER

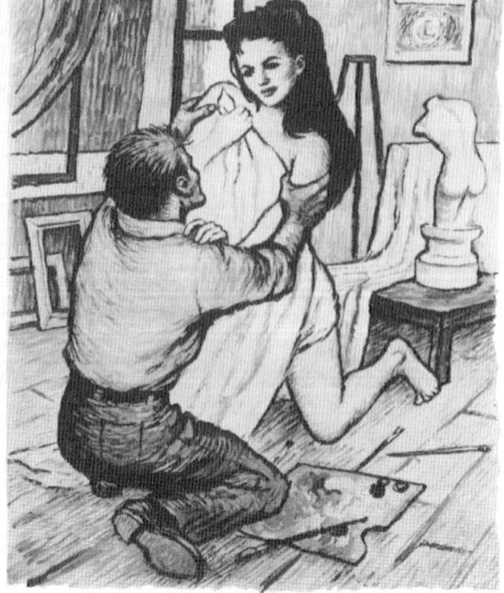

IT MAY SHOCK YOU!
BUT IT WILL THRILL YOU!

"LUST FOR LIFE"

Here is a poster for the MGM film *Lust For Life*, a biographical film about the life of tortured Dutch painter Vincent van Gogh, starring Kirk Douglas. It opened at the Delman on December 4, 1956. The film was nominated for several Oscars, including Best Adapted Screenplay and nominations for Kirk Douglas and Anthony Quinn. Quinn won the Oscar for Best Supporting Actor for his portrayal of French Post-Impressionist artist Paul Gauguin.

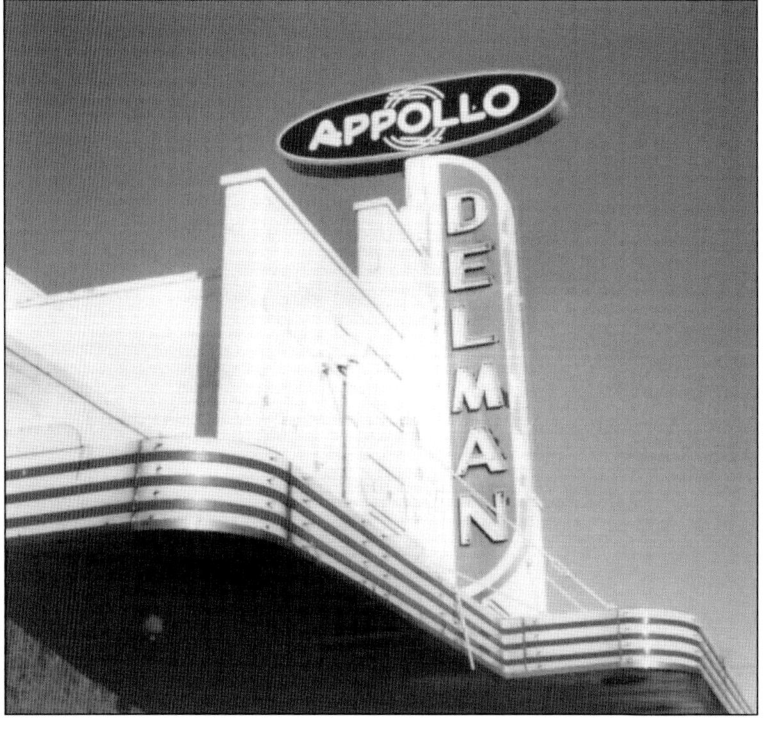

By the 1970s, the Delman was operating as Loew's Delman, joining the California-based Loew's chain. After closing as a movie house, it briefly became a live performance venue, the Appollo Delman, in 1979. National recording artists Chuck Berry and Harry Chapin performed there, as did local musicians Leon Russell and Gus Hardin. The theater closed for good in 1980 and was demolished in January 1989. (Courtesy of Gary Reynolds.)

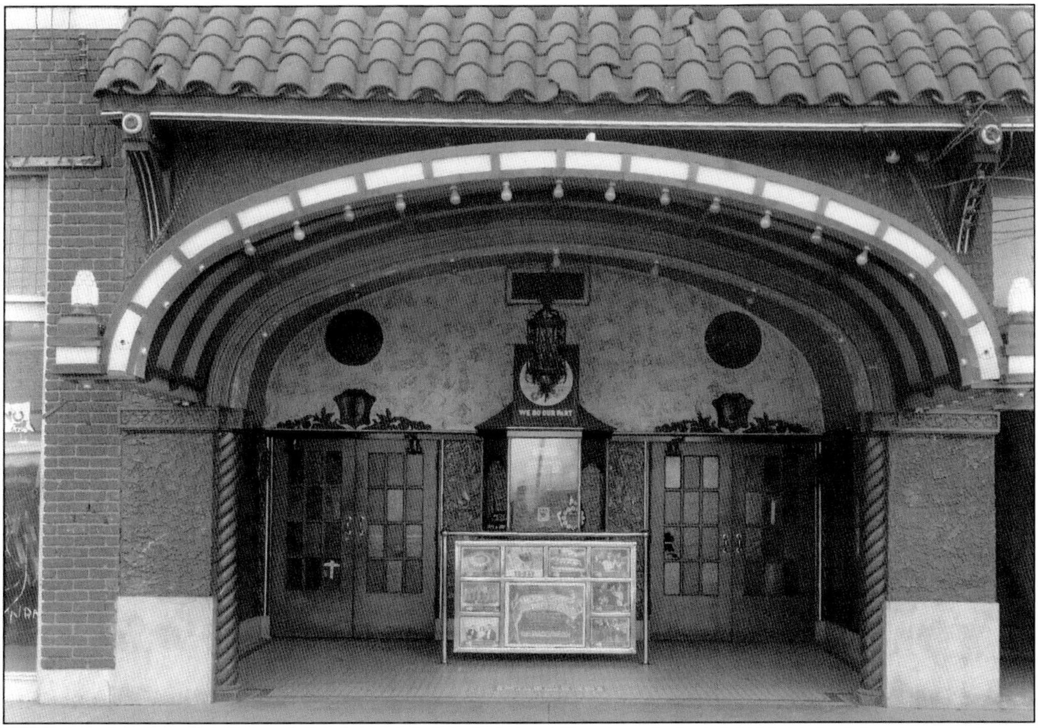

The Cameo theater opened in 1927 at 1315 West Seventeenth Street. Located in west Tulsa, near the entrance to the Mid-Continent Refinery, this Spanish Mission–style movie house featured a reverse layout. Ticket-holders entered the auditorium on either side of the screen. The Cameo is fondly remembered for its Saturday serials and Westerns with Popeye cartoons, and it held lots of promotions, including free carnival glass with admission and, on Friday nights, a giveaway of $50 in groceries. After the Cameo closed in 1955, this location later became a vacant lot near the exit ramp of Interstate 244/US Route 75 at the West Seventeenth Street exit. The Cameo's 370-seat auditorium is shown below. (Both, courtesy of Oklahoma Historical Society.)

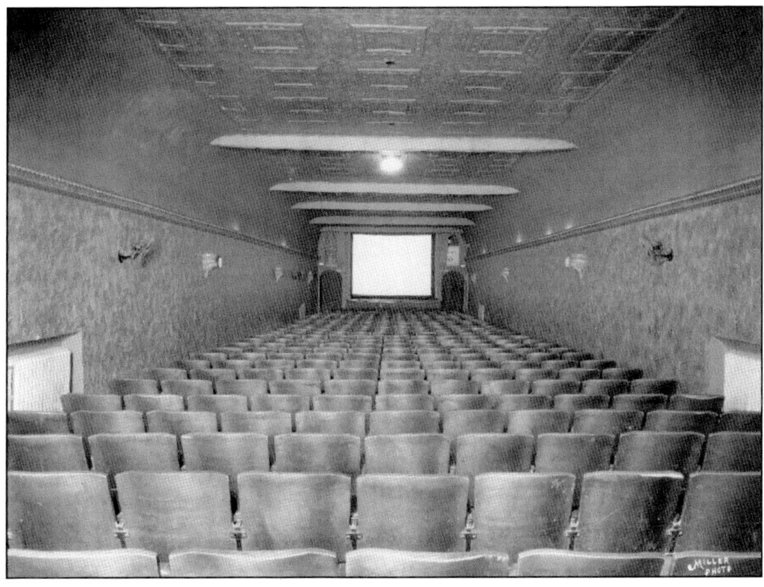

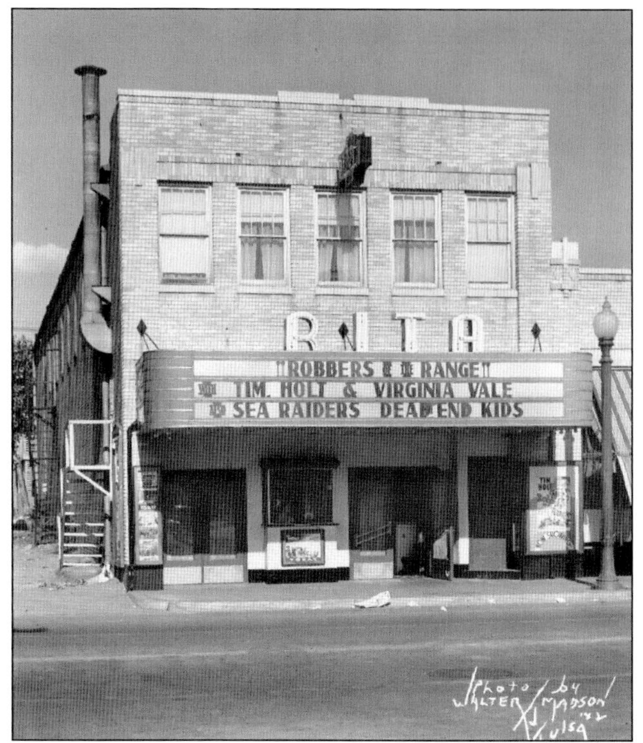

The Rita was a small theater located at 1713 South Quanah Avenue on Tulsa's west side. It had a seating capacity of 318. Playing at the Rita in 1942 was the latest installment of a 12-chapter serial from 1941 called *Sea Raiders*, starring the Dead End Kids and Little Tough Guys. The Rita closed in 1950. (Both, courtesy of Oklahoma Historical Society.)

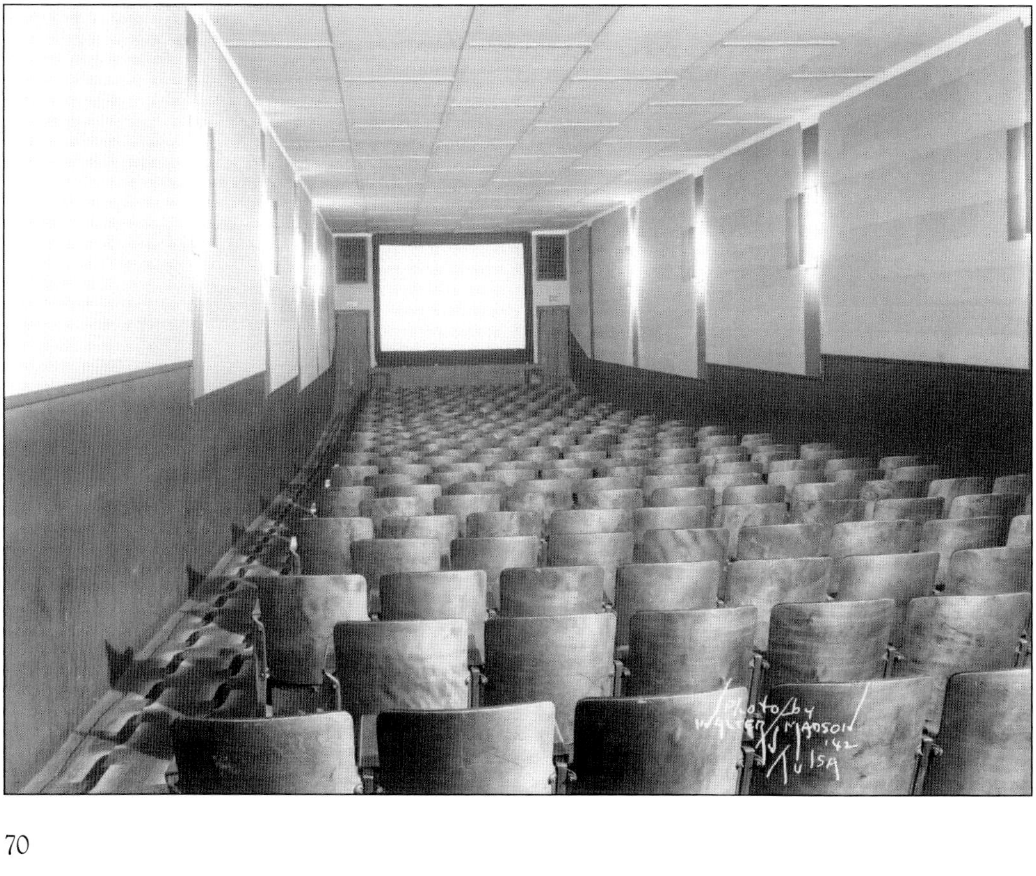

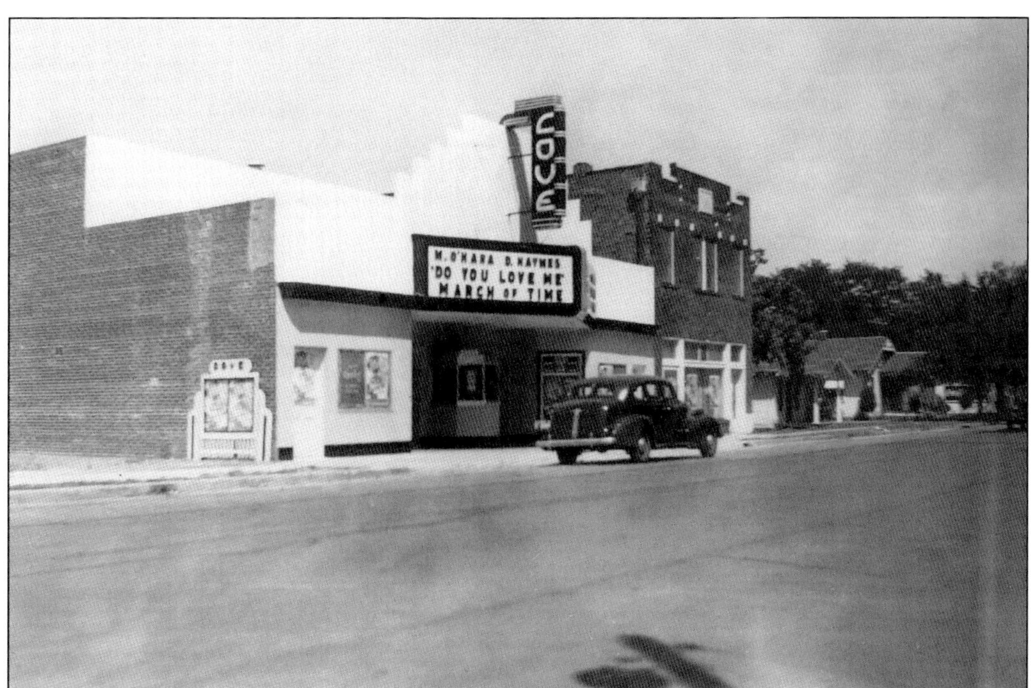

The Cove opened at 2321 West Forty-first Street in Red Fork on August 19, 1946. Although it was only open for a decade, the theater is affectionately remembered by Tulsa westsiders for its films and special crying room where patrons could take their young children and still watch the movie. The Cove received negative publicity surrounding labor violations and damage to the structure by juvenile delinquents in 1954. Despite a new owner and remodeling to include a larger screen, the Cove closed in 1956. The building was later demolished. At right is the Cove lit up at night. (Both, courtesy of Murrel Wilmoth.)

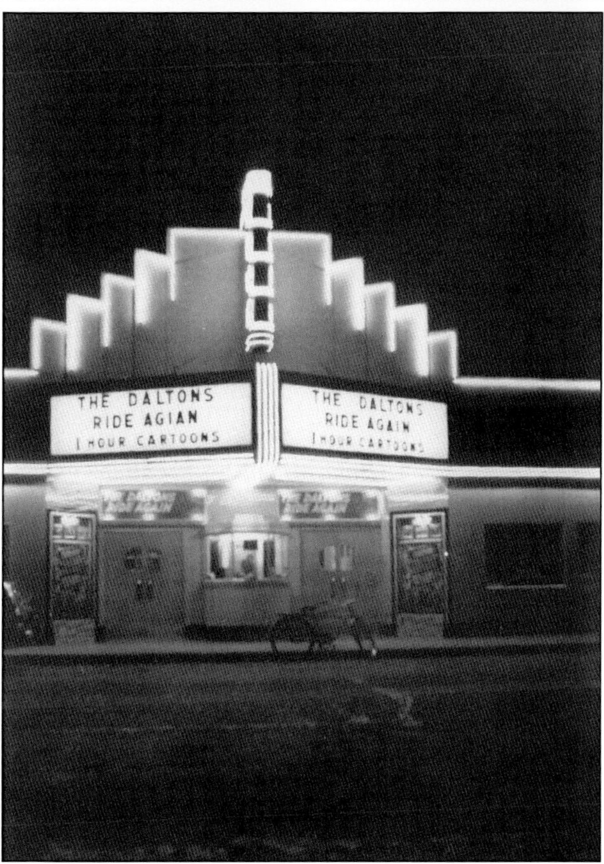

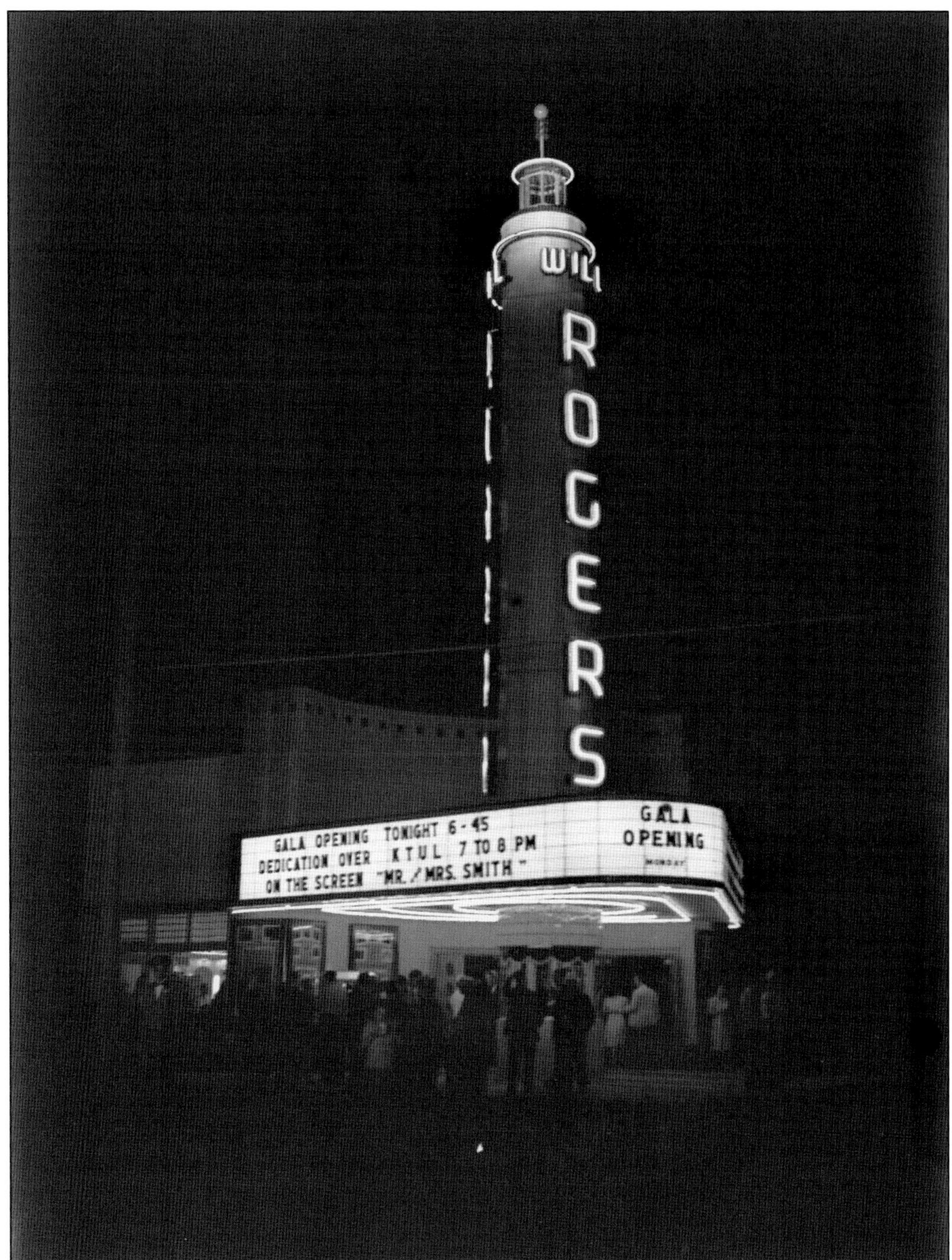

Opening in 1941 at 4500 East Eleventh Street, the Will Rogers Theatre was a Streamline Deco structure with a marquee-wrapped tower. It was designed by famed theater architects Corgan & Moore of Dallas; that company also later designed the Will Rogers Theatre in Oklahoma City. This photograph is from the theater's gala opening-night ceremony, a portion of which was broadcast live over KTUL 1430 AM radio. The first film shown was *Mr. and Mrs. Smith*, the hit romantic comedy directed by Alfred Hitchcock and starring Carole Lombard and Robert Montgomery.

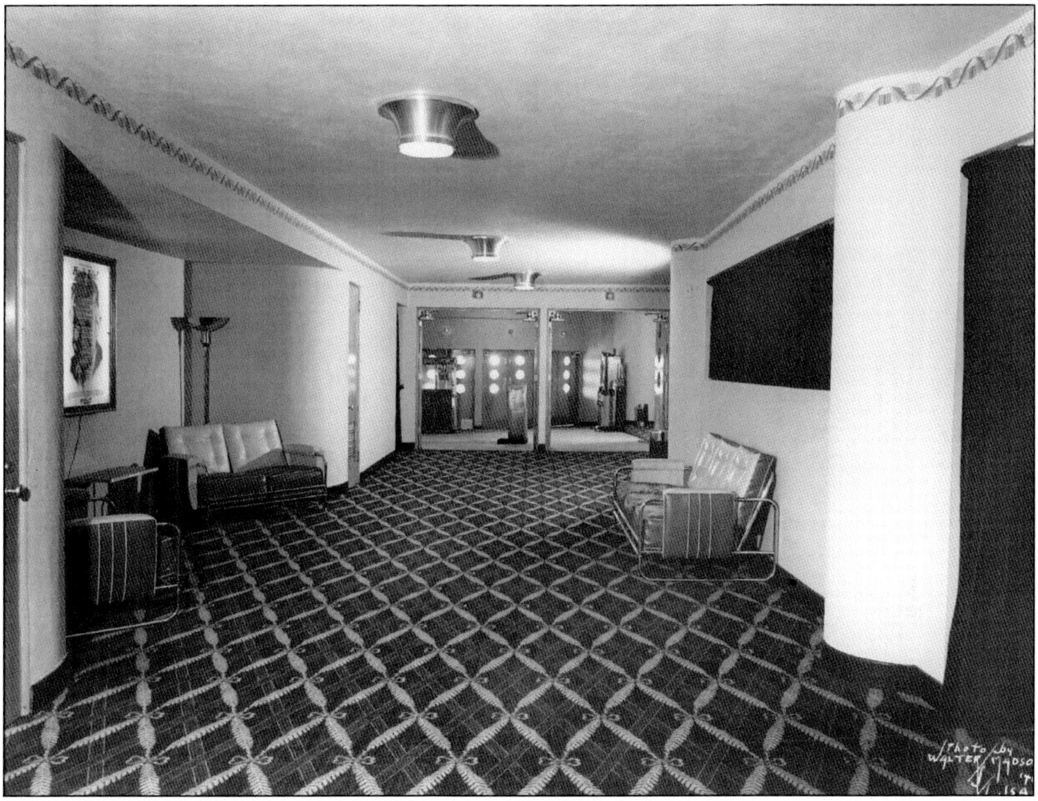

The lobby of the Will Rogers Theatre was updated several times over the theater's 35-year history. A prominent feature was an oil painting of the theater's namesake, Oklahoma native Will Rogers. A young Rogers is depicted on horseback with lasso in hand. An employee from the theater's later years recalled the painting being relocated to an upstairs office after it was vandalized. (Courtesy of Oklahoma Historical Society.)

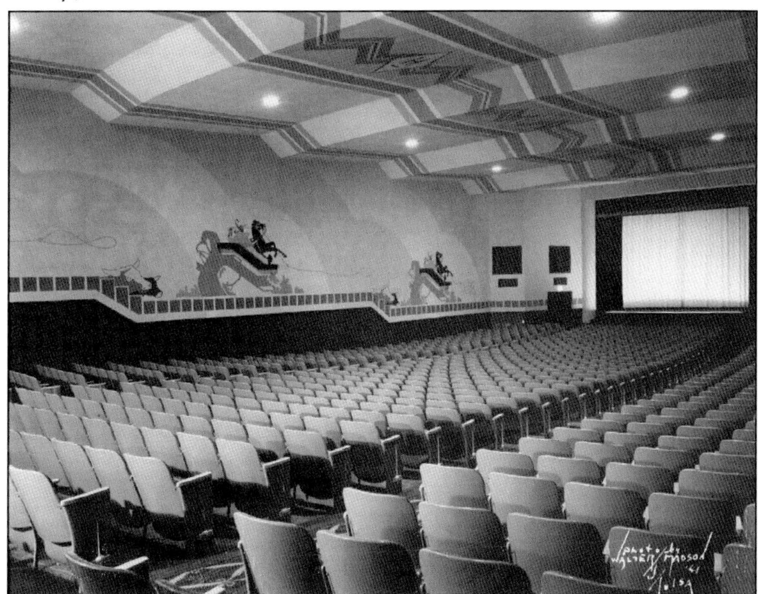

The Will Rogers Theatre auditorium had 719 cloth seats with maroon cushions and seating all on one level. The Western impressionist motif used earth tones with an occasional splash of bright color for accent. Murals of cowboys roping steers adorned the walls. The distinctive tapered ceiling featured a Native American design. (Courtesy of Oklahoma Historical Society.)

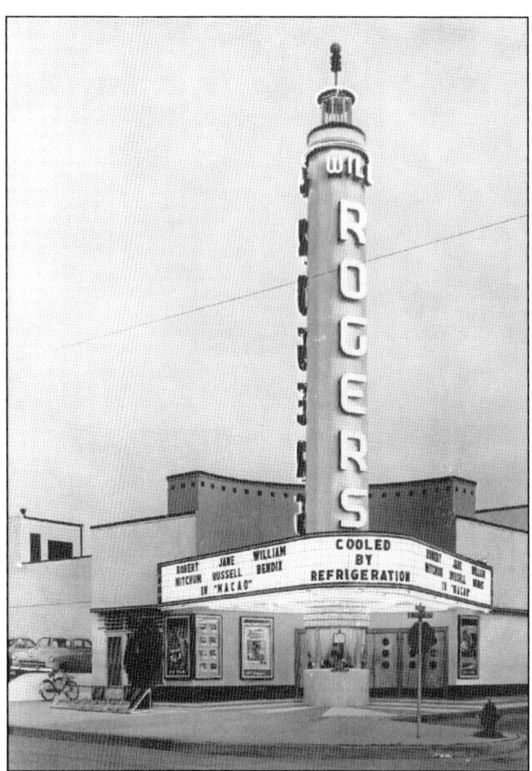

Here is the 1950s photograph from the Beryl Ford Collection that Tulsa-based actor and artist Gailard Sartain references in the foreword of this book. Sartain's bicycle is parked in front of the theater in this image. Sartain first gained fame on local television hosting Saturday night movies in the early 1970s. Sartain's diverse acting credits include *The Outsiders*, *Fried Green Tomatoes*, *The Replacements*, *The Buddy Holly Story*, *The Grifters*, *Mississippi Burning*, and *Elizabethtown*. (Courtesy of Gailard and Mary Jo Sartain.)

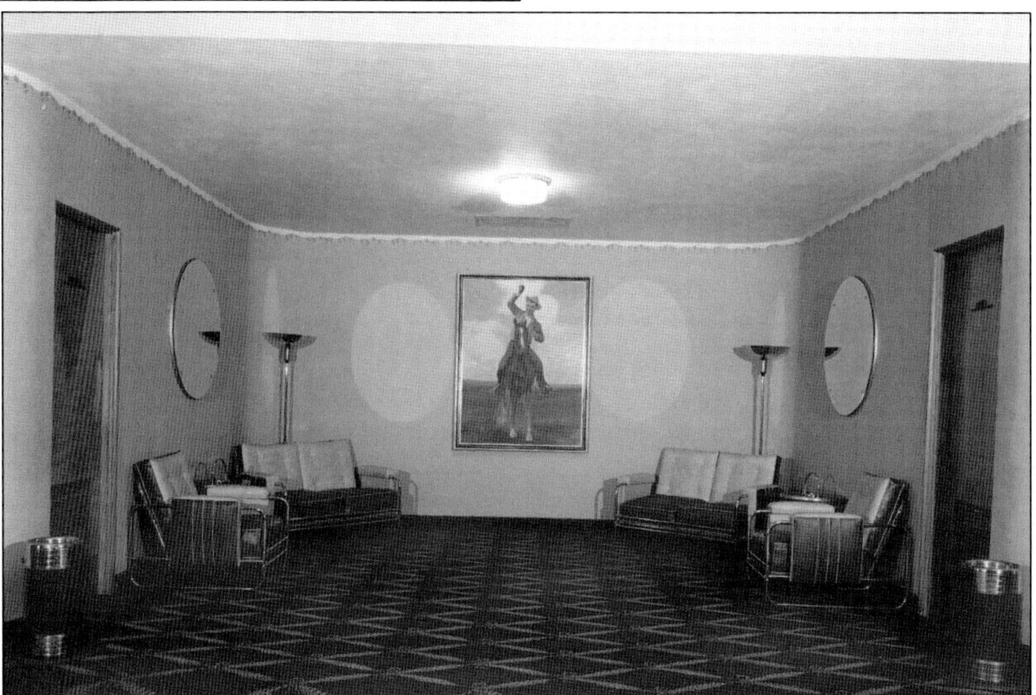

This 1941 image shows the smoking lounge at the Will Rogers Theatre as it appeared at the time of the theater's opening. The painting of the theater's namesake is the featured centerpiece. (Courtesy of Oklahoma Historical Society.)

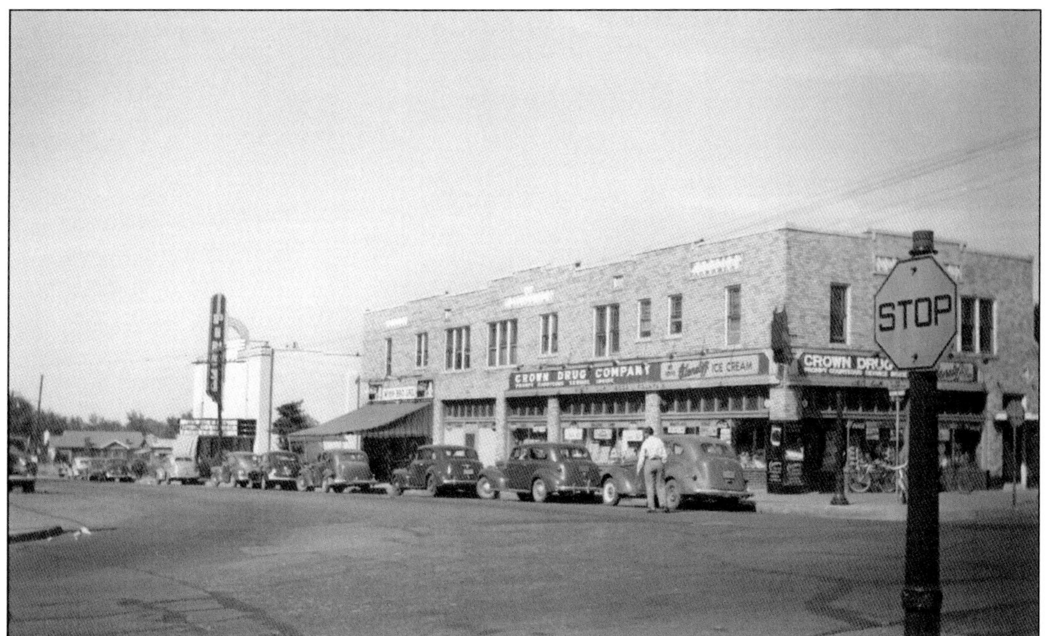

The Pines opened in 1942 at 1515 North Cincinnati Avenue. The theater's Streamline design was created by Corgan & Moore of Dallas. With exterior lines similar to those of the Plaza and Tulsa theaters, the Pines took its name from its location on the corner of Pine Street and Cincinnati Avenue. The Art Deco lines continued inside the 676-seat auditorium. (Below, courtesy of Oklahoma Historical Society.)

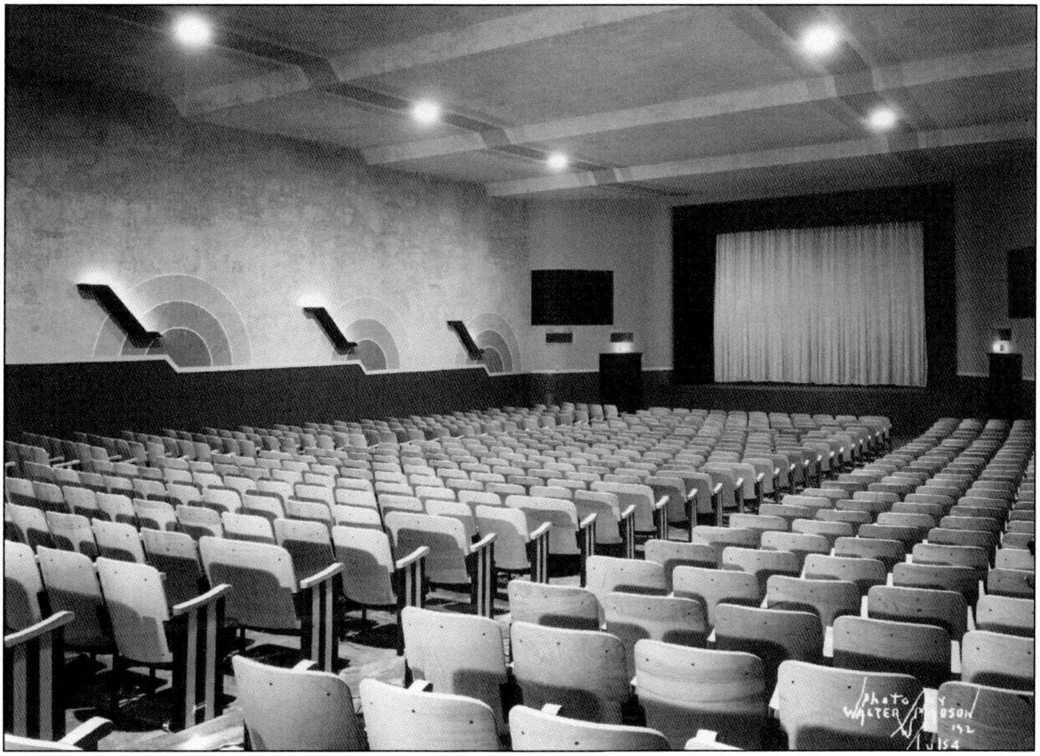

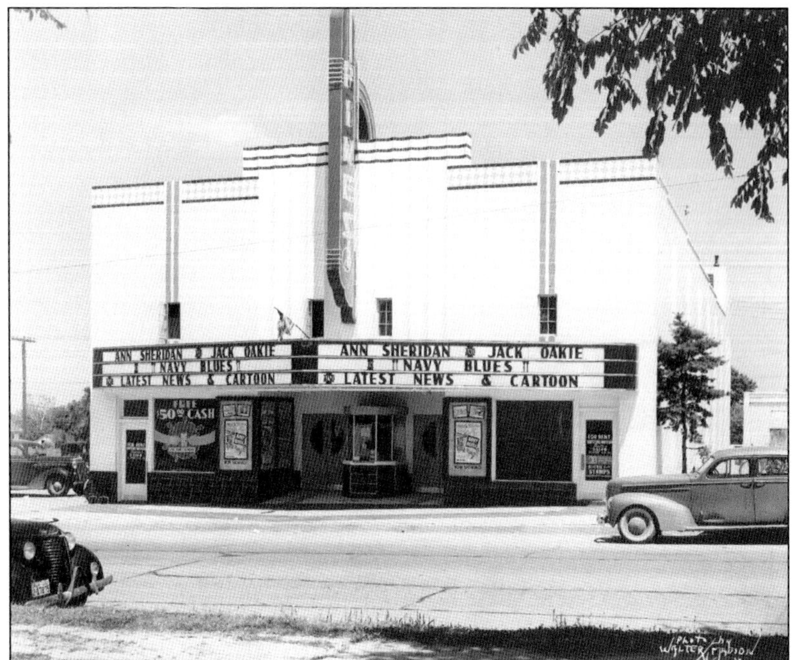

In this image, the Pines marquee highlights the movie *Navy Blues*, starring Ann Sheridan and Jack Dante. It also advertises a newsreel and cartoon that will be featured. (Courtesy of Oklahoma Historical Society.)

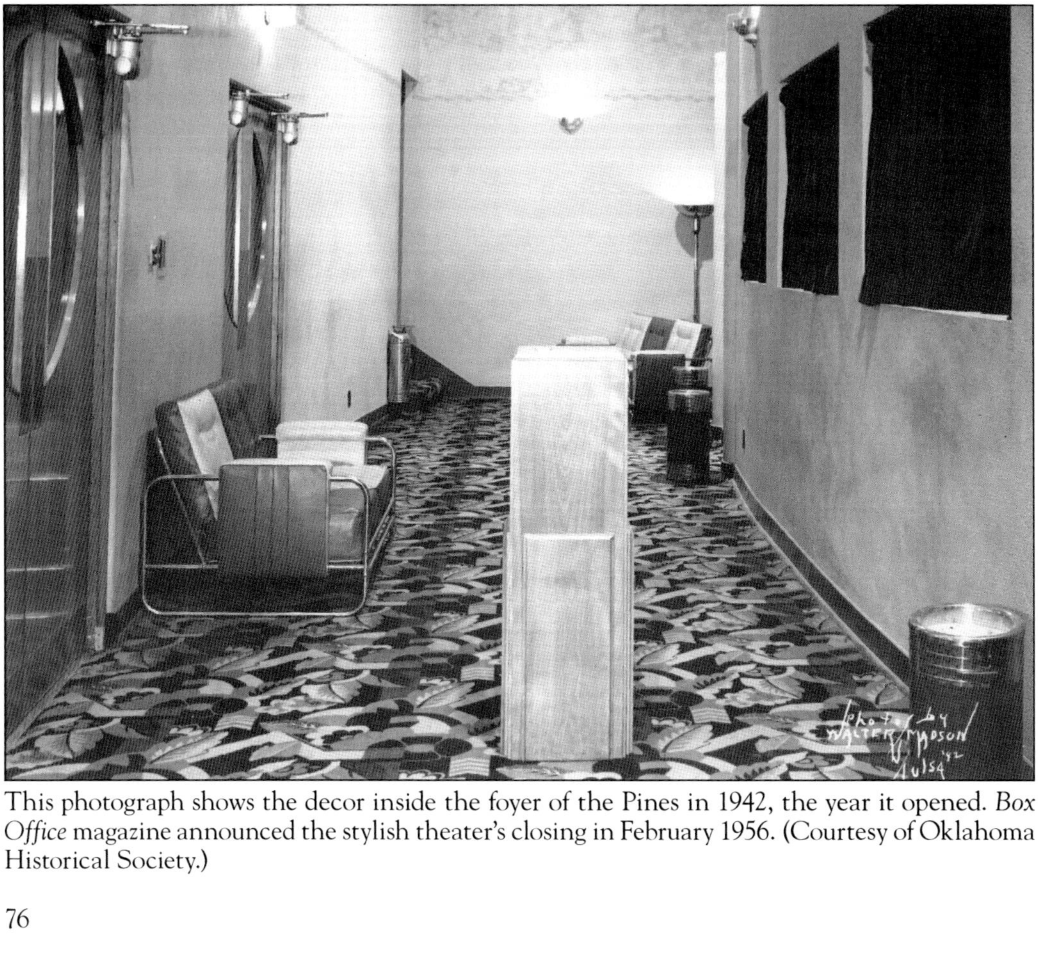

This photograph shows the decor inside the foyer of the Pines in 1942, the year it opened. *Box Office* magazine announced the stylish theater's closing in February 1956. (Courtesy of Oklahoma Historical Society.)

Mary Jo Jones Bradley is shown posing in front of Tulsa's Peoria Theater, located at 2541 North Peoria Avenue. The movie house operated from 1948 to 1957. The theater is listed in Eric Ledell Smith's book *African American Theater Buildings: An Illustrated Historical Directory, 1900–1955*, as being an African American–owned movie house. (Courtesy of Monica Bradley Lamp.)

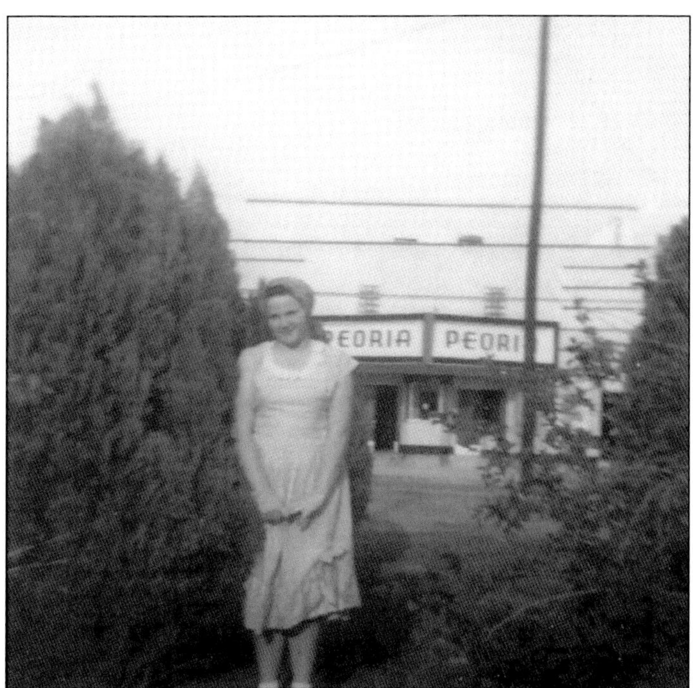

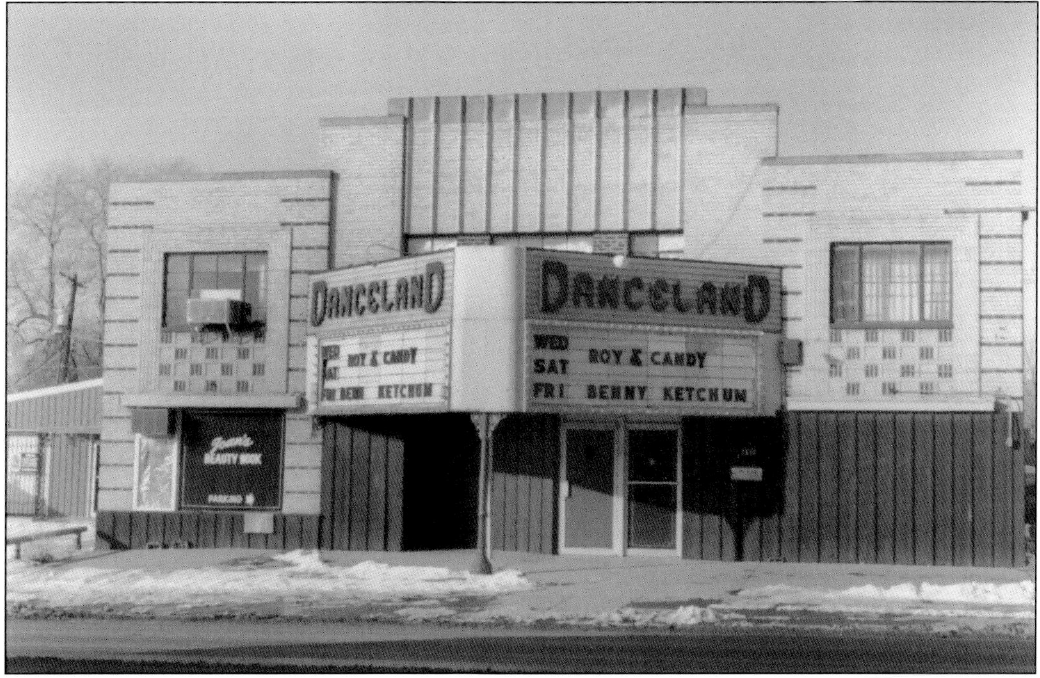

It is not difficult to see that Danceland is located in a former movie theater. The Royal Theater opened in 1948 between Lewis and Delaware Avenues on Eleventh Street, across the street from the Casa Loma Hotel. Eighty-seven-year-old John Holderman fondly remembered his time as an usher at the Royal, when he patrolled the three sections of seats with his flashlight. Holderman said the sure way to fill the theater was to show a Roy Rogers movie. After the Royal closed in 1957, Danceland moved in. The building was later razed for parking for the Bama Companies Inc.

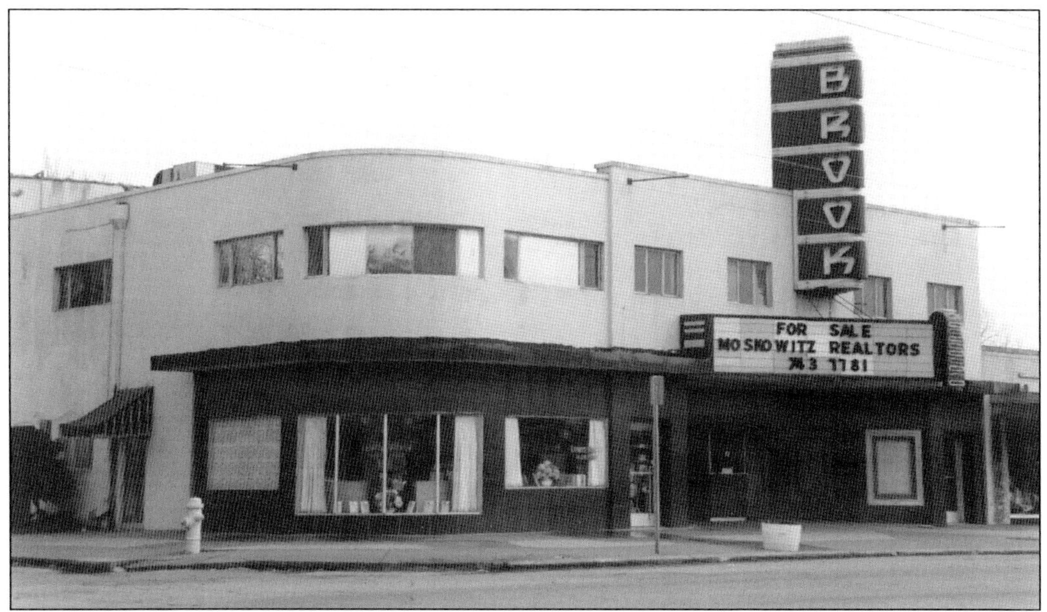

The Deco Moderne–style Brook Theatre, located at 3401 South Peoria Avenue, opened in 1949. In 1965, the Brook was selected to show a rough cut of *The Sound Of Music* and provide feedback to the producers. The movie played at the Brook for over a year! During most of the theater's existence, the building's corner suite was occupied by Lewis Meyer, bookseller. Meyer was a best-selling author and local television celebrity. His Sunday morning program *Lewis Meyer's Bookshelf* ran on KOTV for 40 years, making Meyer nearly as famous as the stars on the screen next door.

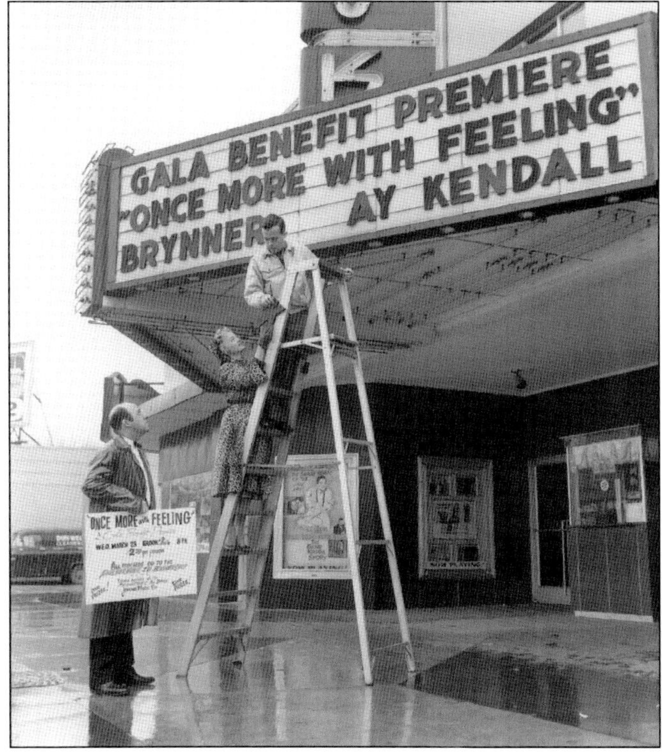

From left to right, manager Bill Donaldson, Betty Bradstreet, and an unidentified man are setting up the marquee for a benefit premiere of *Once More, with Feeling!*, a 1960 romantic comedy starring Yul Brynner and Kay Kendall. Donaldson later became entertainment editor for the *Tulsa Tribune*. While the Brook was known for family fare, it also screened controversial films. *Blow-Up* (1966) and *Last Tango in Paris* (1972) were noted for pushing accepted community standards with nudity and sex scenes, respectively.

This image of the Brook appeared on the cover of Bishop Kelley High School's 1981 *Crest* yearbook. The school received a customized marquee for its photograph. Student photographers for the 1980–1981 year included Erin Strayhorn, Bob Rauner, and Debbie Walters. (Courtesy of Bishop Kelley High School.)

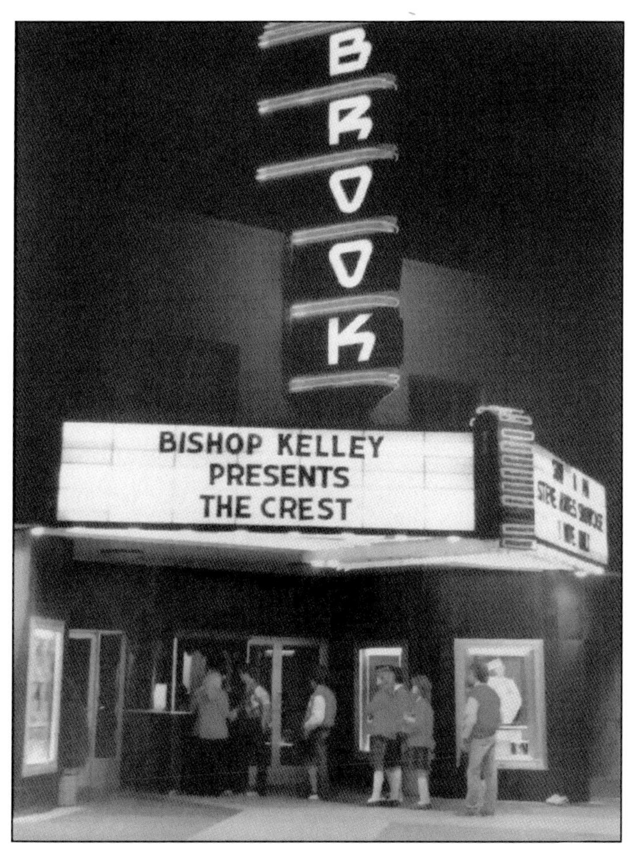

After closing in 1978, the Brook became home to the American Theater Company (ATC), which still occasionally screened films. Children who had enjoyed the Brook's Saturday matinees came back as adults for ATC's cabaret productions, which included Joyce Martel and Eddie and the Eclectics. In recent years, the Brook Restaurant and Bar has occupied the building. The theater's Deco neon sign and marquee remain.

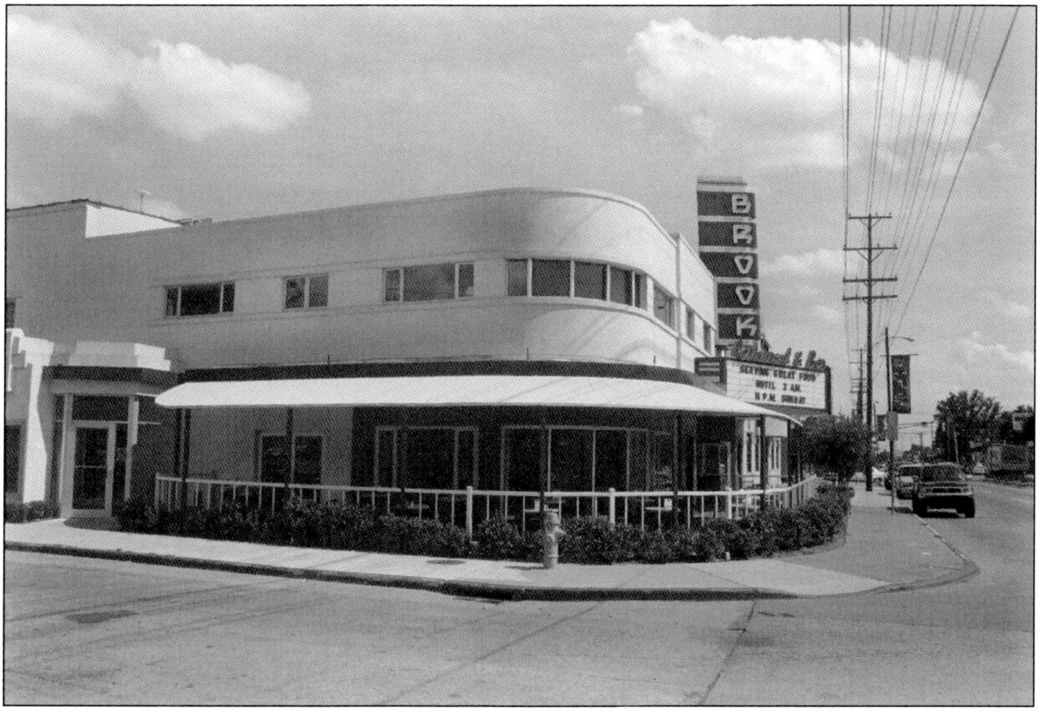

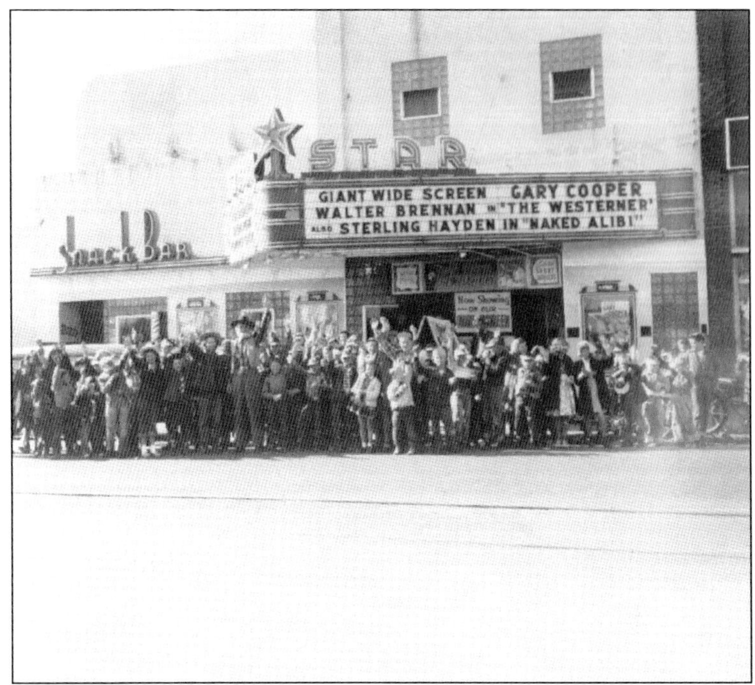

The Star Theatre, located at 114 North Main Street in Sand Springs, opened in 1917 and operated, off and on, until 1979. The Star had a striking Art Deco exterior. This c. 1955 photograph shows a Western-themed crowd gathered for a showing of the 1940 classic *The Westerner*, starring Gary Cooper and Walter Brennan. Moviegoers may recall the high windows in the restrooms where smokers could watch the movies. (Courtesy of Beryl Ford Collection/ Rotary Club of Tulsa.)

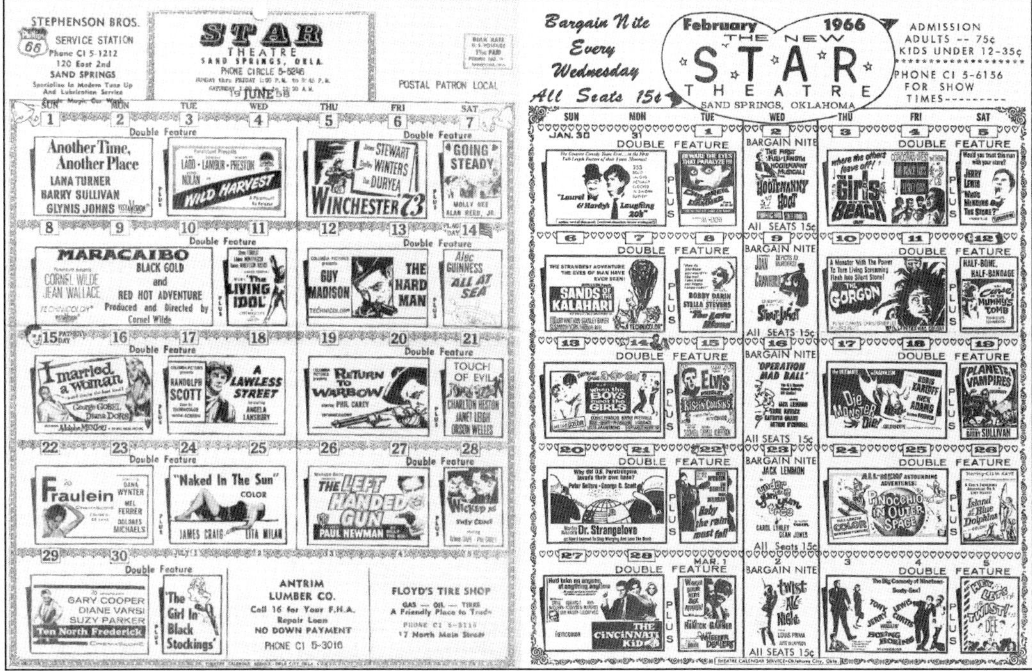

Like many theaters, the Star released flyers featuring the monthly movie schedule. The theater hired kids to distribute them door-to-door in exchange for tickets. These two schedules from 1958 (left) and 1966 illustrate how movies changed in a few short years. There were lots of Westerns on the 1958 flyer, but by 1966, there were more genres aimed at teenagers, including monster and vampire flicks, beach movies, and films with a star who was extremely popular with young girls—Elvis! (Courtesy of Sand Springs Cultural and Historical Museum.)

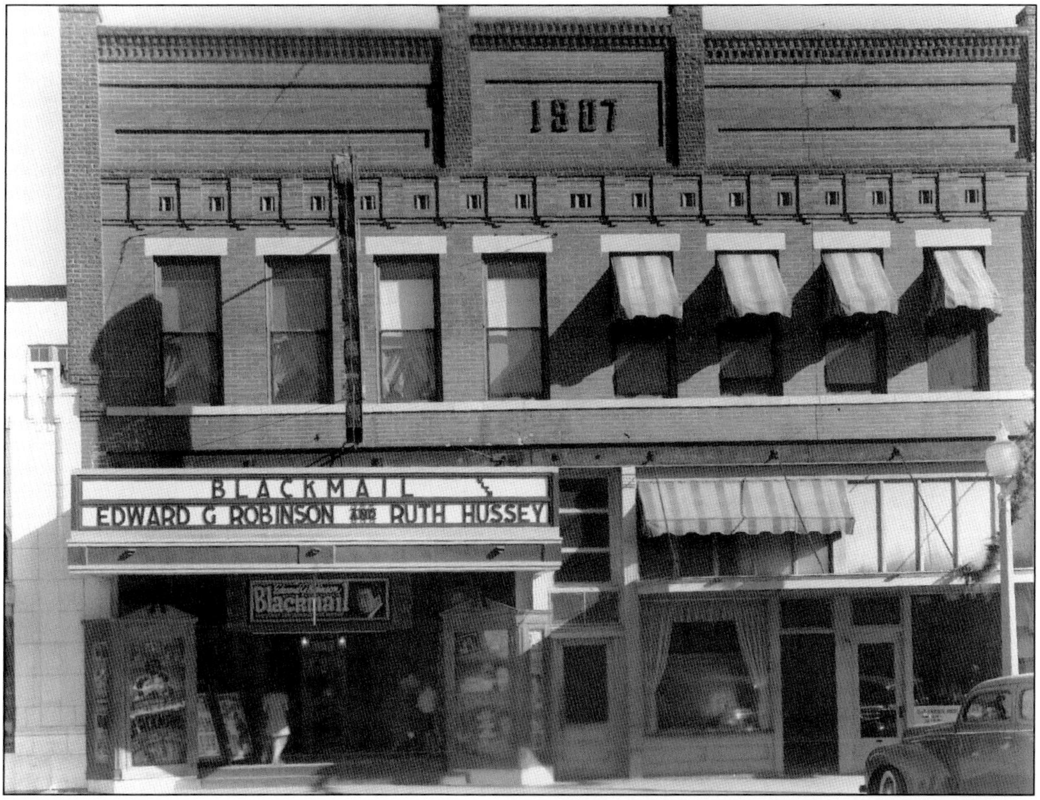

In the first decade of the 1900s, Sapulpa rivaled Tulsa for the title of oil capital. As visitors arrived by train and headed toward downtown, they were greeted by an elaborate sign that spanned the roadway and proclaimed, "Sapulpa: Oil City of the Southwest." The Yale Theatre opened in 1907 at 7 South Main Street in Sapulpa. The early style of the theater was described as conservative Gothic. Some time later, the first-run movie house received a new facade. Although it had a somewhat plain concrete appearance in the daylight, it looked nice illuminated at night, as shown in the c. 1945 image at right. (Both, courtesy of Oklahoma Historical Society.)

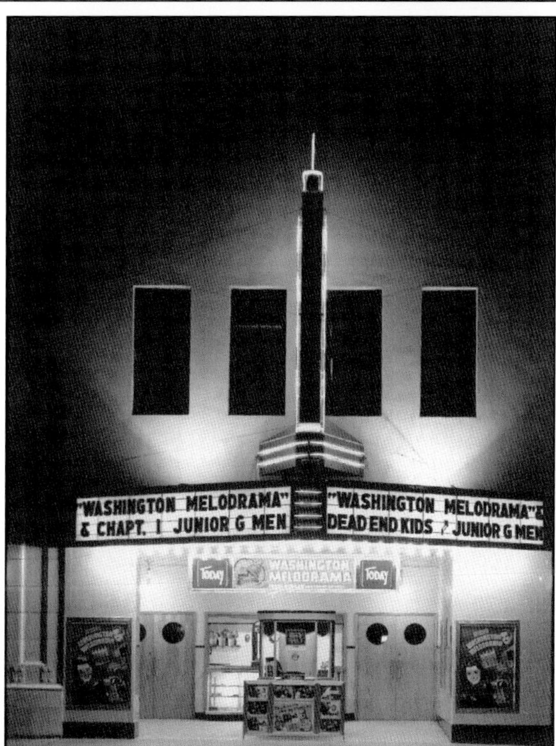

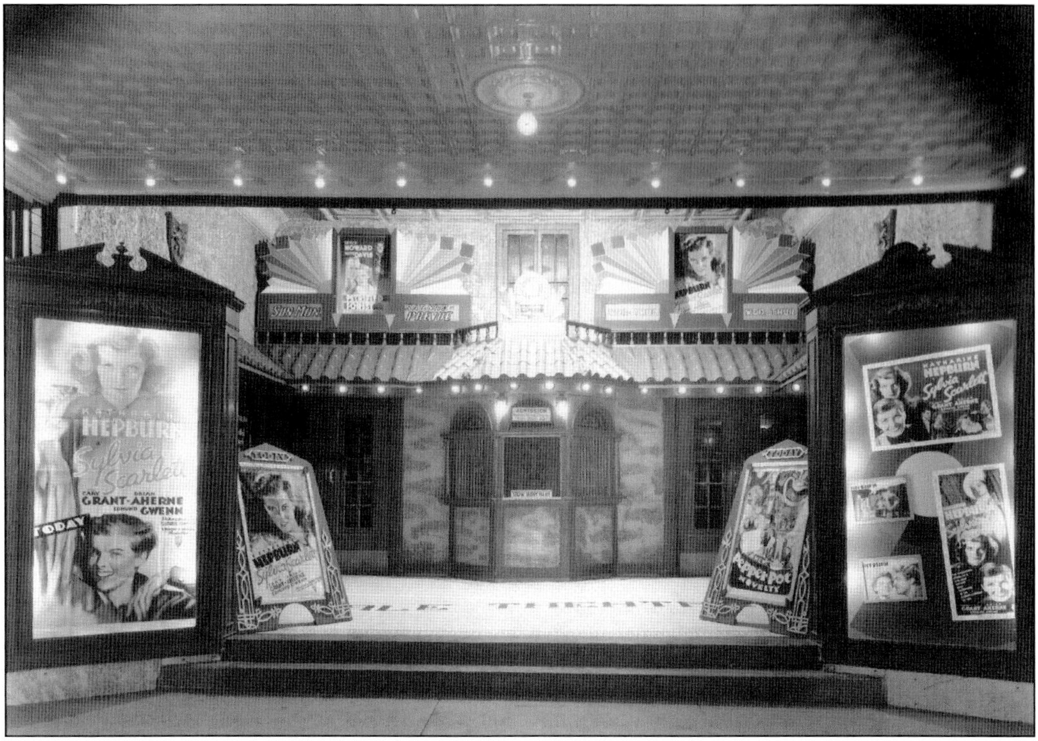

Here are two views of the first-run Yale Theatre in Sapulpa as it appeared in the 1930s. The elaborate display in the front of the theater is for the 1935 film *Sylvia Scarlett*, starring Katharine Hepburn and Cary Grant. The coming attraction is *Petrified Forest*, a 1936 film starring Leslie Howard, Bette Davis, and Humphrey Bogart and based on the Robert E. Sherwood Broadway drama of the same name. Note the inlaid tile spelling out Yale Theatre in front of the 1907 building—a common practice in the early 20th century. Below is an image of the Yale's fashionable auditorium with seating for 699. The Yale Theatre burned in 1954 and did not reopen. (Both, courtesy of Oklahoma Historical Society.)

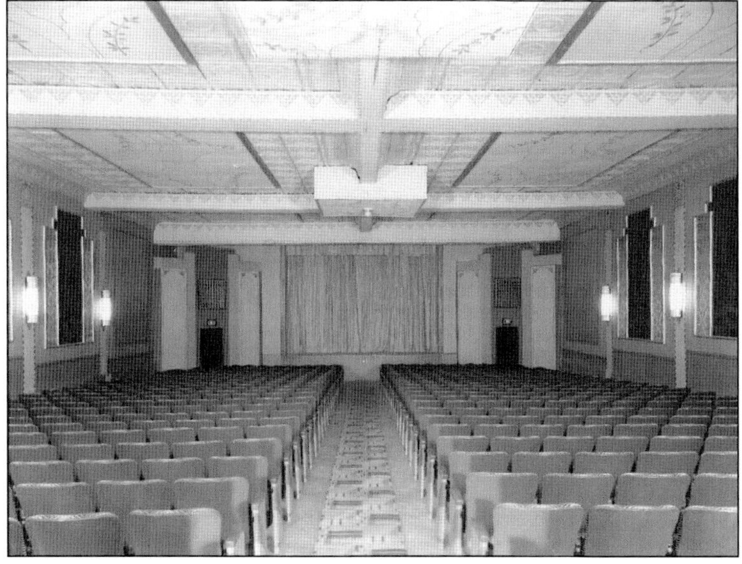

Griffith Amusement Company opened the State Theater at 118 East Dewey Street in Sapulpa in 1939. It was a B movie theater (as opposed to Griffith's first-run theater, the Yale). In the image at right, the marquee announces the 1937 crime drama *The Last Gangster*, starring Edward G. Robinson and James Stewart. In 2021, the building still looked remarkably similar to this photograph. After the TeePee Drive-In opened in 1950, the State only operated during cold-weather months when the drive-in was closed. The State closed for good in 1956. In recent years, the building has housed a portrait studio. The below photograph shows that the interior of the State, a second-run movie house, was not as fancy as that of its sister theater, the Yale. (Both, courtesy of Oklahoma Historical Society.)

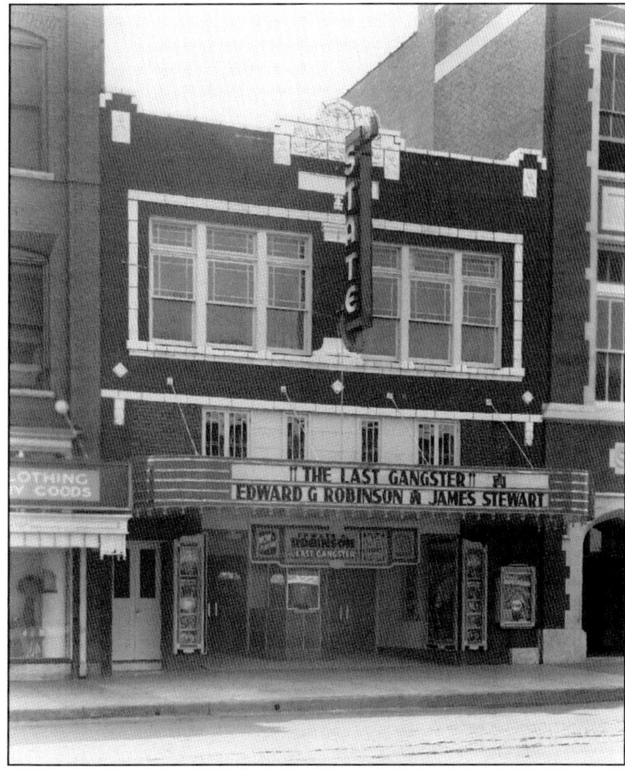

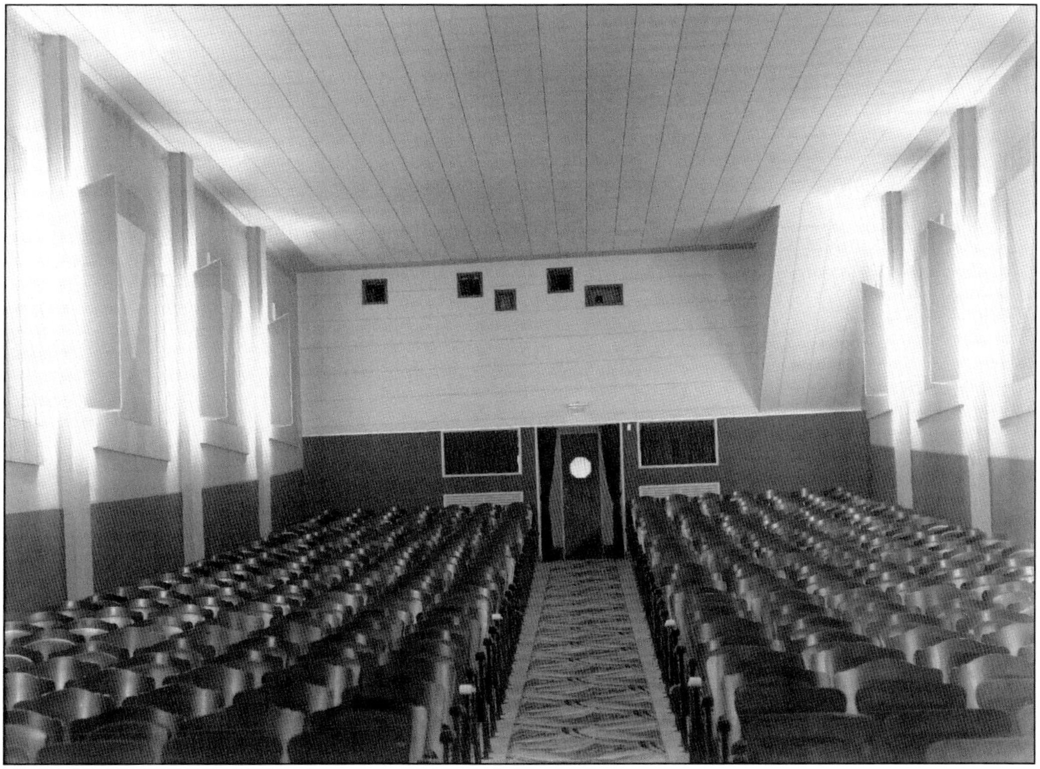

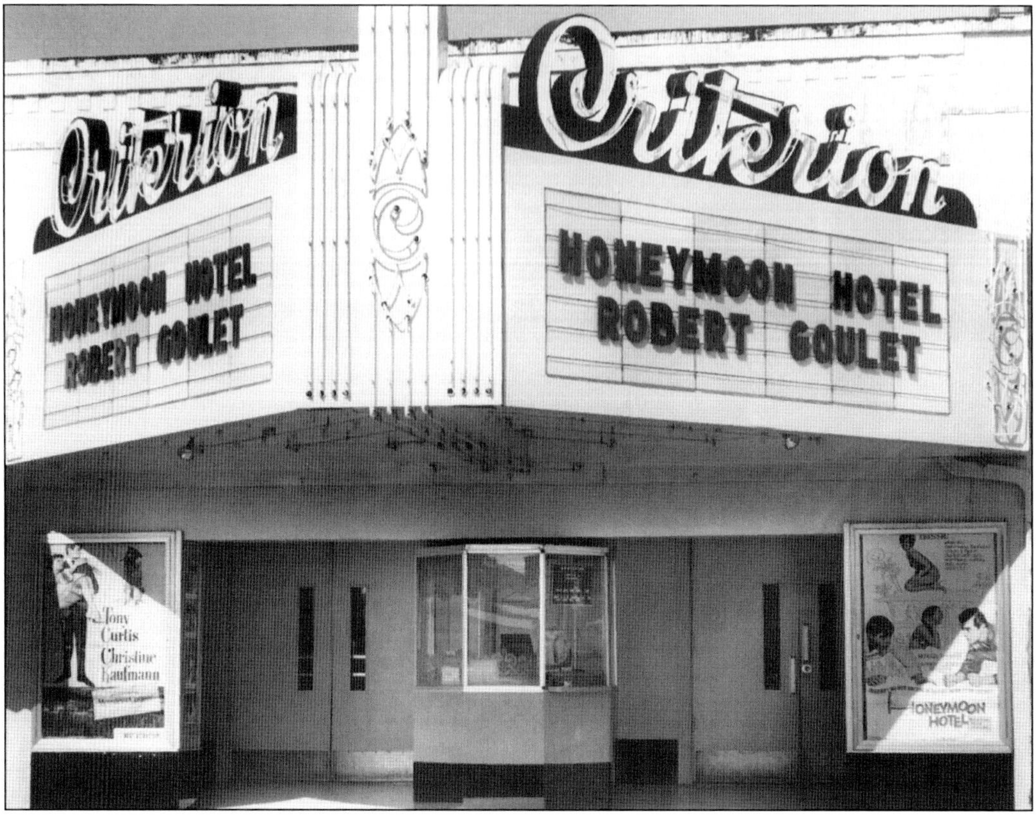

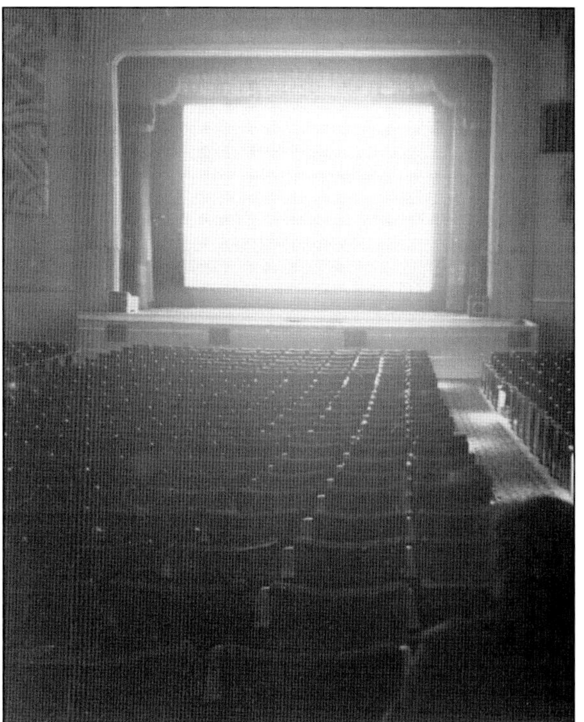

Sapulpa's Victorian Theatre debuted in 1924 at 10 South Water Street with a Wurlitzer pipe organ to accompany its silent films. After it was closed at the end of the decade and outfitted for sound, it reopened in 1930 as the Criterion. The exterior received a Streamline Deco makeover in 1947, which remained in place until the end of the theater's run. The c. 1964 photograph above shows the comedy *Honeymoon Hotel* on the marquee. The Criterion's auditorium was demolished in 1976, leaving only the front of the building. Since then, restaurants and a tattoo parlor have occupied that space. (Both, courtesy of Oklahoma Historical Society.)

Five

Drive-Ins
The Outdoor Experience

It begins with the sound of car tires on gravel, headlights off. Once inside the open-air theater, drivers maneuver to gain the perfect viewing angle. Children scramble toward the playground as parents set up the portal—a tinny-sounding speaker that will transport them via the giant screen. Enticing aromas of perfume and popcorn alternate with those of car exhaust and cigarette smoke. This is all part of the vintage drive-in experience.

The drive-in theater phenomenon arose from post–World War II car culture. Americans felt they had earned the right to have some fun, and they were on the move. With the typical outdoor theater occupying at least 10 acres of land, drive-ins filled the wide-open spaces on the outskirts of Tulsa and its suburbs.

Tulsa's Hi-Way 66 Drive-In opened east of Tulsa, at Eleventh Street and Mingo Road, in the summer of 1947. By the following year, three more had opened: Riverside (on Seventy-first Street near the Arkansas River) and the Apache and the Skyline (both on Tulsa's north side).

These early drive-ins offered inexpensive family entertainment. Parents watched the movie in the front seat while kids crashed in the back. Many of them, including Riverside, Sand Springs, and Airview, had elaborate playgrounds beneath the screen. The drive-in became the domain of those same young people as they grew up and the baby boomer generation reached dating age.

By 1955, a dozen drive-ins dotted the Tulsa landscape. These included the Sheridan, TeePee in Sapulpa, and Broken Arrow Drive-In as well as the Bellaire, across from the Pepsi plant, just west of the Arkansas River.

Tulsa's most famous drive-in began as the Modernaire on May 24, 1951. One year later, it was renamed the Admiral, and following the addition of a second screen, the Admiral Twin. After providing generations of entertainment, the Admiral Twin's screen tower burned down in September 2010. When owner Blake Smith announced that there was no insurance and that rebuilding was unlikely, public donations covered the cost. On June 15, 2012, the Admiral Twin reclaimed its place as a local icon.

Eventually, the land occupied by automobile amphitheaters became valuable for residential and retail development, and most of them disappeared. However, thanks to the generosity of Tulsans and their love for the movies, the Admiral Twin Drive-In continues to introduce new generations to the drive-in experience.

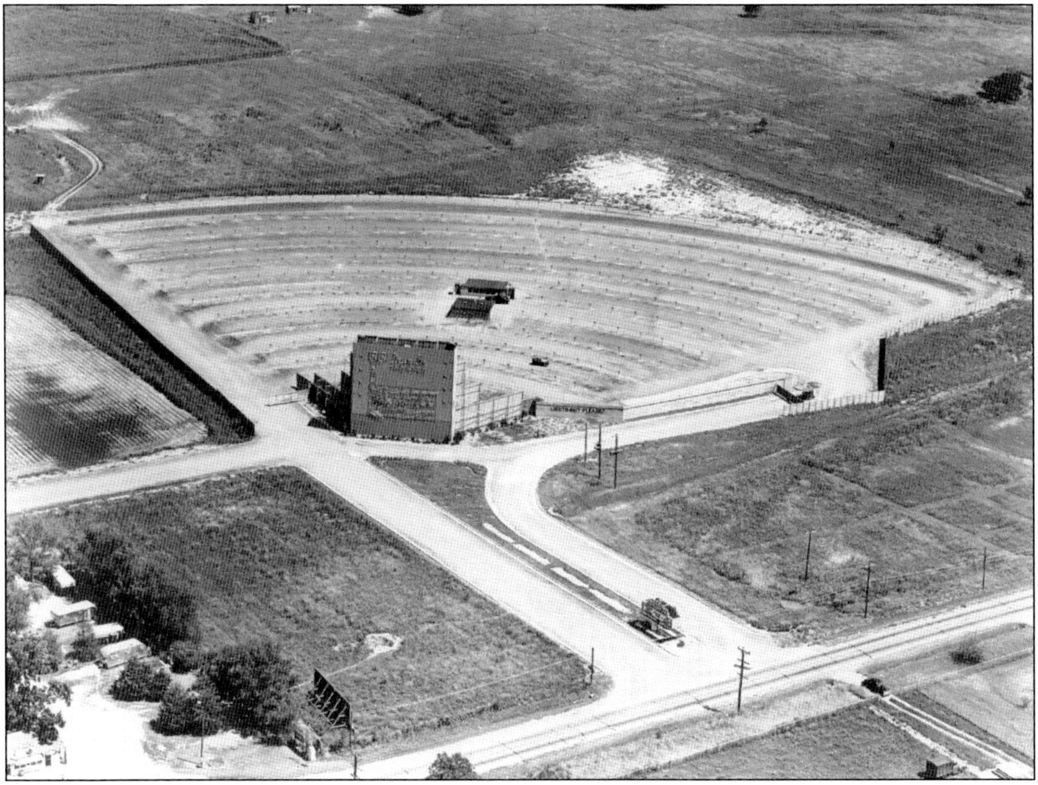

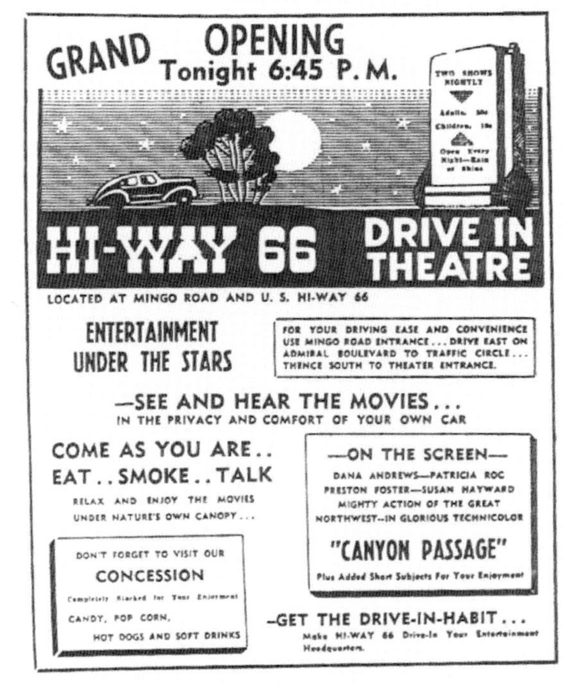

Tulsa's first drive-in theater, the Hi-Way 66 Drive-In, opened on August 21, 1947, on Route 66 east of Tulsa. The opening night feature was *Canyon Passage*, starring Dana Andrews and Susan Hayward. Many Tulsans would get to see Hayward in person just two years later (see chapter six). (Courtesy of Oklahoma Historical Society.)

When the Hi-Way 66 Drive-In opened on Tulsa's outskirts shortly after World War II, the drive-in experience was brand-new. Early advertisements, like this one for the grand opening, invited moviegoers to "Come as you are . . . eat . . . smoke . . . talk." This helped to educate the public about how the drive-in theater operated. (Courtesy of Wesley Horton.)

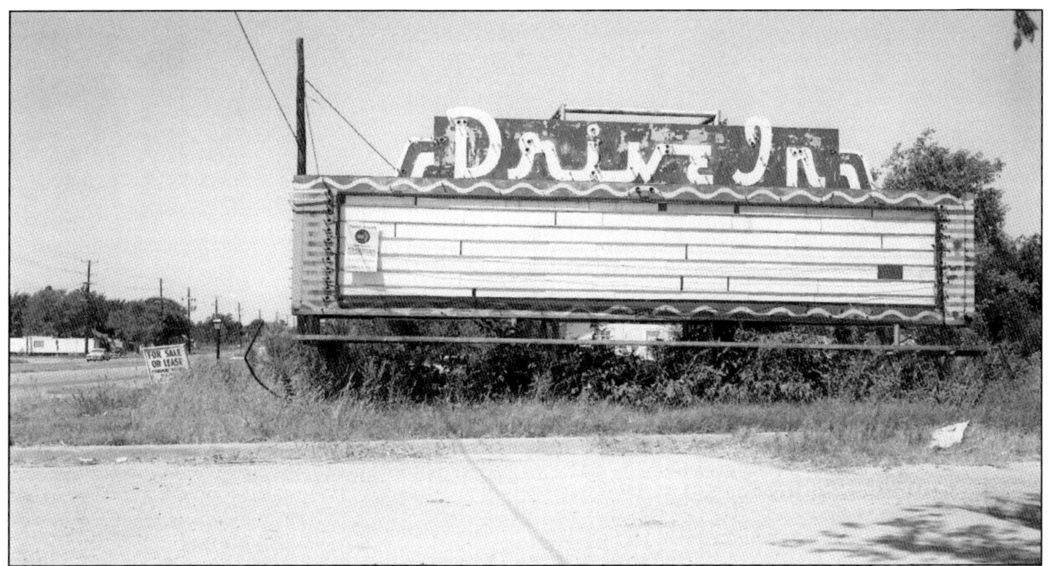

If the classic marquee for the Hi-Way 66 Drive-In looks a little run down in this 1962 image, it is because the automobile amphitheater had been dormant for three years. However, the theater soon saw new life as the 11th Street Drive-In and was also "twinned," adding a second screen in 1967. After the theater was demolished in 1983, God's Shining Light Church later occupied a portion of that land.

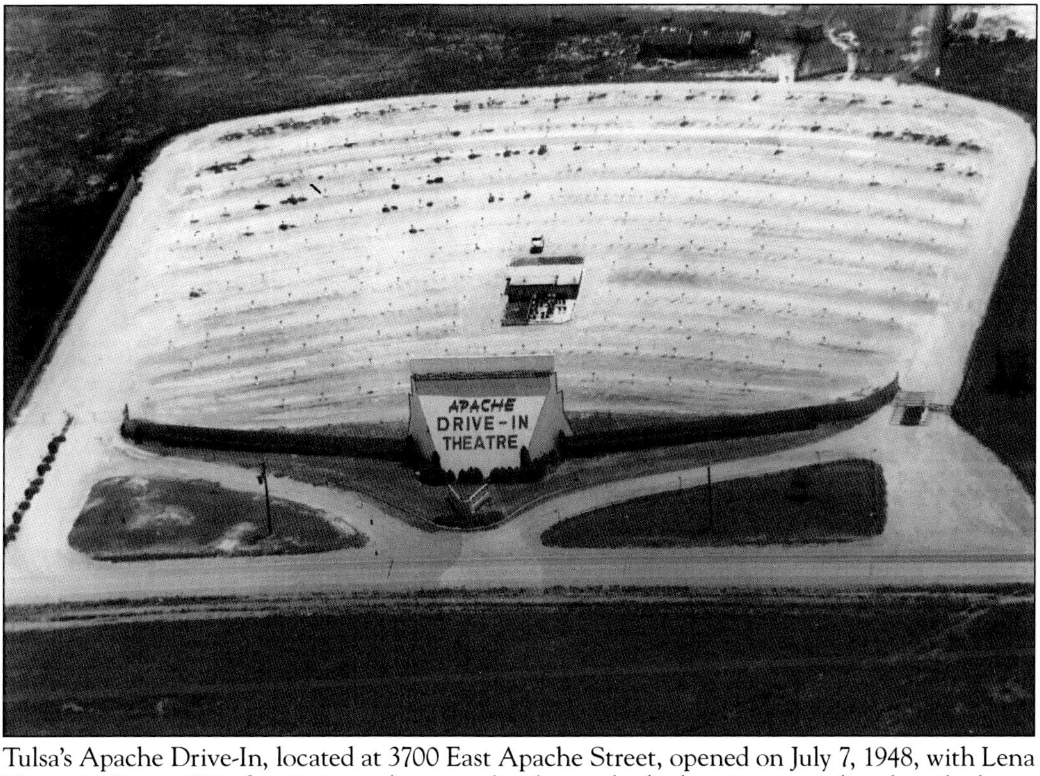

Tulsa's Apache Drive-In, located at 3700 East Apache Street, opened on July 7, 1948, with Lena Horne in *Stormy Weather*. In its early years, the theater had advertisements that described it as being an African American theater. The Apache operated until 1979 and was demolished.

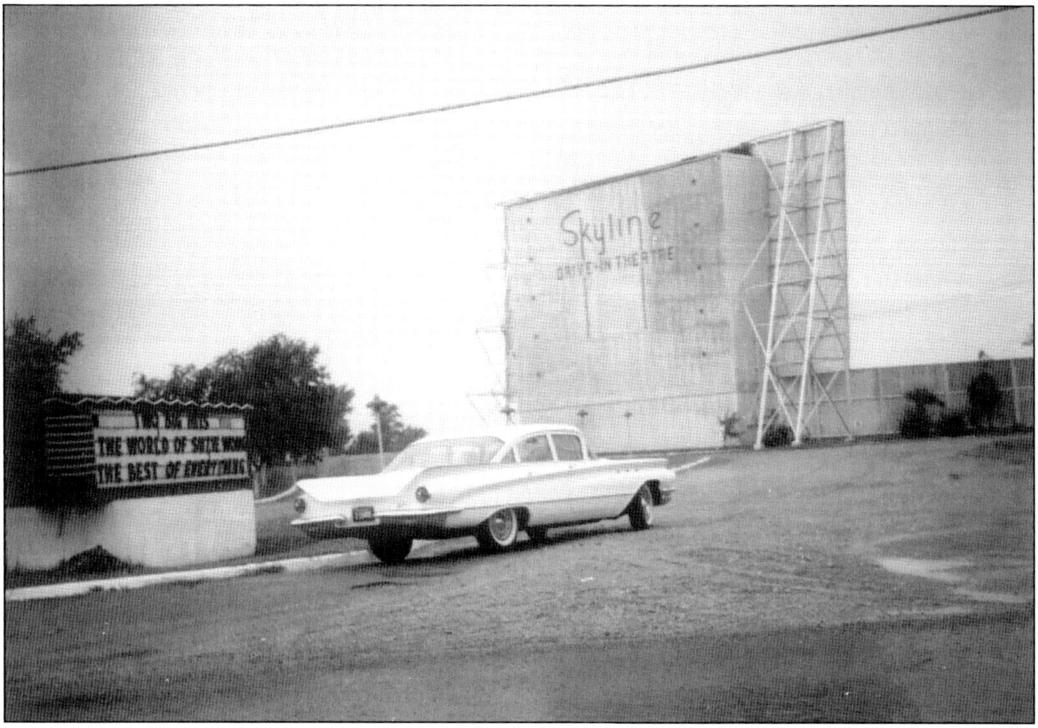

Another early entry in the drive-in theater scene was Video Independent Theaters' Skyline Drive-In. A newspaper advertisement for the Skyline's opening night said that Tulsa's newest drive-in was located "high on the hilltop on north Cincinnati." It enticed moviegoers to "enjoy the cool breezes in the privacy of your own car while you see the movies." (Courtesy of Oklahoma Historical Society.)

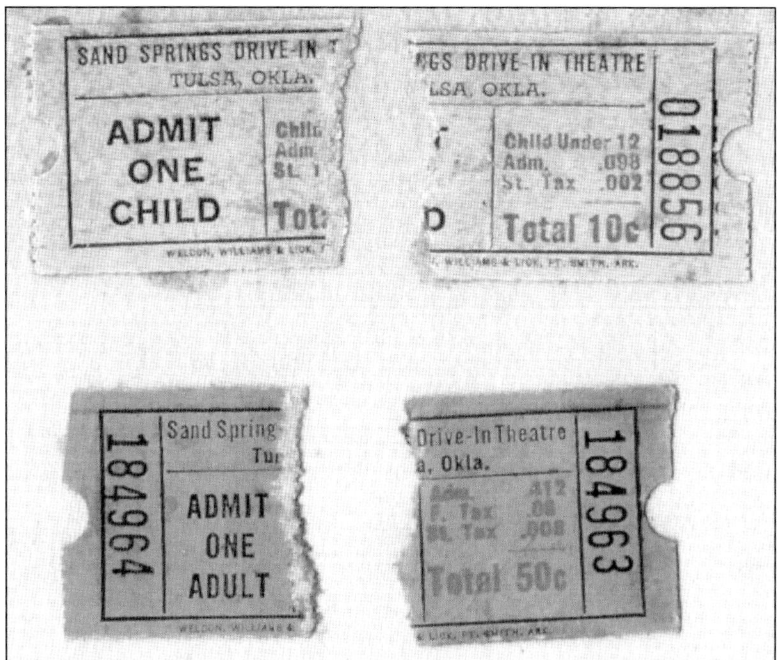

The Sand Springs Drive-In, located seven miles west of Tulsa, opened on April 27, 1950. After Doris Fisher of Sand Springs attended a movie there, she saved her tickets in a scrapbook, as shown here. On Monday, May 21, 1951, her companions to see *Lullaby of Broadway* were Fred, Gerry, and Billy. At that time, admission was 50¢ for adults and 10¢ for children. (Courtesy of Steve Clem.)

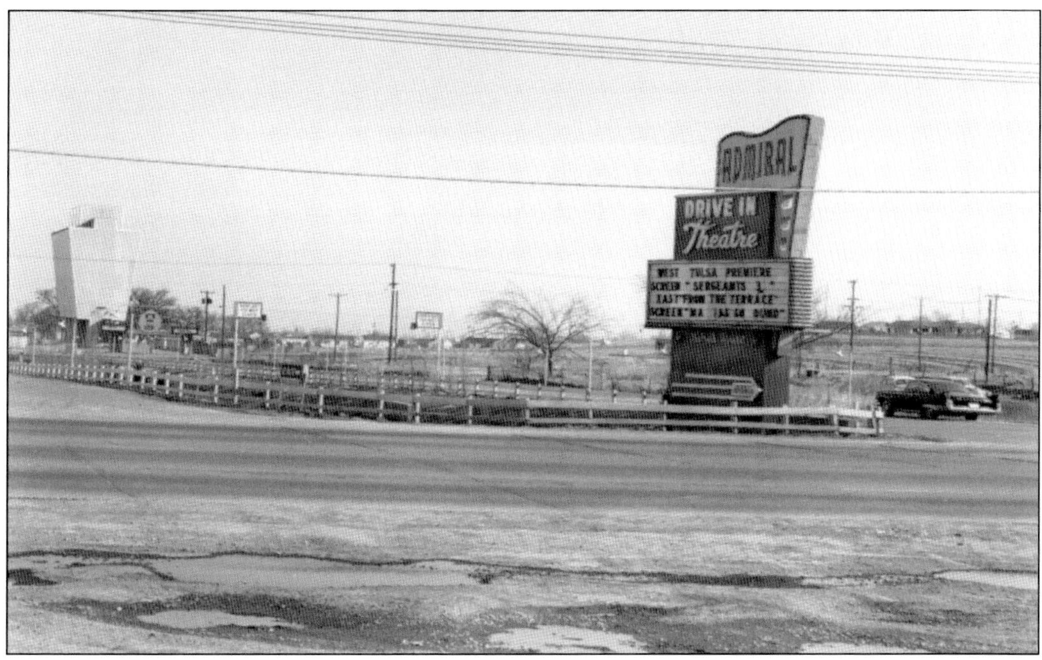

Tulsa's most famous drive-in opened in 1951 as the Modernaire. The name was changed to Admiral Drive-In the following year. There was a lot of star power in the movies playing when this picture was taken on a summer evening in 1962. The entire "Rat Pack"—Frank Sinatra, Dean Martin, Sammy Davis Jr., Peter Lawford, and Joey Bishop—were featured in the Western *Sergeants 3*. On the other screen, real-life husband and wife Paul Newman and Joanne Woodward appeared in *From the Terrace*. (Courtesy of Beryl Ford Collection/Rotary Club of Tulsa.)

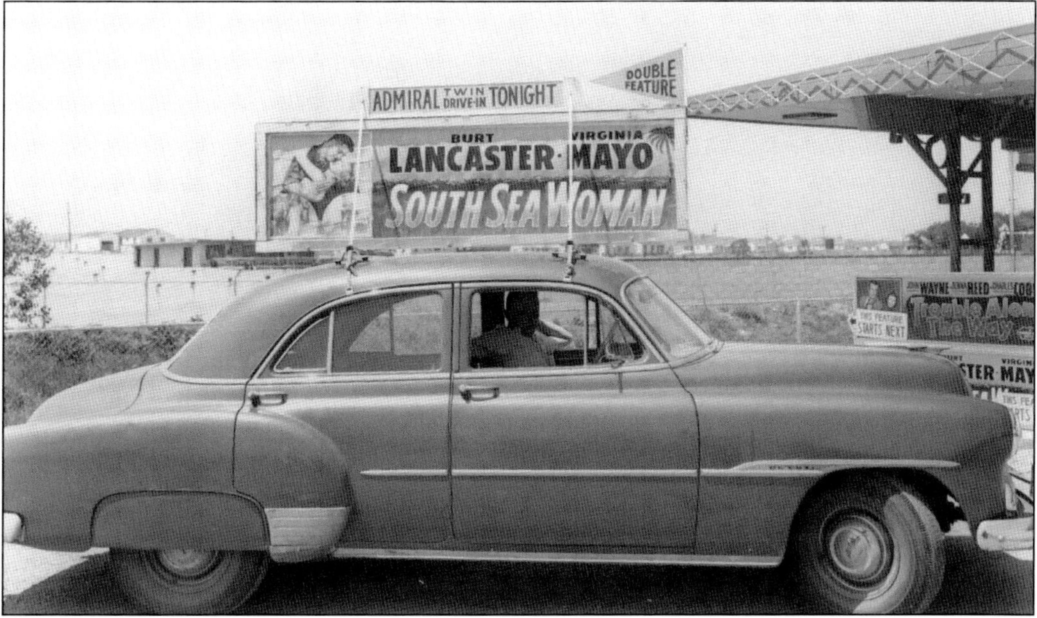

In this c. 1955 photograph, a man is posing in his car beside the Admiral Twin's ticket booth. The movie posters promote the 1953 movie *South Sea Woman*, a comedy starring Burt Lancaster and Virginia Mayo.

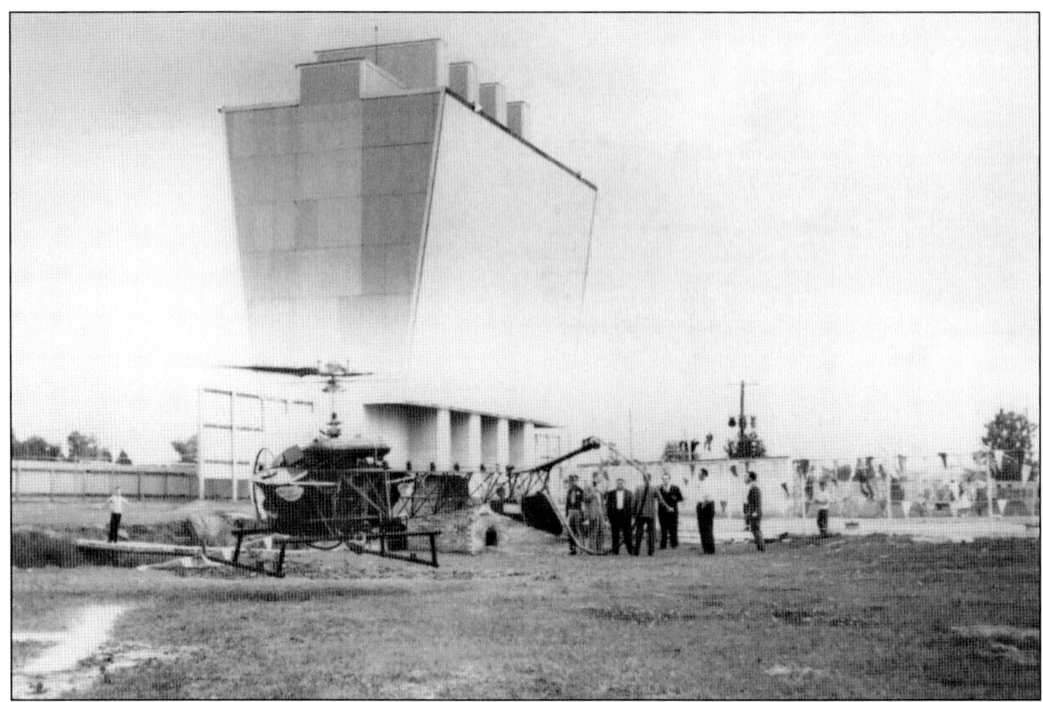

The Admiral Drive-In was twinned in 1955. Its screen tower, shown in this publicity photograph when it was new, stood nine stories high. The addition of a second screen increased the amphitheater's combined capacity to 1,350 cars. This screen tower burned down in 2010, but donations from the public helped build new screens, and the theater reopened in 2012. (Courtesy of Mary Ann Blue.)

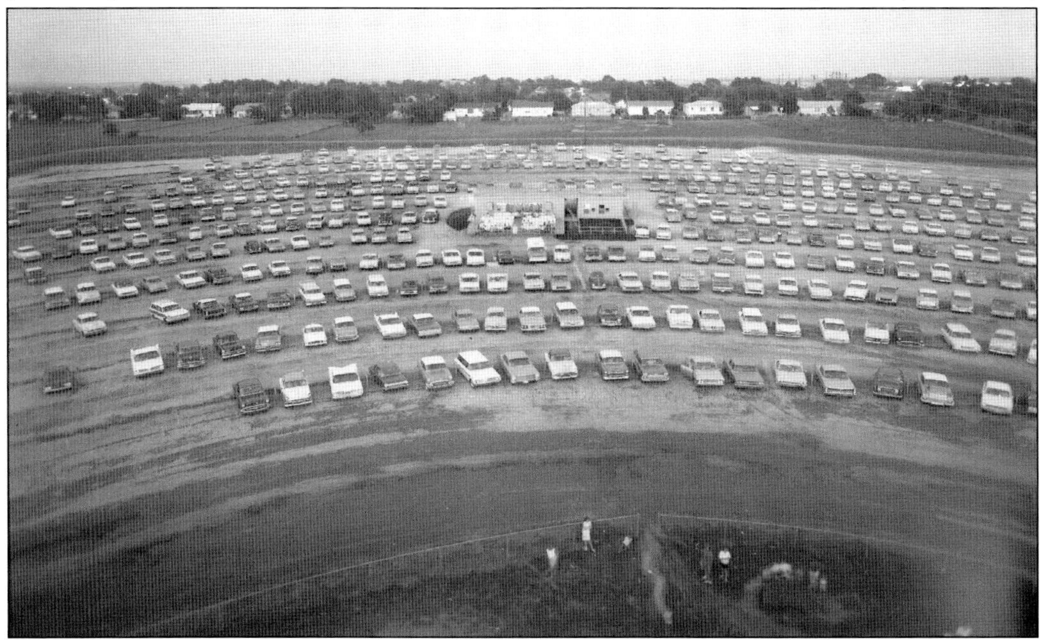

The Admiral Twin's west screen had a near-capacity crowd on this summer evening in 1965. Ahead of the evening's features, a few customers are sitting in front of the concession stand, while others are enjoying the playground near the screen.

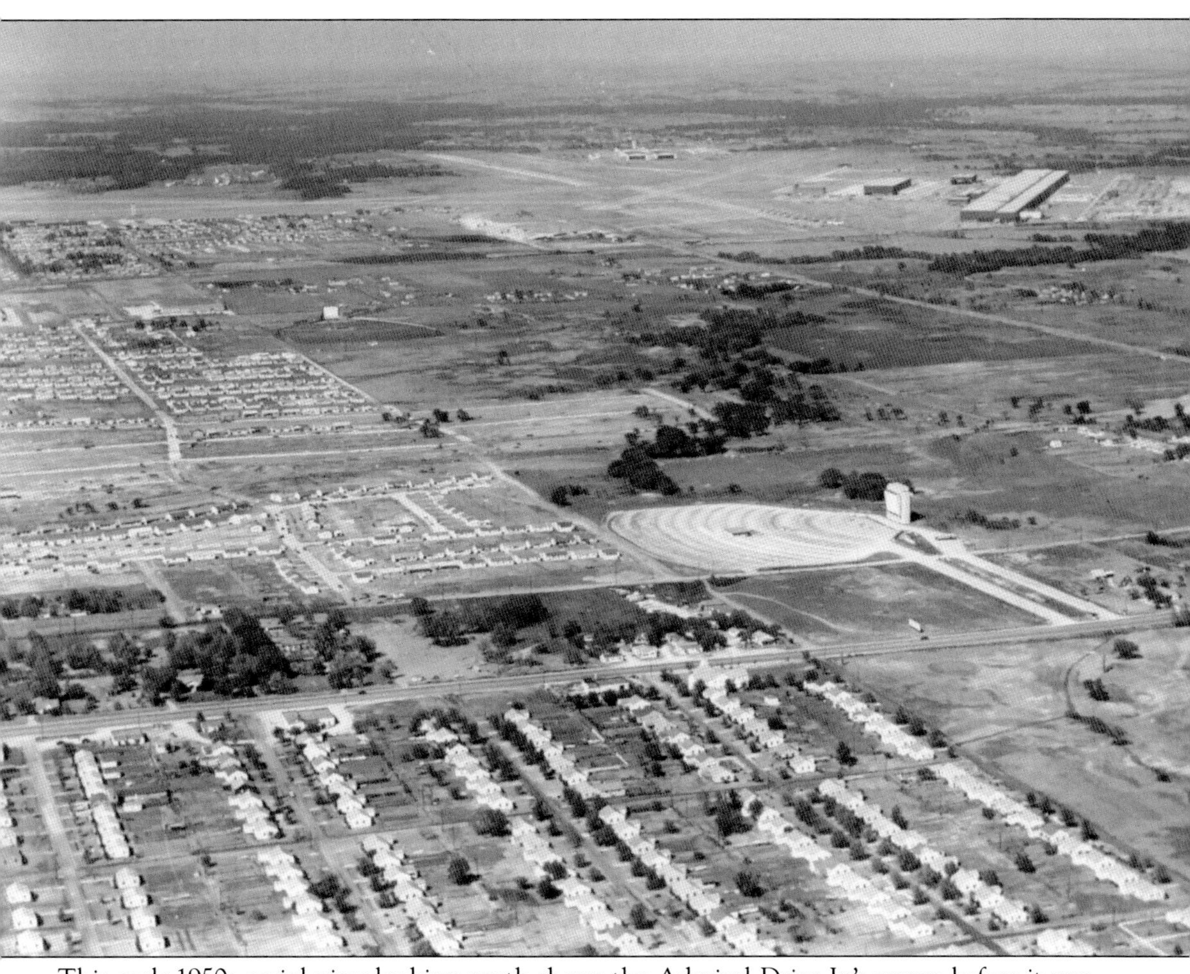

This early-1950s aerial view looking north shows the Admiral Drive-In's screen before it was twinned. Another drive-in theater, the Airview, located only a couple of miles north of the Admiral, is visible near the top center of the photograph. (Courtesy of Mary Ann Blue.)

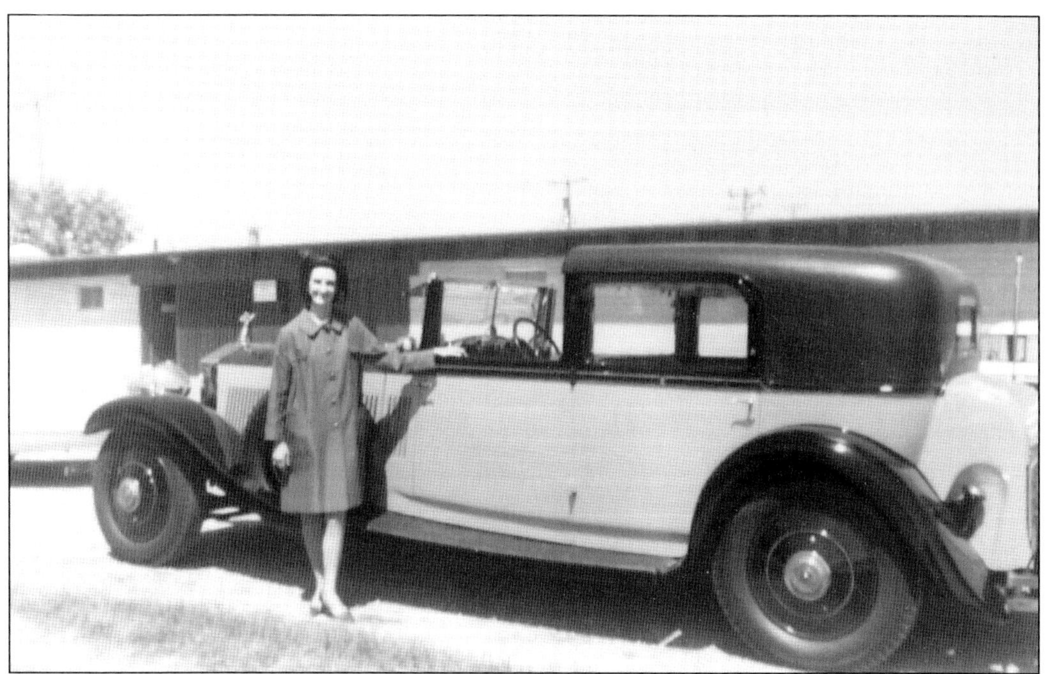

The Yellow Rolls-Royce was a 1964 British anthology about three different owners of a car. The film's all-star cast included Ingrid Bergman, Rex Harrison, Shirley MacLaine, Omar Sharif, George C. Scott, and Art Carney. To promote the film in the United States, a model was hired to take a yellow Rolls-Royce around the country to theaters showing the film. Her entourage included a chauffeur and a security guard for the car. The unidentified model is shown with the luxury car on the day they arrived in Tulsa to visit the Admiral Twin. (Courtesy of Mary Ann Blue.)

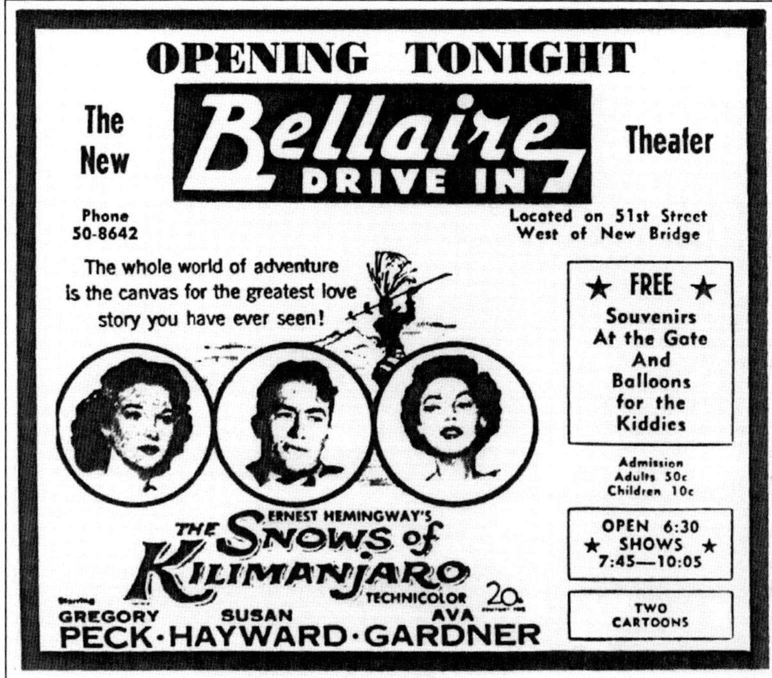

The Bellaire was a popular drive-in theater located just across from the Pepsi plant on West Fifty-first Street on the west bank of the Arkansas River. The June 1953 opening night feature was *The Snows of Kilimanjaro*, starring Gregory Peck, Ava Gardner, and an actress who was familiar to Tulsa audiences—Susan Hayward. (Courtesy of Wesley Horton.)

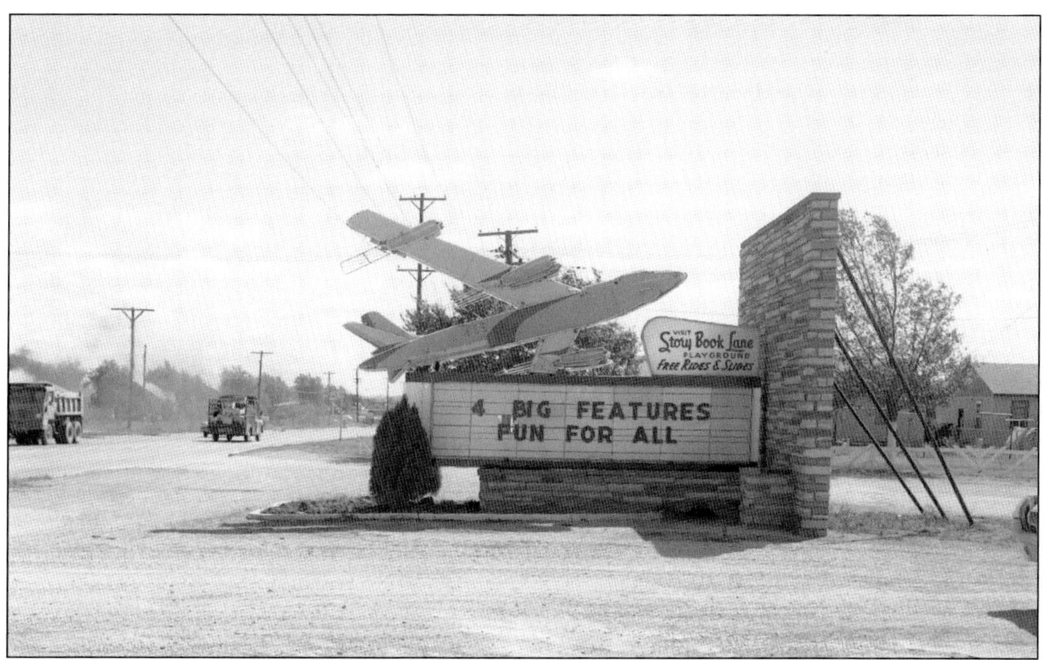

Tulsa's Airview Drive-In, located at 7500 East Pine Street, opened on June 7, 1951. It featured a striking mid-century modern sign and marquee. The Airview and the Modernaire (later known as the Admiral Twin) opened for business in the same summer season just a couple of miles apart.

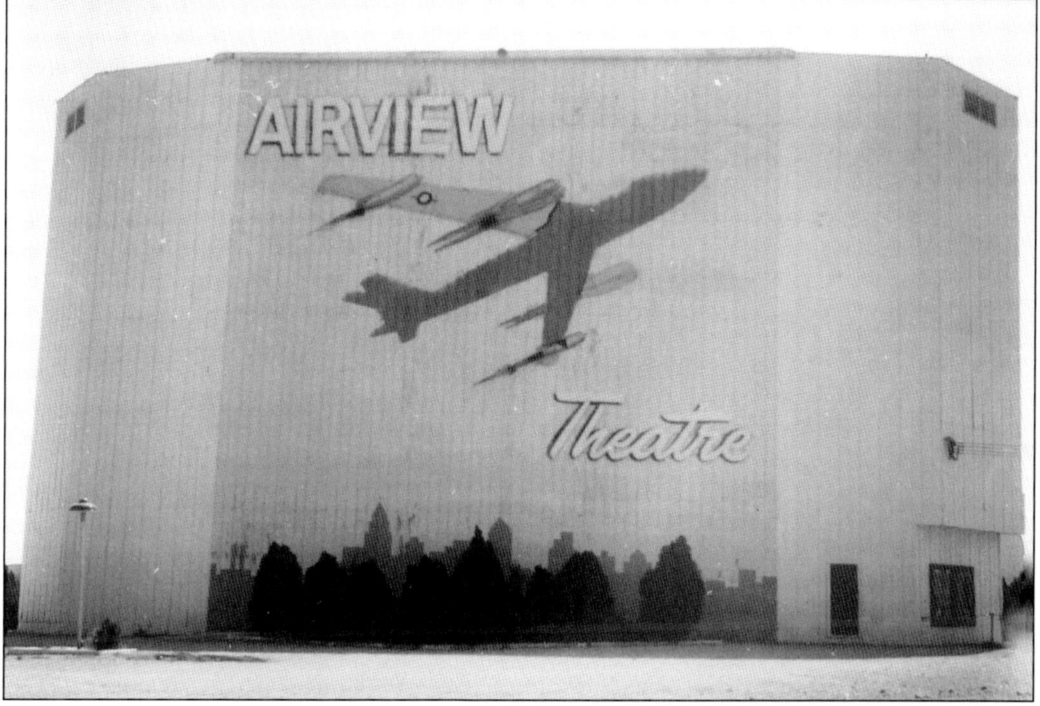

The Airview had a capacity of 700 cars. Its clever name promoted its proximity to Tulsa's aviation hubs, including Tulsa Municipal Airport and, later, Tulsa International Airport. (Courtesy of Oklahoma Historical Society.)

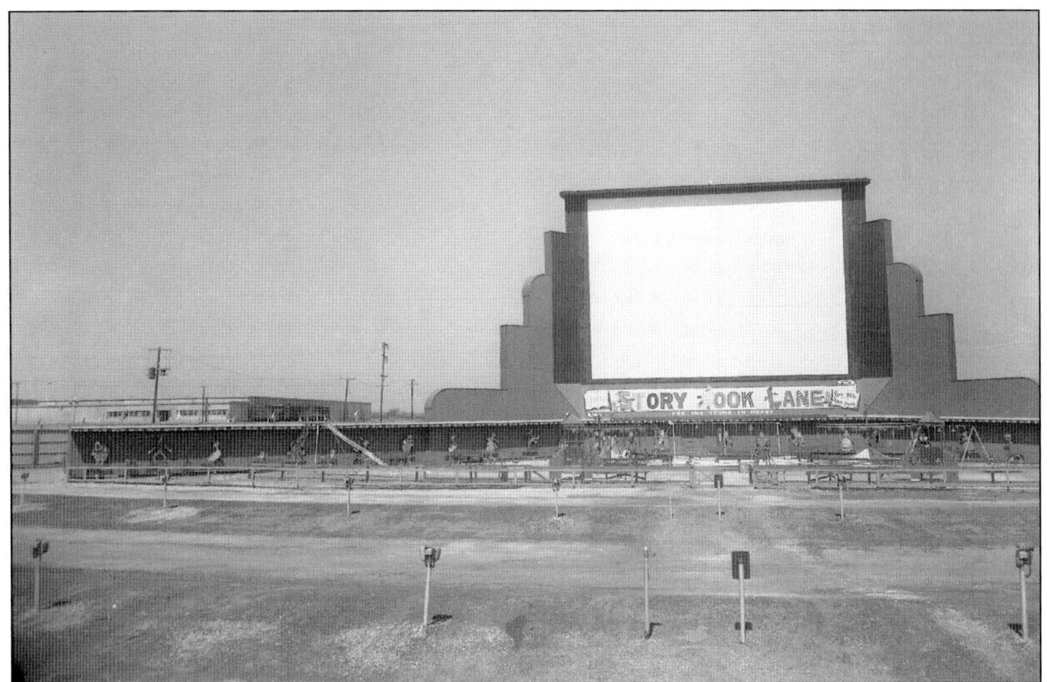

Like most early drive-ins, the Airview catered to families. The above image shows the Airview's elaborate Story Book Lane playground beneath the screen, which was promoted as "truly a child's paradise." That utopia included a miniature train and what was described as a "giant ocean wave." The Airview's opening night festivities in June 1951 included a live Western band for the adults and an appearance by Toto the Clown for the children, who were admitted for free. (Above, courtesy of Beryl Ford Collection/Rotary Club of Tulsa.)

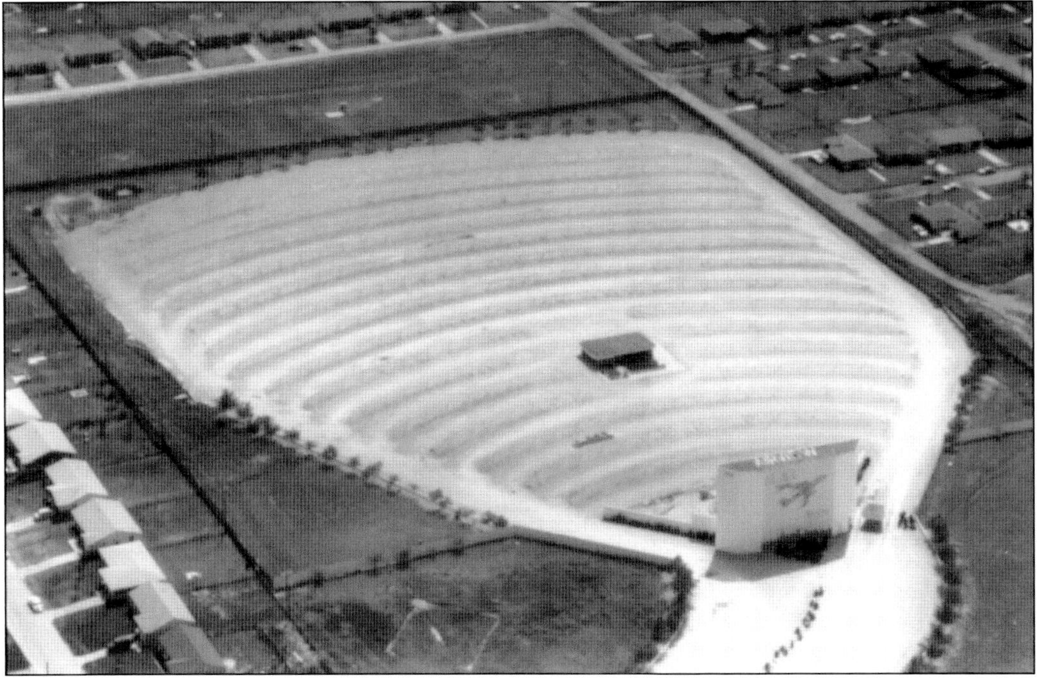

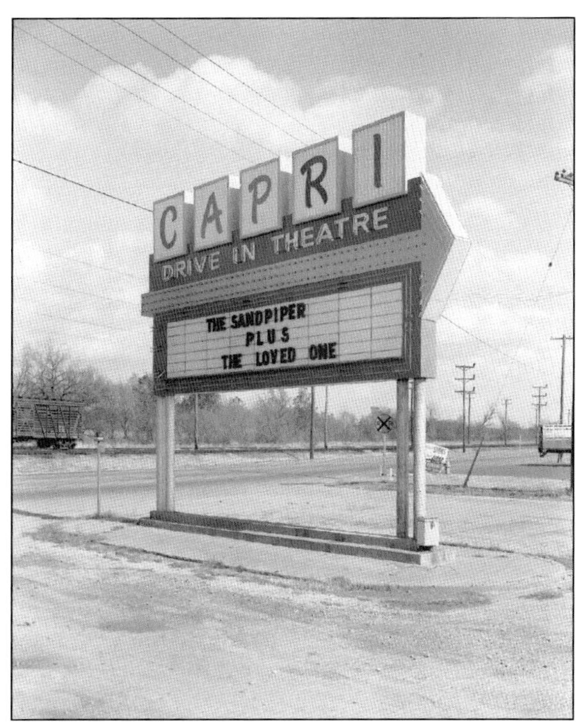

The Sand Springs Drive-In opened in 1950. Its name was changed to the Capri in the 1960s. After initially focusing on family entertainment, the Capri switched to adult films in the 1970s. During that era, a popular pastime for area teenagers involved parking at Chandler Park's overlook to try to get a free peek at the theater's screen, which was visible just across the Arkansas River. The Capri ceased operation in 1983. The land has since housed an auto parts salvage and a recycling company. (Right, courtesy of Beryl Ford Collection/Rotary Club of Tulsa.)

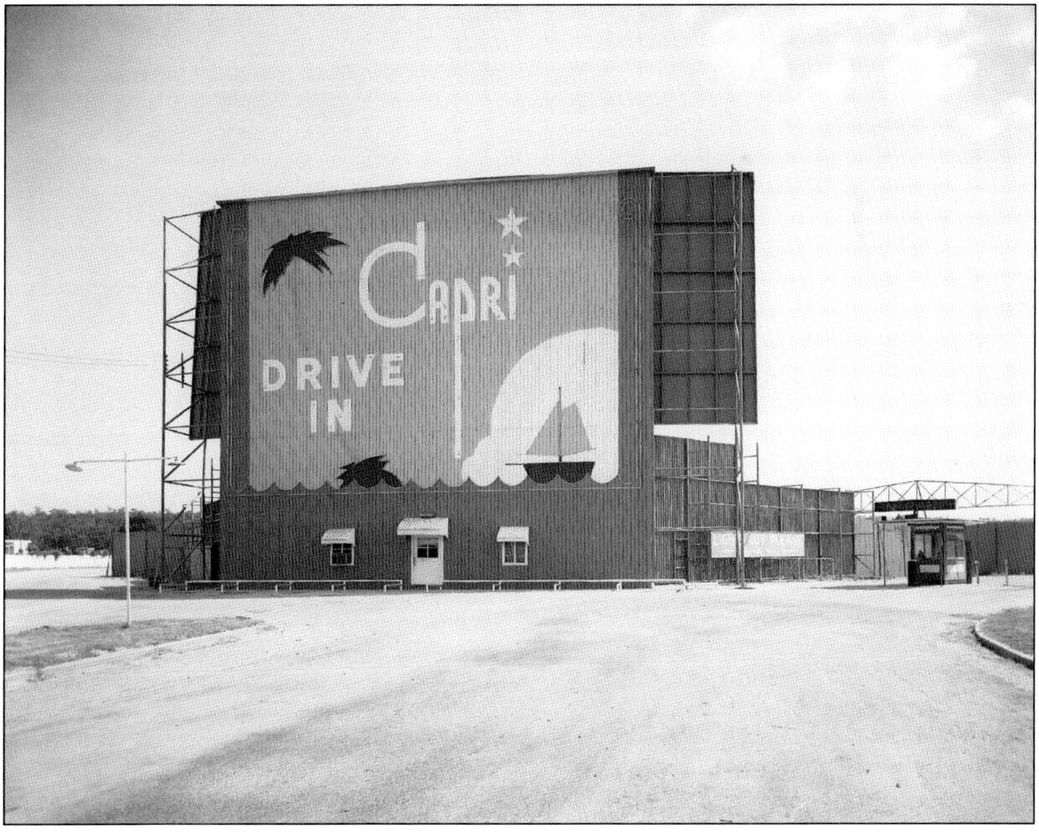

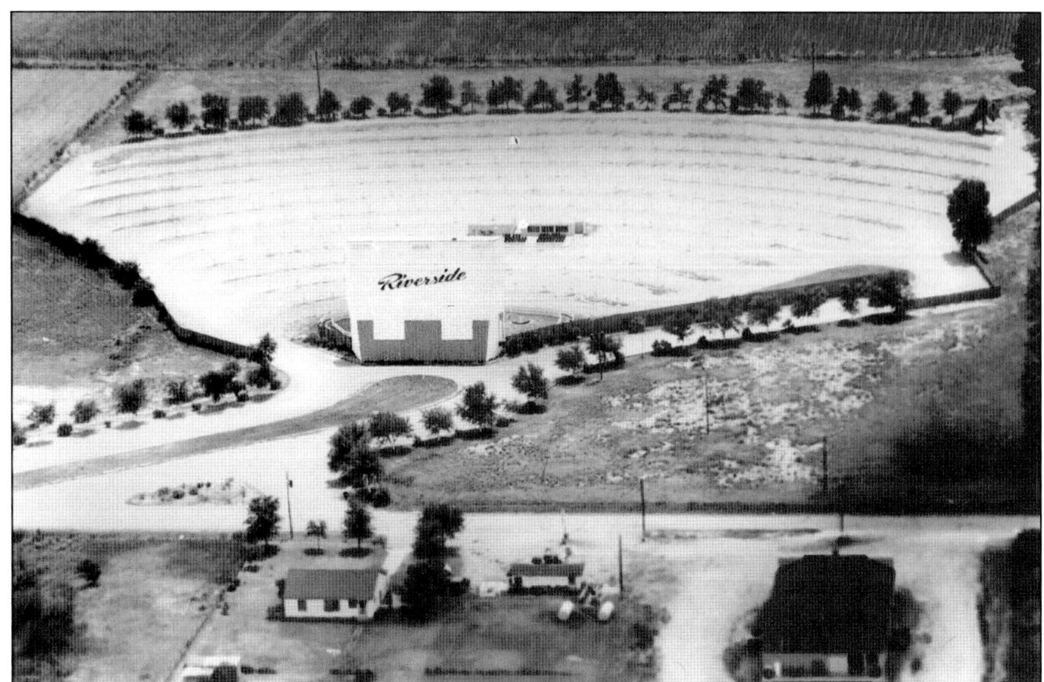

The Riverside Drive-In opened in 1948 outside of town on the south side of Seventy-first Street, east of the Arkansas River. In the 1956 image below, giant cut-out cartoon figures are visible around the perimeter of the playground beneath the screen. Kids could play before falling asleep in the back seat as their parents watched the movie. (Below, Oklahoma Historical Society.)

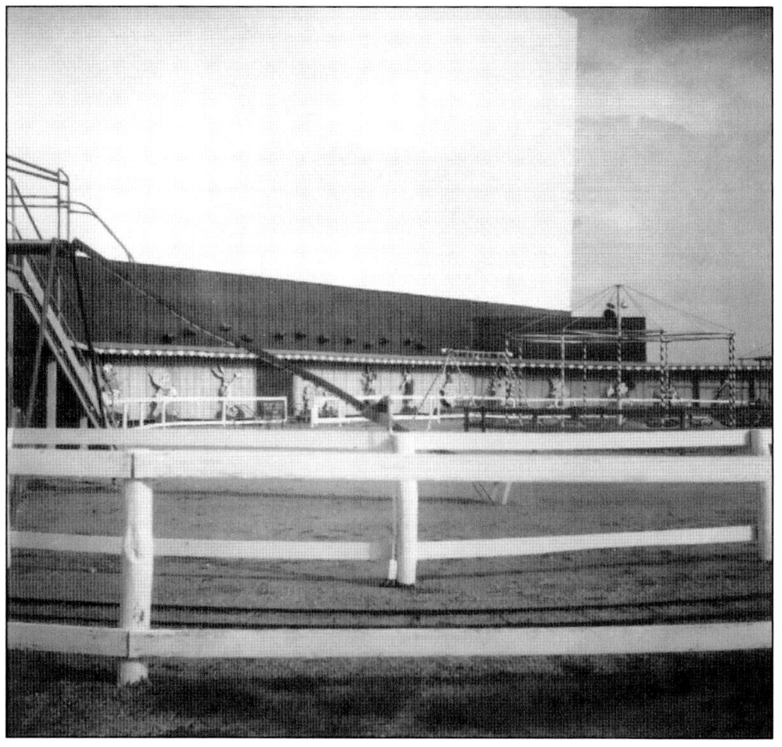

The Sheridan Drive-In opened on April 20, 1951, with *Vengeance Valley*, starring Burt Lancaster, and operated until 1963 at 4500 South Sheridan Road. Early advertisements for the theater claimed the Sheridan had the largest screen in Tulsa. It was known for its G-rated double features and the free kids' carnival beneath the screen. The theater was in the path of rapid residential and commercial development in the 1960s, which hastened its closing.

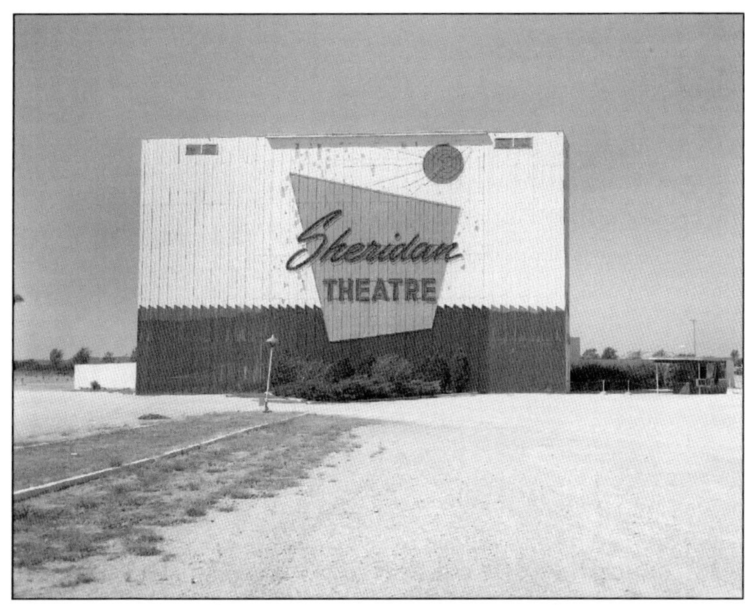

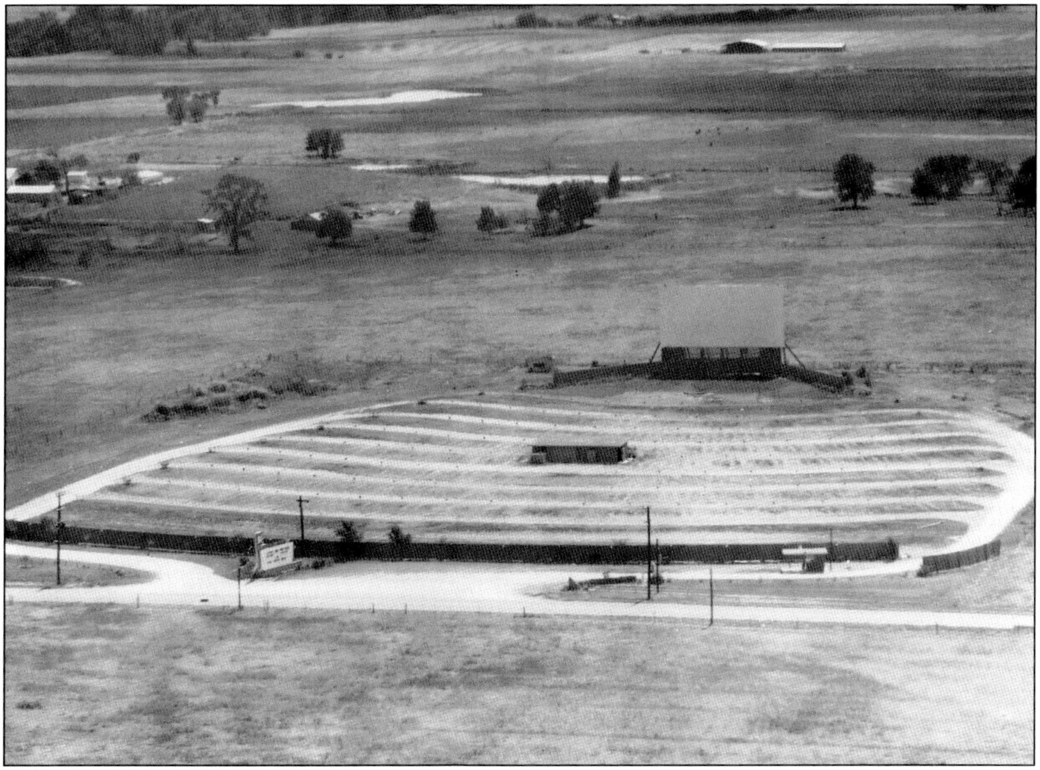

The Broken Arrow Drive-In, later known as the 51 Drive-In, was located on Seventy-first Street between 129th and 145th Streets. The theater, which operated for nearly 40 years, had an unusual opening and closing. The day of its advertised opening, July 31, 1953, a large truck loaded with gravel fell through the theater's septic tank and could not be moved in time for the theater to open. Nearly 40 years later, in May 1993, shortly after the theater closed for the night, a small tornado demolished the screen, and the theater never reopened.

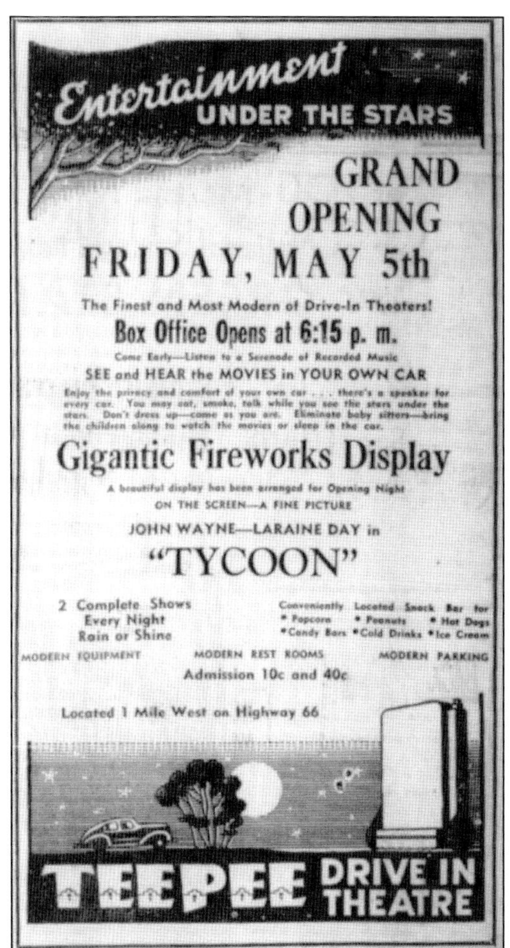

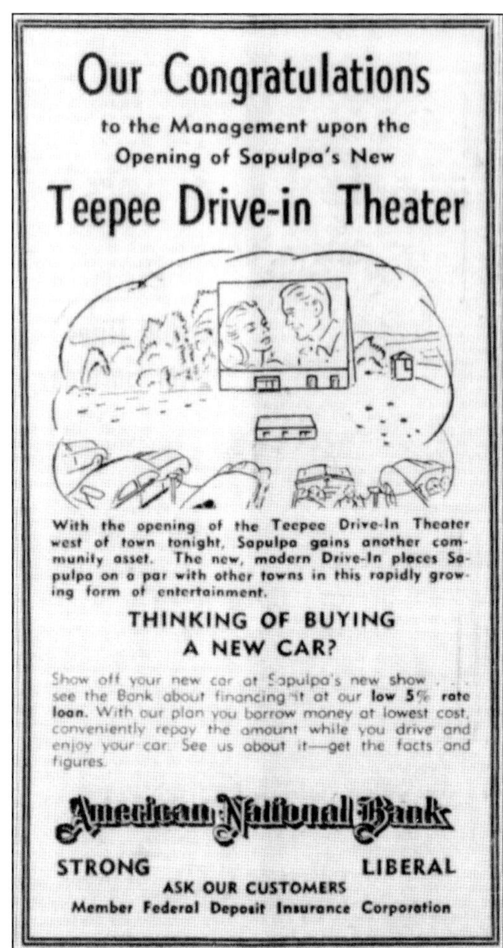

Pictured are a pair of advertisements related to the grand opening of the TeePee Drive-In in Sapulpa. The TeePee opened in May 1950 just west of Sapulpa on Route 66. The first advertisement promises "entertainment under the stars" and a gigantic fireworks display. The advertisement for American National Bank, at right, invites the public to finance a new car with them and show it off at the TeePee. (Both, courtesy of *Sapulpa Daily Herald*.)

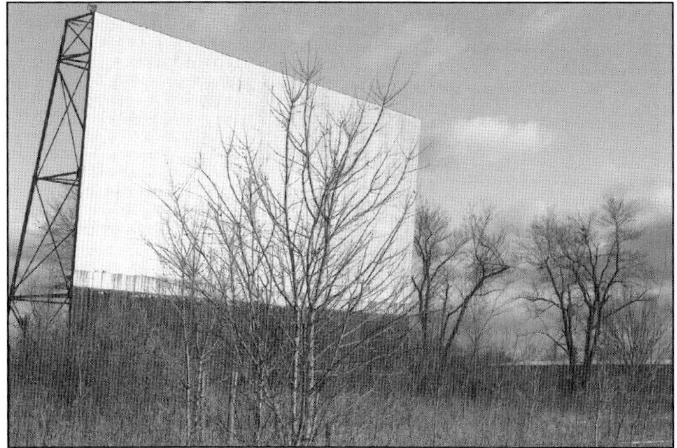

The TeePee Drive-In screen is shown as it appeared in February 2021, shortly before a renovation began. After being dormant since 1999, the drive-in, located on an original alignment of Route 66 west of Sapulpa, was purchased by a group planning to reopen the theater in 2022. The drive-in sits just west of a historic 1921 bridge over Rock Creek, a popular attraction on the Mother Road. (Courtesy of Steve Clem.)

Six

Premieres
Glitz, Glamour, and Hollywood Stars

Tulsa may be far removed from Hollywood, but it has had its share of star-studded glitz and glamour. In the early days of film, the motion-picture industry was spread more widely across the country, with movies made by local companies in many communities. In Tulsa, early theater owner William Smith started a movie studio along the Sand Springs Railway Line near Vern Station. Local films sometimes brought in nationally known talent or used locals. And, naturally, these movies premiered in Tulsa theaters.

In 1919, *The Wrecker* was described as "Tulsa's first home talent motion picture." It was filmed locally and had a cast of Tulsans, including a number of well-known community leaders. *The Wrecker* premiered at the Majestic on August 20, 1919. *The Crossroads of Tulsa*, produced locally to be shown as a prologue to *The Crossroads of New York*, premiered at the Rialto on August 18, 1922. Although these premieres were exciting to locals, the films had little lasting appeal. As time passed and Hollywood solidified its position as the center of the movie industry, premieres with Tulsa connections became grander events.

In February 1944, actress Jennifer Jones, who grew up in Tulsa as Phyllis Lee Isley, returned home for a premiere of the movie *The Song of Bernadette*. Both the Ritz and Orpheum played host as Jones spoke to hometown crowds. Just a week later, she won an Academy Award for her role.

One of the biggest events in Tulsa history was the parade held in conjunction with the premiere of the film *Tulsa* in 1949. An estimated 100,000 people gathered downtown on April 13, 1949, for a day of celebration, including a parade featuring the stars of the movie and miles of oil-field equipment. Susan Hayward, Robert Preston, and Chill Wills attended the film's premiere at the Big Four theaters downtown. Although the premiere was originally scheduled for only two theaters, more had to be added because of a quick sellout. However, there were not enough copies of the film. Reportedly, during the premiere, when a reel was finished at one theater, someone had to run it down the street to the next one.

Another well-known film with a Tulsa connection is *The Outsiders*. Based on the book by native Tulsan S.E. Hinton, the movie was filmed in the Tulsa area with a cast of up-and-coming stars, including Tom Cruise, Patrick Swayze, and Rob Lowe. Directed by Francis Ford Coppola, *The Outsiders* premiered at the Williams Center Cinema on March 22, 1983.

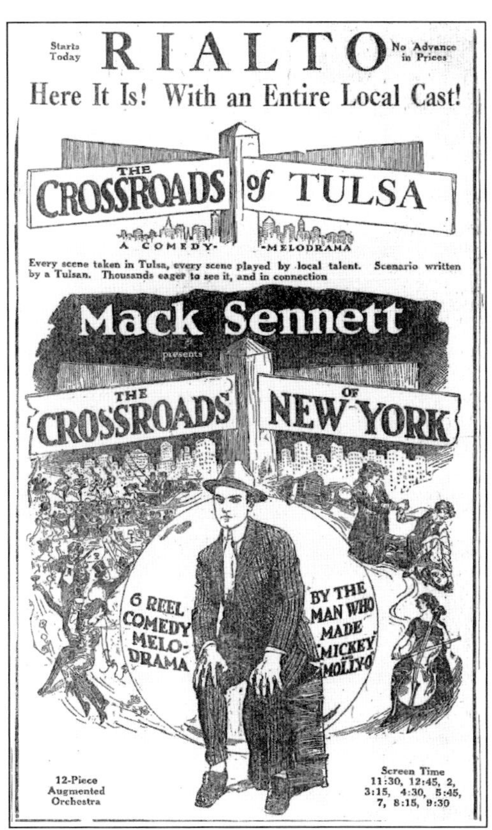

On August 18, 1922, *The Crossroads of Tulsa* premiered at the Rialto. The film was produced by William Smith, who owned several theaters in the area and started his own local film company. The impetus for creating *The Crossroads of Tulsa* was to show it in conjunction with *The Crossroads of New York*. Discussions in the local papers offered many suggestions for ways to create a good film and include Tulsans as actors.

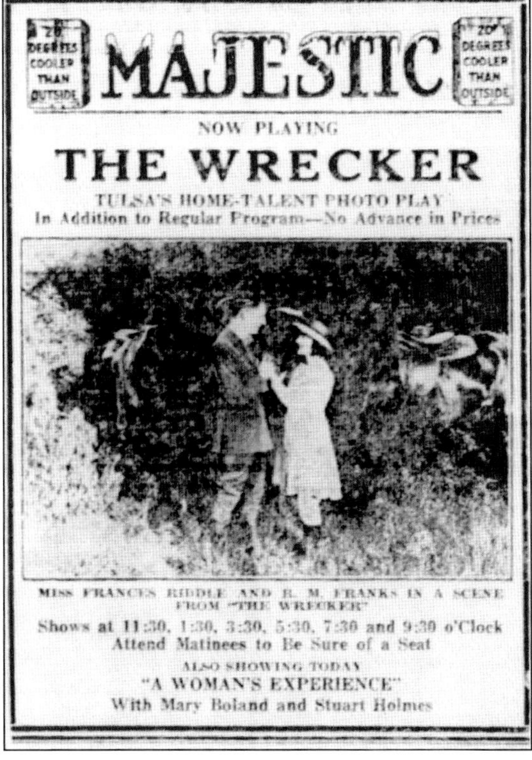

The Wrecker, filmed in Tulsa in 1919, extensively advertised its local cast. Many of the advertisements listed the names of the most prominent Tulsans appearing in the film, including the mayor, Charles Hubbard. The newspaper described the project as "three weeks of pistol fights, automobile smash-ups, downtown fires, train wrecks, love-making, and hard work." *The Wrecker* premiered at the Majestic on August 20, 1919, to a sold-out crowd that elicited apologies from the theater for a lack of space. (Courtesy of *Tulsa World*.)

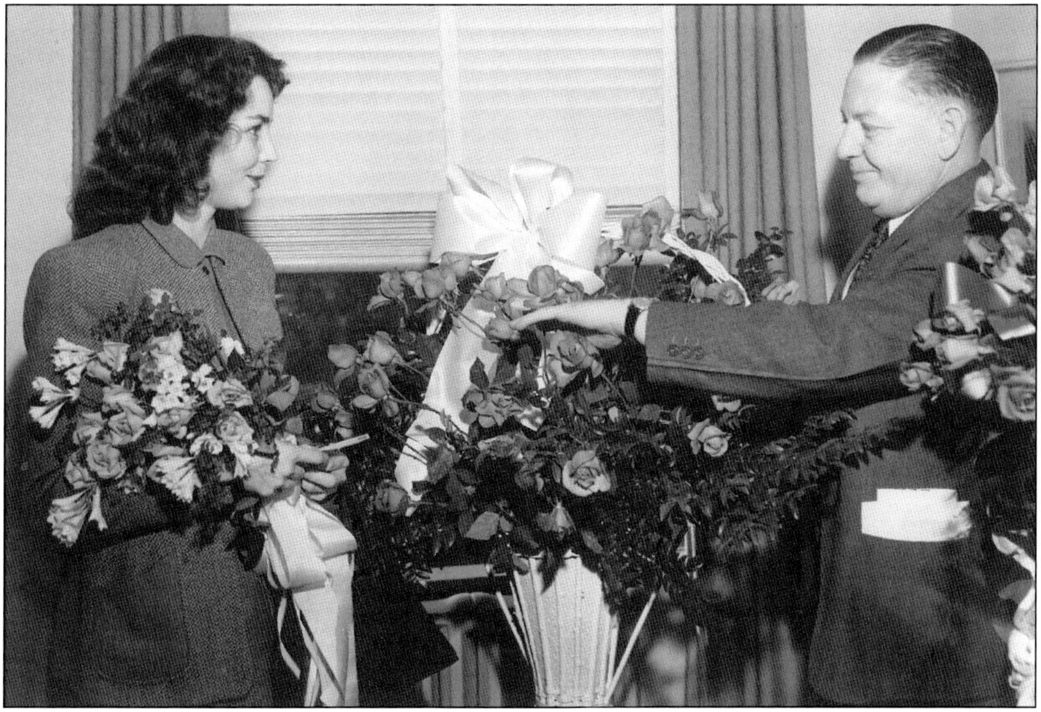

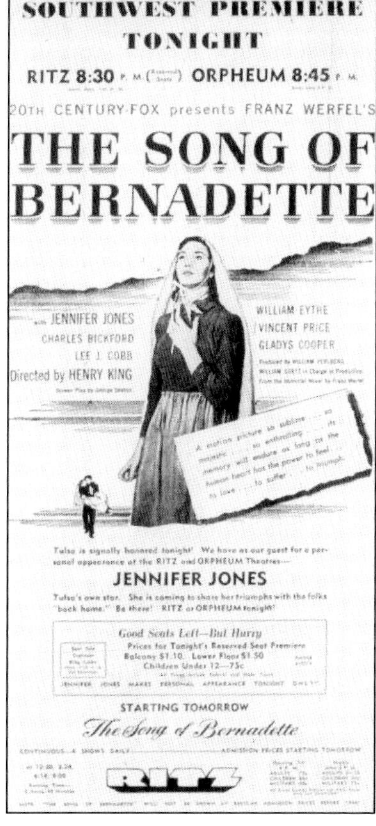

On February 24, 1944, Jennifer Jones returned to Tulsa for the Southwest premiere of *The Song of Bernadette*. She arrived at Tulsa's Union Depot to a crowd of fans, and welcome banners hung above Main Street. The *Tulsa World* described the scene: "Wearing a yellow and brown tweed suit and alligator pumps . . . Jones smiled and waved to the crowd, exclaiming 'I'm so glad to be here, I could almost die!'" Jones is pictured above with Glenn Condon before her evening appearances at the Ritz and Orpheum. Condon, who worked as both a radio and newspaper journalist, also managed the Majestic theater early in his career. (Both, courtesy of *Tulsa World*.)

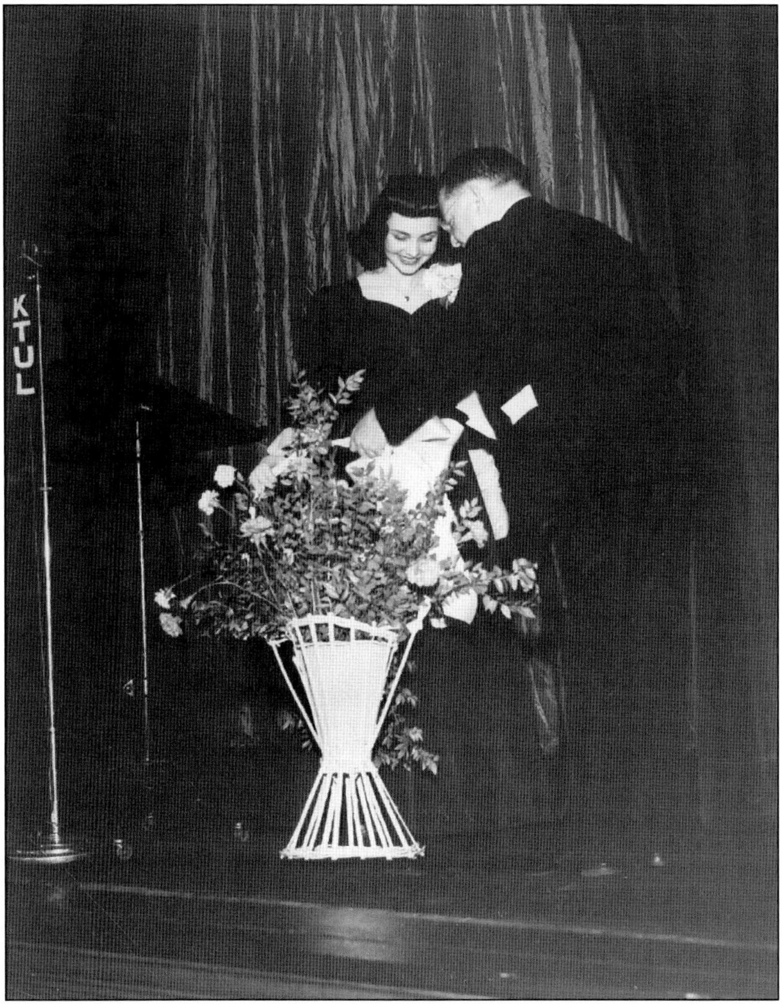

Jennifer Jones wore a black taffeta dress for her appearances at the Ritz and Orpheum in 1944. Glenn Condon introduced her to the audiences at both theaters. Tickets for *The Song of Bernadette* included the following note: "Honoring the star who will make the only personal appearance with the picture here in Tulsa—her 'hometown.'" The next day, Jones unveiled a statue of herself as Bernadette at her alma mater, Monte Cassino School. (Courtesy of *Tulsa World*.)

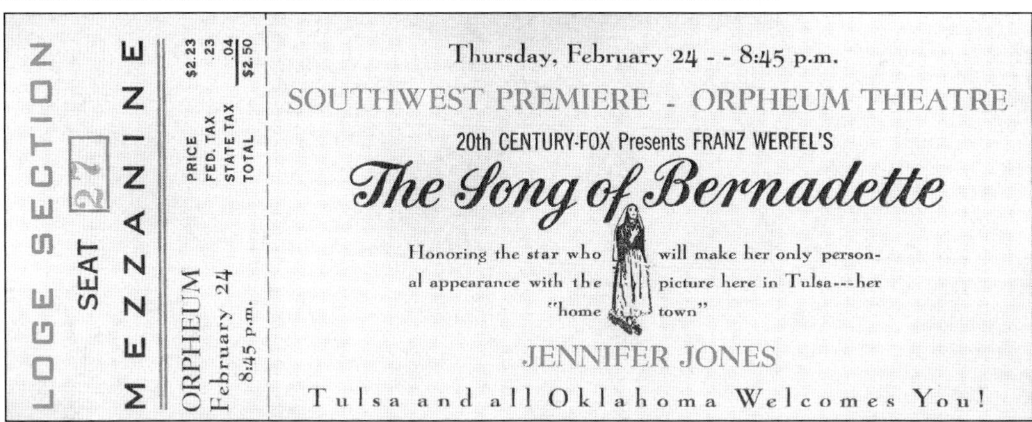

LOGE SECTION

SEAT 27

MEZZANINE

PRICE $2.23
FED. TAX .23
STATE TAX .04
TOTAL $2.50

ORPHEUM
February 24
8:45 p.m.

Thursday, February 24 - - 8:45 p.m.

SOUTHWEST PREMIERE - ORPHEUM THEATRE

20th CENTURY-FOX Presents FRANZ WERFEL'S

The Song of Bernadette

Honoring the star who will make her only personal appearance with the picture here in Tulsa---her "home town"

JENNIFER JONES

Tulsa and all Oklahoma Welcomes You!

A week after being welcomed home by Tulsa fans, Jennifer Jones received an Academy Award at Grauman's Chinese Theatre in Hollywood. Many were amazed that she won the award for her first role. As of 2021, Jones remains the only Tulsan to have won an Oscar. She also appeared on the cover of *Life* magazine's July 24, 1944, issue.

Tulsa still held the nickname "Oil Capital of the World" in April 1949, when the film *Tulsa* premiered in its namesake city. The metro area population was just under 200,000, and half of that population would end up gathering downtown for the biggest event in the city's history—Tulsa Day. An entire day of activities was planned for April 13, 1949, including a parade, an afternoon square dance, and a number of private parties at which the city's elite could mingle with the movie's stars. Susan Hayward and Robert Preston are prominently featured on this poster for the film.

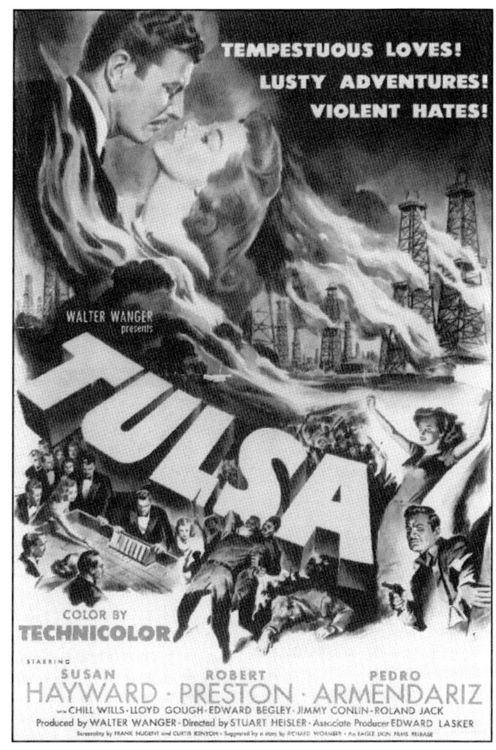

With financial backing from the oil industry, the Tulsa Day parade and festivities grew bigger and bigger. Oil companies decided the parade would be the perfect opportunity to show off their equipment and technology. The parade ended up including more than $10 million of oil equipment representing 100 different companies.

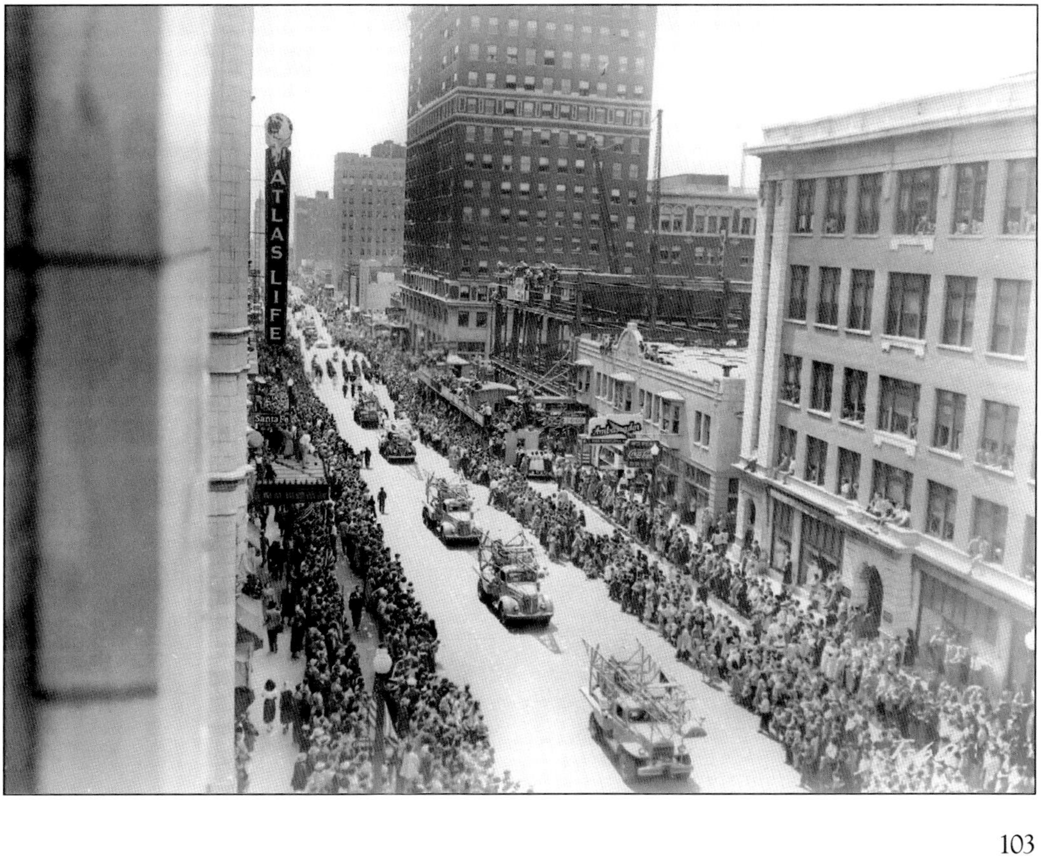

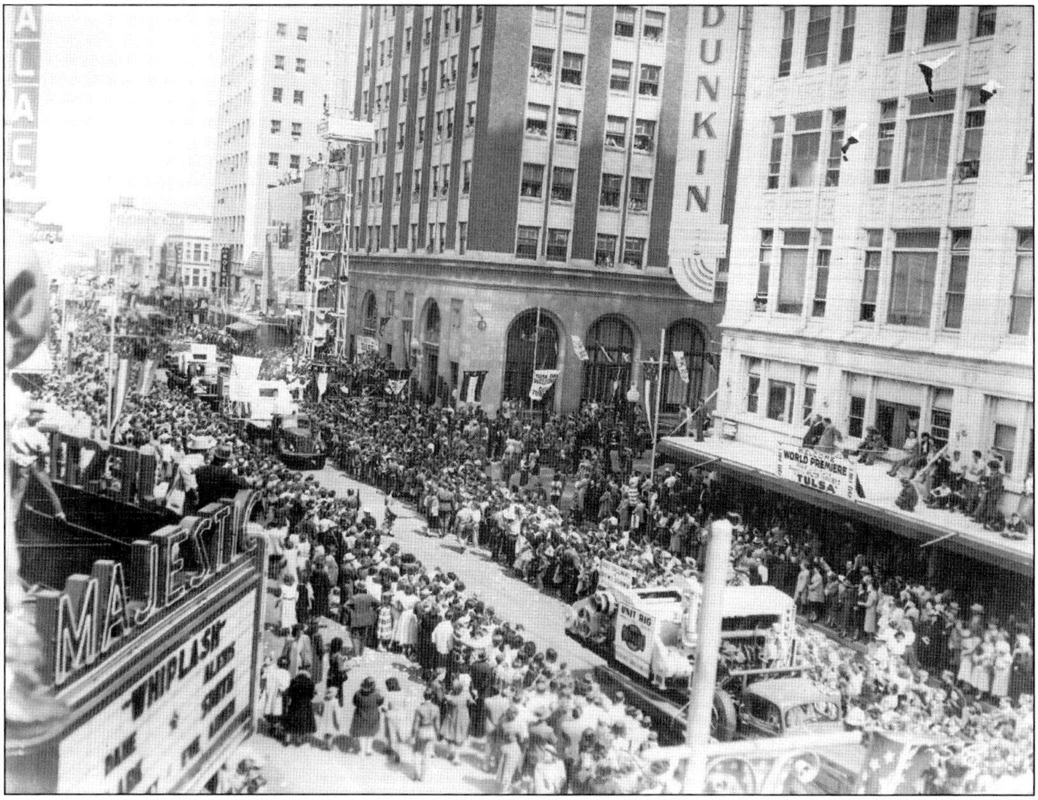

In addition to featuring oil equipment, the Tulsa Day parade on April 13, 1949, included 22 marching bands from area high schools. The entire spectacle ended up being five miles long and lasted for somewhere between two and a half to three hours as it zigzagged through the streets of downtown. In this view, the Majestic marquee is visible in the foreground at left.

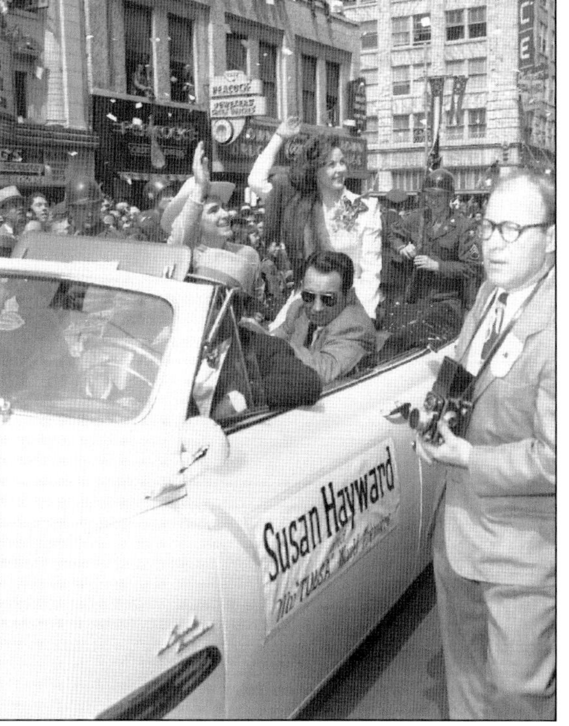

The stars of the film—Susan Hayward, Robert Preston, and Chill Wills—each waved to the crowd from their own convertibles. Chill Wills had a tendency to jump out of his car to sign autographs and talk to children along the way.

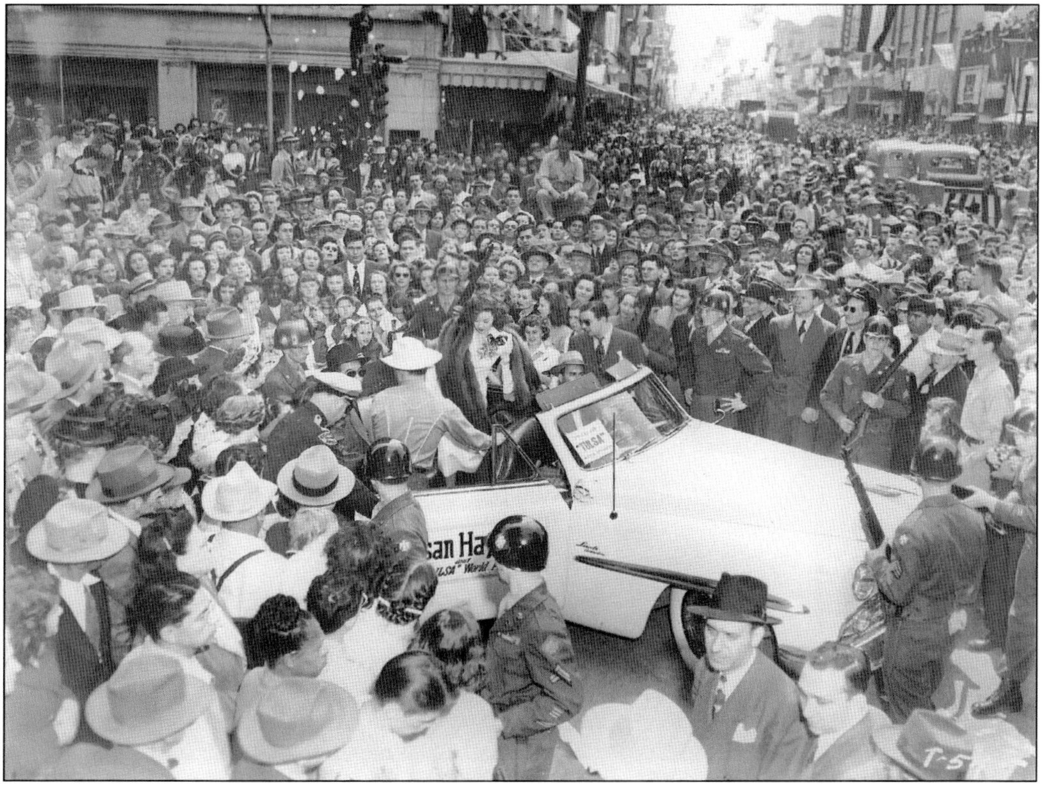

A reviewing stand, in the form of a 127-foot-tall portable oil rig, was set up next to the First National Bank at Fourth and Main Streets. As the parade passed that point, Susan Hayward exited her car and was immediately surrounded by the crowd. Next, she was lifted 75 feet in the air on the oil rig's platform to speak to the crowd. Hayward was reportedly unaware of this plan and was terrified the entire time. As the platform ascended, many of those working in the building leaned out of the windows to greet Hayward. Others scaled the rig to get closer to the star. Hayward responded by smiling and explaining that she was too scared to look down. Upon reaching the top, she exclaimed to the crowd, "I've just had the most terrifying ride of my life." In answer to a question about whether she would like to work on an oil rig for a living, she exclaimed, "Oh no!"

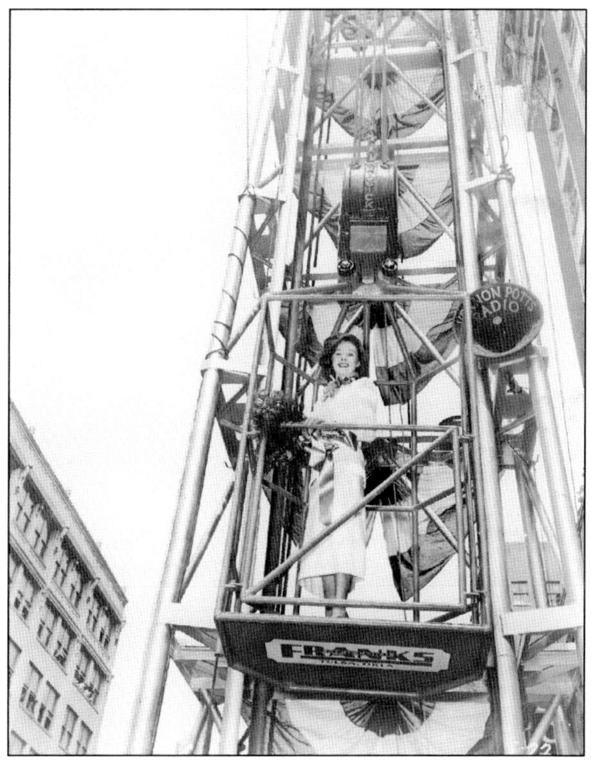

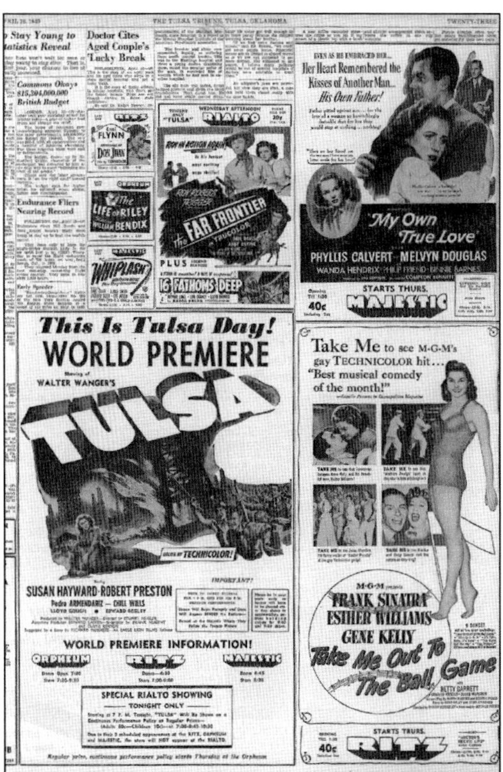

THE TULSA TRIBUNE, TULSA, OKLAHOMA

TWENTY-THREE

Stay Young to Statistics Reveal

Doctor Cites Aged Couple's Lucky Break

Commons Okays $15,304,000,000 British Budget

Endurance Fliers Nearing Record

Early Speeder

RITZ
Errol FLYNN
DON JUAN

ORPHEUM
The LIFE of RILEY
WILLIAM BENDIX

MAJESTIC
WHIPLASH

TONIGHT ONLY "TULSA"
WEDNESDAY AFTERNOON
RIALTO
30¢
ROY IN ACTION AGAIN!
ROY ROGERS TRIGGER
The FAR FRONTIER
in TRUCOLOR
PLUS
16 FATHOMS DEEP

EVEN AS HE EMBRACED HER...
Her Heart Remembered the Kisses of Another Man... His Own Father!
'My Own True Love'
PHYLLIS CALVERT · MELVYN DOUGLAS
WANDA HENDRIX · PHILIP FRIEND · BINNIE BARNES
STARTS THURS.
MAJESTIC
40¢

This Is Tulsa Day!
WORLD PREMIERE
WALTER WANGER'S
TULSA
TECHNICOLOR!
SUSAN HAYWARD · ROBERT PRESTON
Pedro ARMENDARIZ — CHILL WILLS
LLOYD GOUGH · EDWARD BEGLEY
IMPORTANT!
WORLD PREMIERE INFORMATION!
ORPHEUM · RITZ · MAJESTIC
SPECIAL RIALTO SHOWING
—— TONIGHT ONLY ——
Regular price, continuous performance policy starts Thursday at the Orpheum

Take Me to see M-G-M's gay TECHNICOLOR hit...
"Best musical comedy of the month!"
M-G-M presents
FRANK SINATRA
ESTHER WILLIAMS
GENE KELLY
Take Me Out To The Ball Game
with BETTY GARRETT
STARTS THURS.
RITZ
40¢

Oklahoma governor Roy Turner declared April 13, 1949, as Tulsa Day. In preparation, there were Tulsa Day sales to encourage people to attend events dressed in Western attire. Businesses and schools closed to allow as many people as possible to celebrate the day. (Courtesy of Beryl Ford Collection/Rotary Club of Tulsa.)

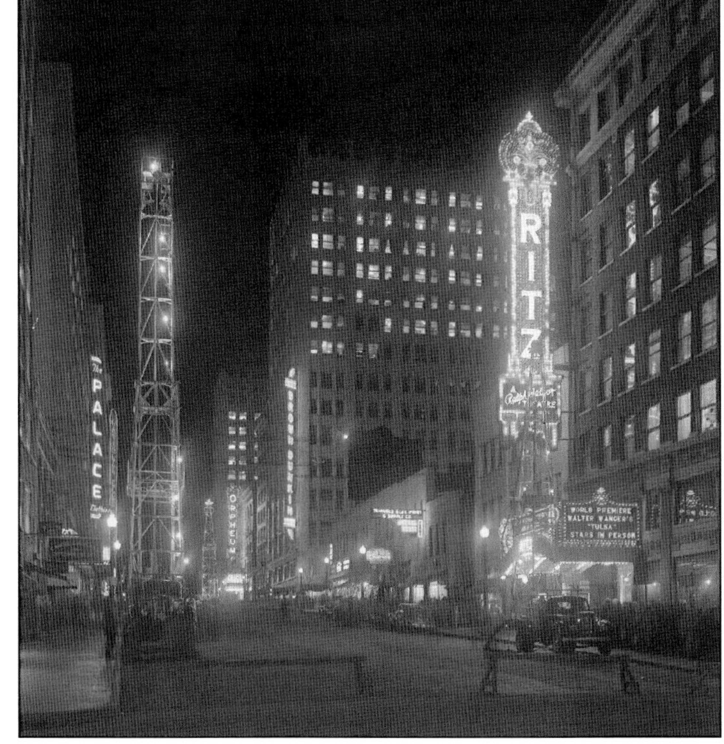

A total of 7,000 people were lucky enough to see *Tulsa* on the night it premiered—April 13, 1949. The stars of the film spoke to crowds at each of the Big Four theaters. There ended up being eight showings that evening, which led to the actors having to travel from theater to theater. In this view of Fourth Street, both the Ritz and Orpheum are visible. Lighted oil rigs were set up along the street as part of the celebration.

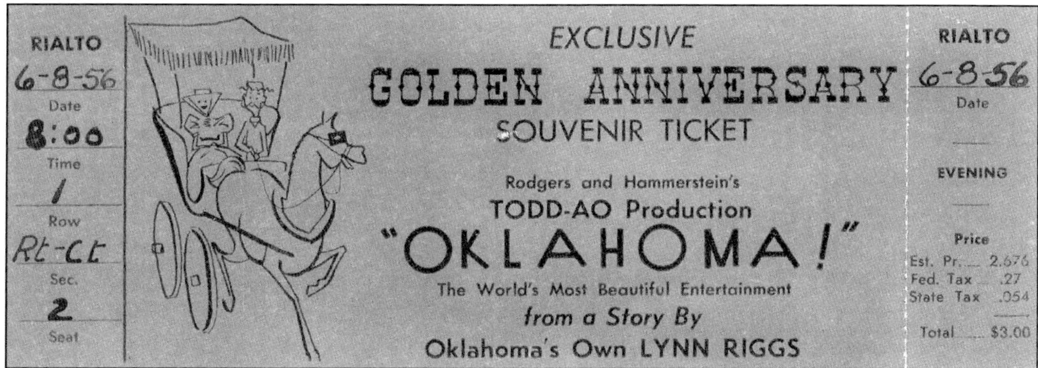

On June 8, 1956, the Southwest premiere of the film *Oklahoma!* was held at the Rialto. In order to earn the right to host the event, the owners paid $56,000 for a state-of-the-art Todd-AO screen and sound system. *Oklahoma!* was the first movie photographed using the 70-mm wide-screen process. At the time of the premiere, it was reported that only 20 theaters in the country had been outfitted with Todd-AO technology; the Rialto was the only theater between Chicago and Dallas equipped to show the film. The movie *Oklahoma!* was based on a 1931 stage play written by Oklahoman Lynn Riggs called *Green Grow the Lilacs*. Following the June 8, 1956, premiere of *Oklahoma!* to a standing-room-only audience, the film played at the Rialto for months, which was very unusual at the time. Newspapers reported that people from all over Oklahoma journeyed to Tulsa to see the film at the Rialto, even leading to plans for some communities to provide bus trips to the theater.

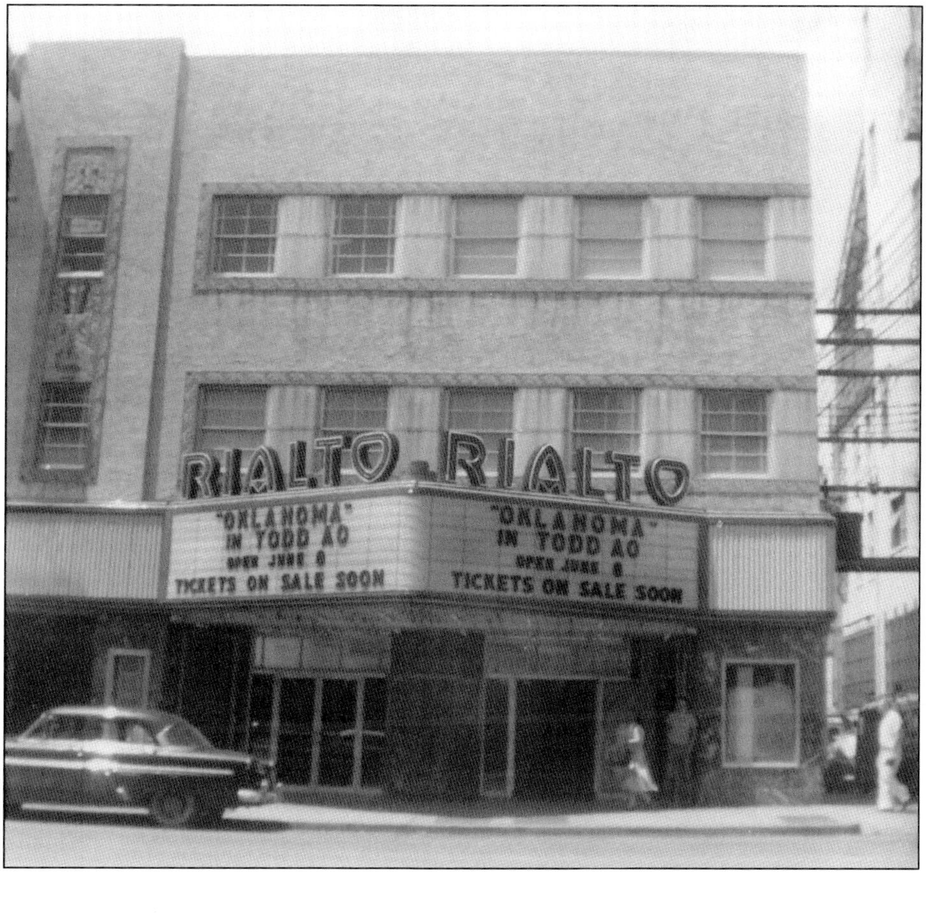

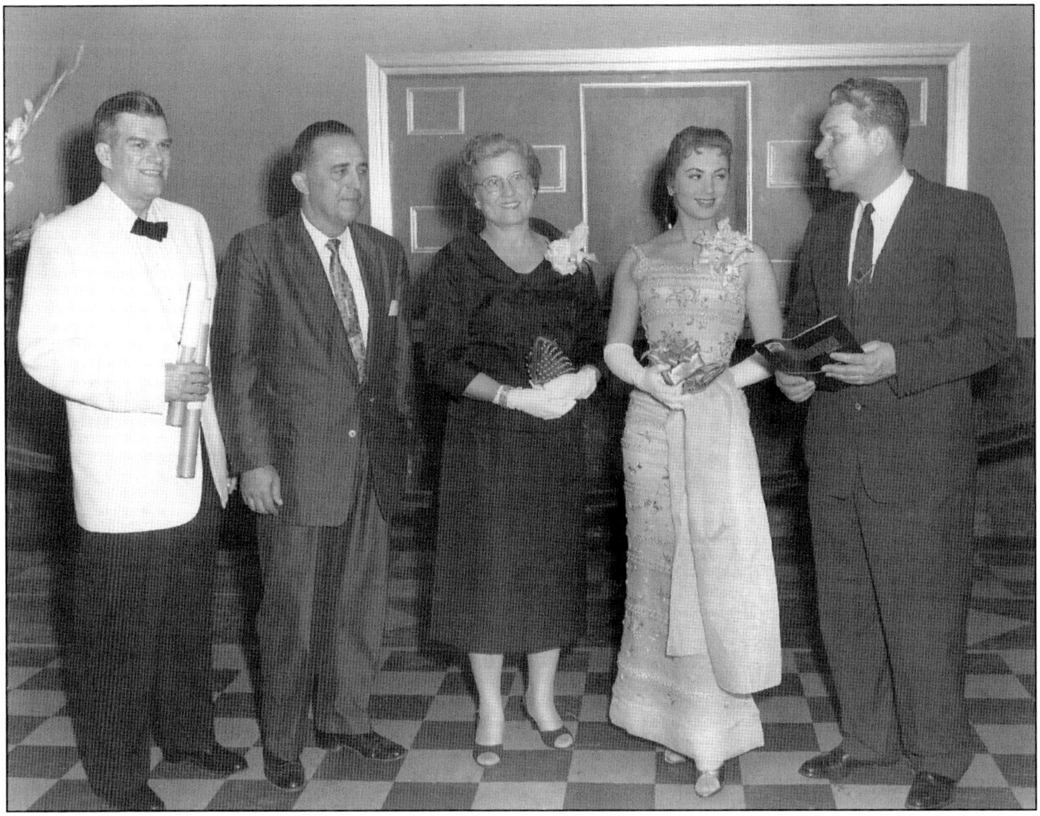

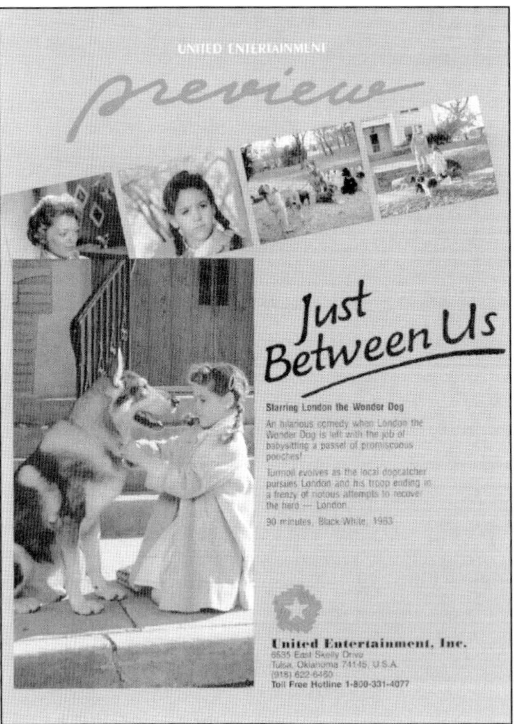

Oklahoma! featured actress Shirley Jones in her first role. Jones, who played Laurey, attended the premiere. Tulsa was the first city to show a specially produced film entitled *The Miracle of Todd-AO*, which explained the technology. It also provided an exciting Todd-AO journey to the crowd as they experienced a roller coaster, skiing, and even a police chase. In this image, Jones and Gov. Raymond Gary are at right.

Just Between Us is a 1961 low-budget comedy that was shot in Tulsa. It starred a German shepherd named London the Wonder Dog and featured future Golden Girl Rue McClanahan. London was one of the highly trained canines of Chuck Eisenmann, a former minor-league baseball player who had, for a time, played for the Tulsa Oilers. London had already racked up movie credits for *The Littlest Hobo* and *My Dog Buddy* when Eisenmann brought the dog and his two stand-ins to Tulsa to film *Just Between Us*. Eisenmann also wrote the script about the adventures of a young girl and London.

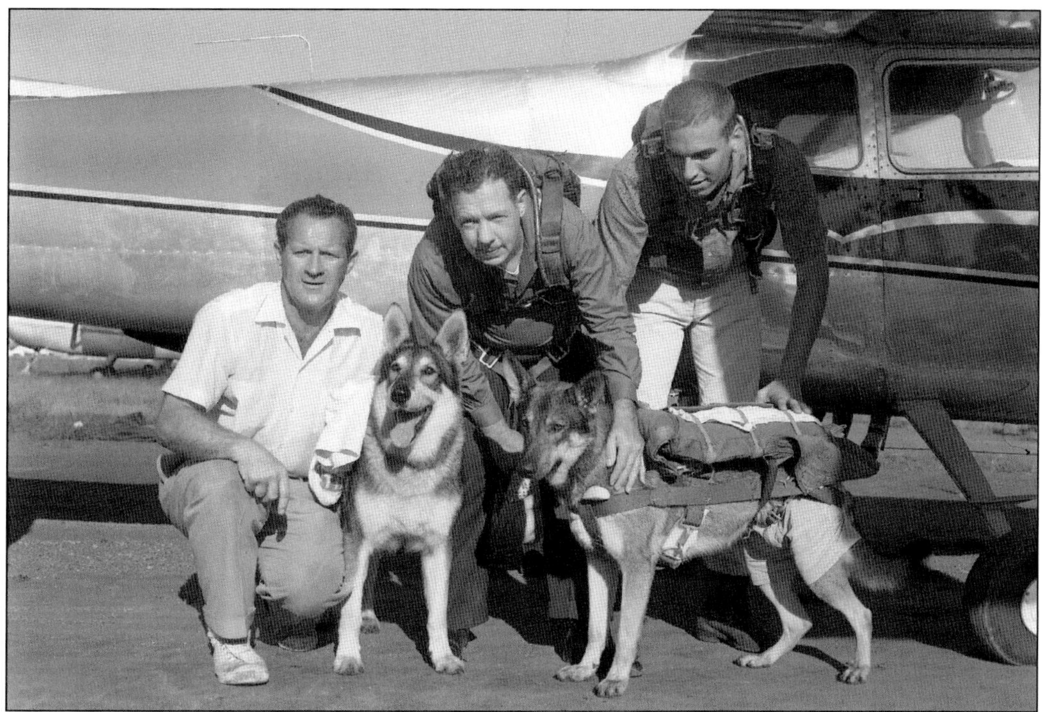

Just Between Us was financed and cast in Tulsa. Eight-year-old Marcia Becton, a talented young dance student, won the role of the little girl, while recent University of Tulsa graduate Rue McClanahan was cast as her mother. The film was shot at various locales, including the Tulsa Zoo. The premiere was held on June 25, 1961, at Tulsa's Premiere Theater and Airview Drive-In. London the Wonder Dog performed tricks before the screenings. As a publicity stunt to promote the premiere, one of Eisenmann's canines parachuted from a light plane at Tulsa's Harvey Young Airport. The parachuting dog was carried off course by the wind and landed in a commercial frog pond but was uninjured. Ultimately, the film of that stunt may have been seen by more people than the movie, as *Just Between Us* did not get picked up for major distribution. However, a later Eisenmann project incorporated footage of a parachuting dog into its end credits. London (or one of Eisenmann's other canines that went by that name) later starred in a Canadian television series also named *The Littlest Hobo*. (Both, courtesy of Beryl Ford Collection/Rotary Club of Tulsa.)

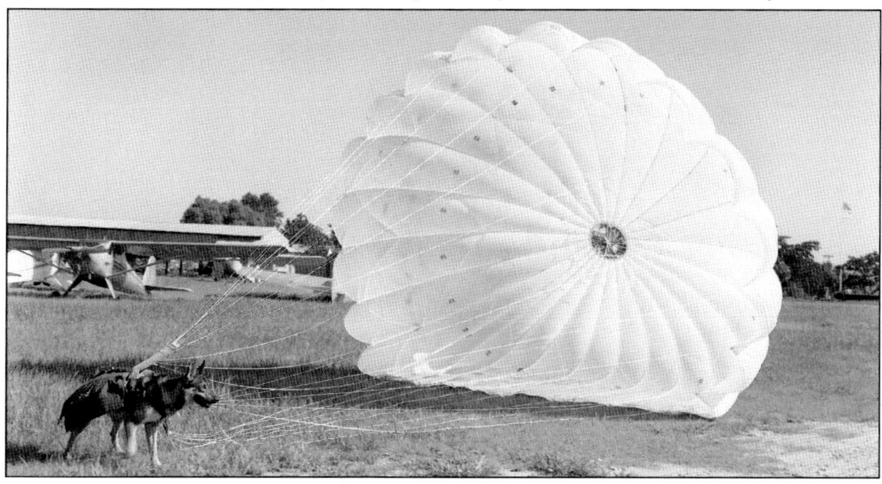

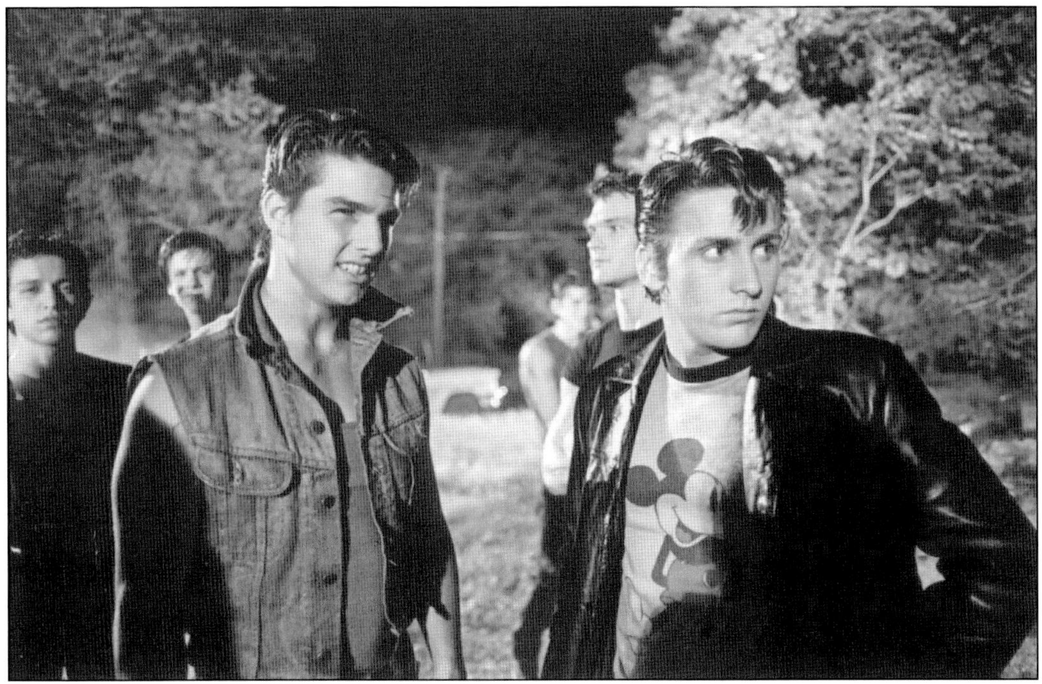

In 1982, Francis Ford Coppola brought a crew to Tulsa to film the screen version of S.E. Hinton's bestseller *The Outsiders*. The much-loved story of "greasers and socs" spotlighted many of the Tulsa locations the author originally included in her story, like the Admiral Twin Drive-In and Will Rogers High School. Many of the young actors in the film were on the verge of stardom. Pictured here between takes are Tom Cruise, Emilio Estevez, Patrick Swayze, and C. Thomas Howell.

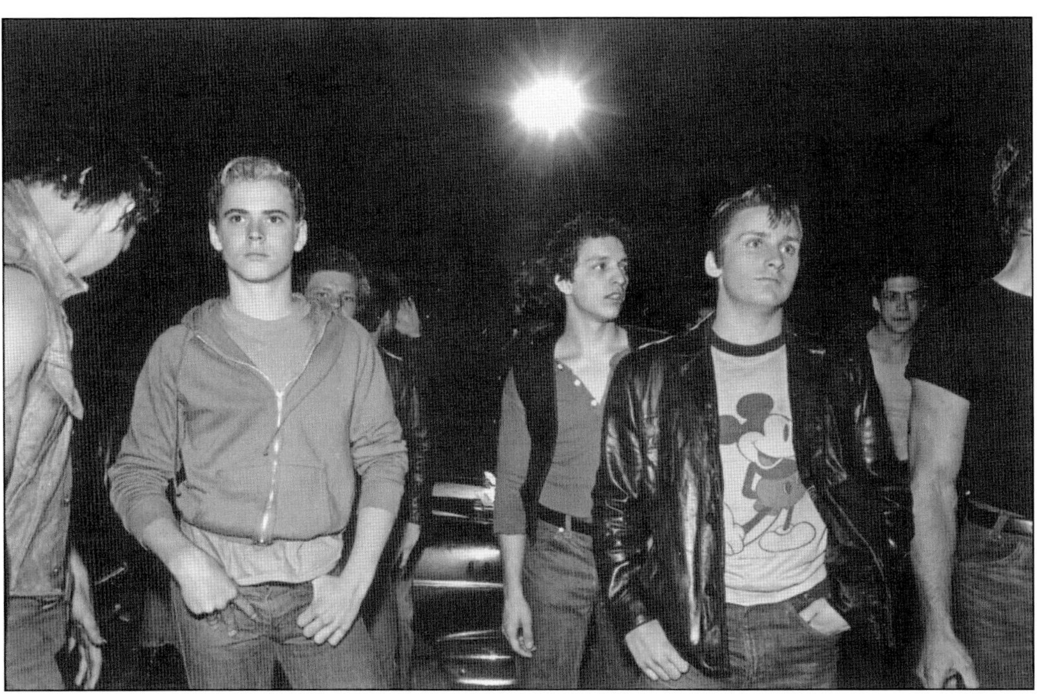

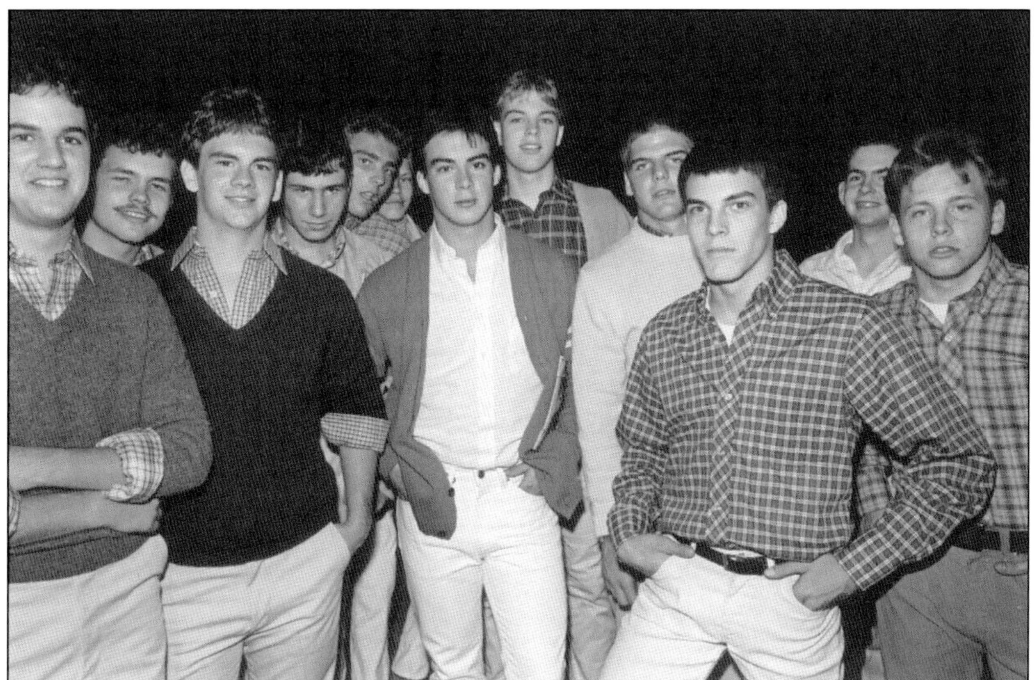

Many Tulsans remember when *The Outsiders* was filmed in Tulsa in 1982. The project gave locals the chance to be extras by playing greasers and socs (above). *The Outsiders* was only one of three movies based on books by S.E. Hinton that were filmed in Tulsa in close succession. The other two, *Tex* and *Rumble Fish*, allowed for even more participation from Tulsans as they took their turns working as extras or stand-ins.

The Outsiders premiered in Tulsa on March 22, 1983, at the Williams Center Cinema several days before its national release. The premiere was a benefit for a local charity, with movie tickets priced at $25, and was followed by a reception at Charlie's Nostalgia. Author S.E. Hinton (pictured here holding a drink), Patrick Swayze, and C. Thomas Howell attended the premiere.

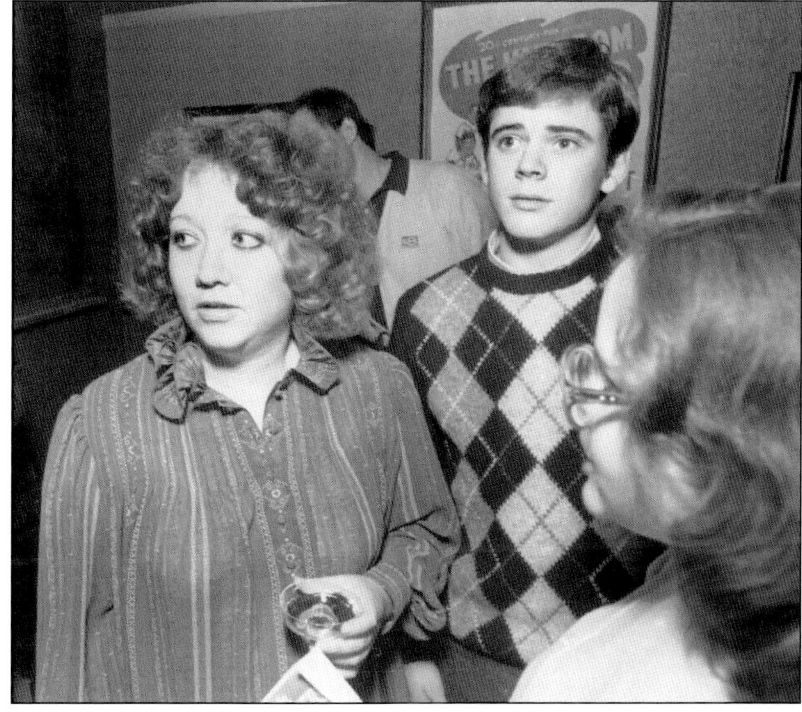

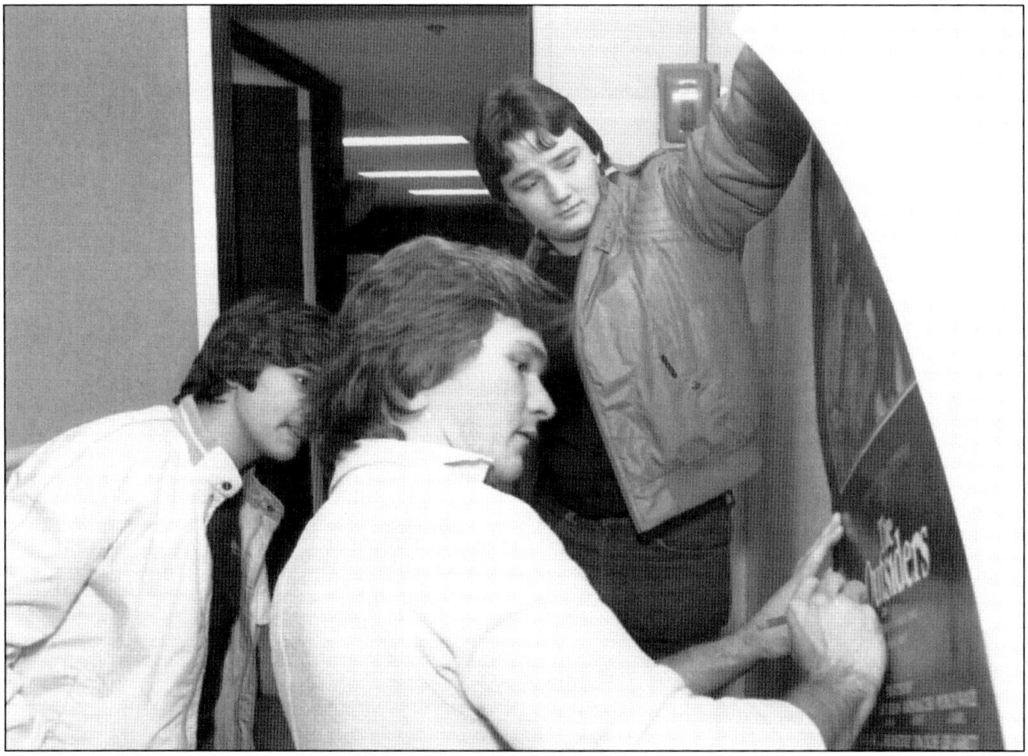

Patrick Swayze, who played Darrel Curtis in the film, and C. Thomas Howell, who starred in the lead role of Ponyboy Curtis, were swarmed by fans asking for autographs at the premiere. Although it was advertised that Matt Dillon would also be there, he was not available. Many of those who attended the premiere appeared in the film. Patrick Swayze (center) is pictured signing a movie poster during the premiere.

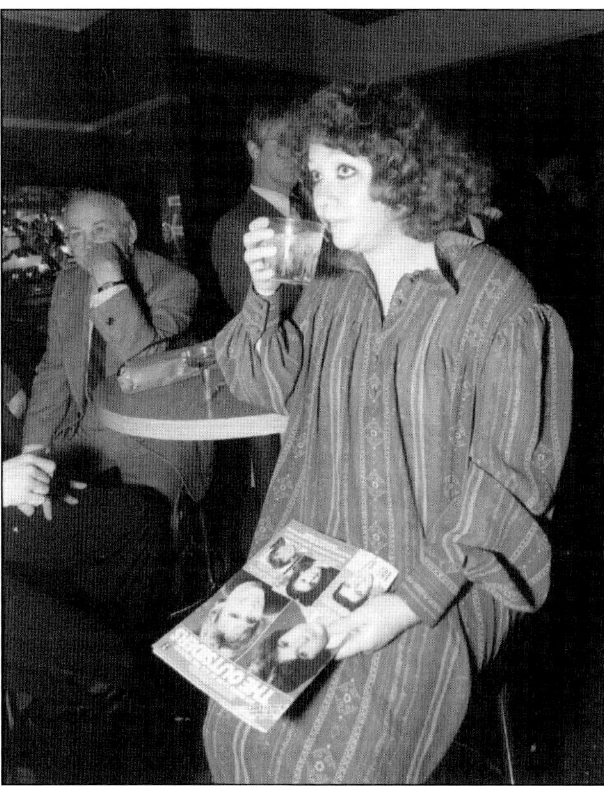

The Outsiders provided early roles for many in its cast who were just beginning very successful careers. The cast was featured in a magazine targeted to preteens around the time of the film's release. In this image, author S.E. Hinton is holding a copy of that magazine with Matt Dillon, Ralph Macchio, C. Thomas Howell, Diane Lane, and Rob Lowe on the cover.

Seven

Multiplexes

Blockbusters and Big Sound

A new era in movie theaters began in Tulsa in 1965 with the appearance of the multiplex. The word "multiplex" simply refers to multiple screens in a single theater complex. When the Boman Twin opened in 1965 with two auditoriums sharing a central lobby, the future had arrived.

The single-screen cinemas that opened later, including Southroads Cinema, Park Lane, and Fox, all added additional screens in order to compete. Even small Tulsa multiplexes that opened with two or three screens, including UA Annex 3, would add more screens in this new era. The sacrifice was auditorium size, as rooms were split in half to accommodate more screens. Improved sound technology brought big sound to smaller, boxy auditoriums.

One theater bucked that trend. Barton Theaters of Oklahoma City built single-screen houses—both called the Continental—in Tulsa and Oklahoma City. Designed for roadshow films, the Tulsa Continental opened in 1966 and featured state-of-the-art sound, 35-mm and 70-mm projection, and a giant curved screen. However, the huge and cavernous Continental was no match for the multiplex, and Tulsa's Continental closed in 1981.

The multiplex was the venue of the first summer blockbusters. *Indiana Jones*, *Star Wars*, and the *Terminator* and *Die Hard* movies played on multiplex screens. Rocky Balboa, the Brat Pack, and Tom Cruise appeared there. Likewise, *Terms of Endearment*, *Titanic*, and *The Princess Bride* enchanted audiences at the multiplex. And then there were midnight movies. Some theaters, including the Fox 4 and Village I and II, built weekend midnight movies around the cult classic *The Rocky Horror Picture Show*.

Over time, some multiplexes became dollar theaters, including Fontana 6, Southside Cinema Twin, and Super Saver Cinema. These theaters filled the time gap between a film's theatrical release and its arrival at video stores.

By the mid-1990s, many multiplexes were beginning to show their age. Digital technology began to offer new ways for people to enjoy movies at home, and dollar theaters and video stores started to vanish.

As a new millennium approached, a generation raised on computers and flashy video games would have their own cinemas in which to experience the latest installments of *Harry Potter*, *The Avengers*, and the *Star Wars* series—and they would not even have to stand in line to buy a ticket.

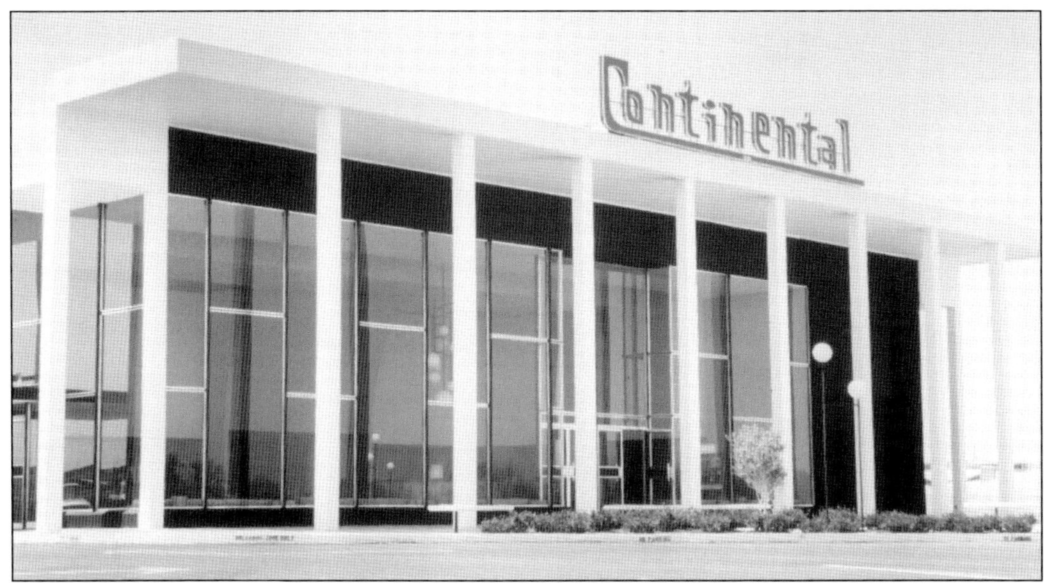

In 1965, Barton Theaters wanted to bring glamour back to going to the movies. With a focus on aesthetics, it built Continental Theaters in Tulsa, Oklahoma City, and Denver. Tulsa's Continental, located on East Skelly Drive near Memorial Drive, opened in March 1966. Featuring contemporary black-and-white and chrome decor, the 900-seat theater had a giant curved Cinerama screen, spacious rocking seats, and plush draperies. Featuring 35-mm and 70-mm projection, the theater was acoustically designed for large-screen roadshow films like *2001: A Space Odyssey*, which played in 1968.

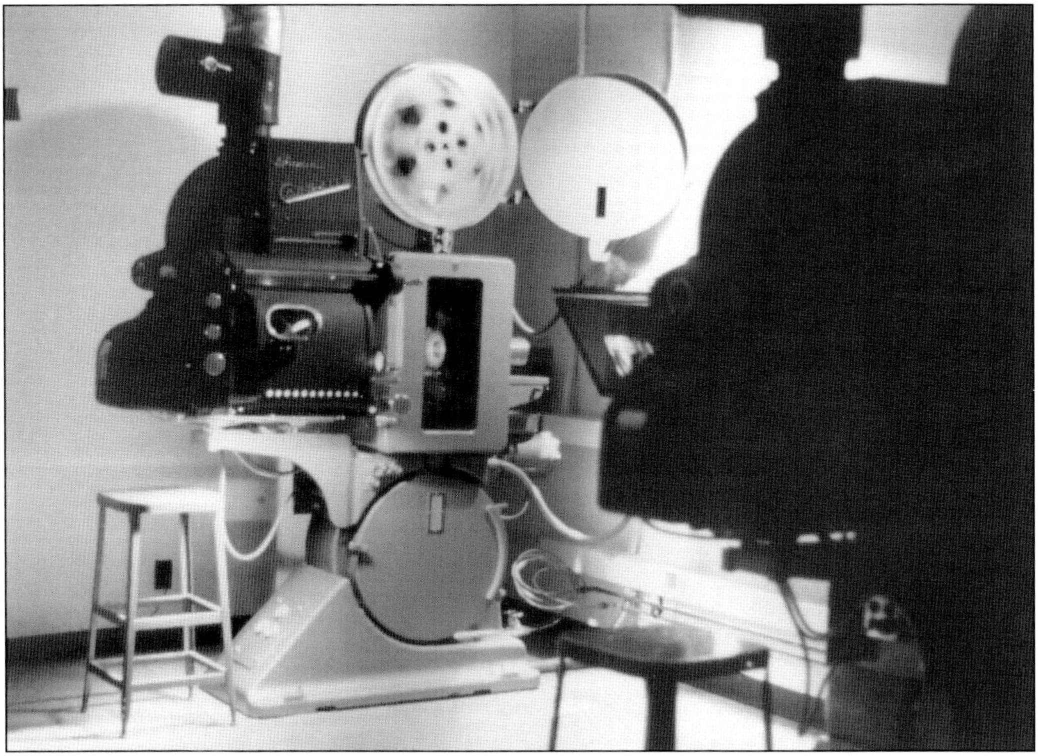

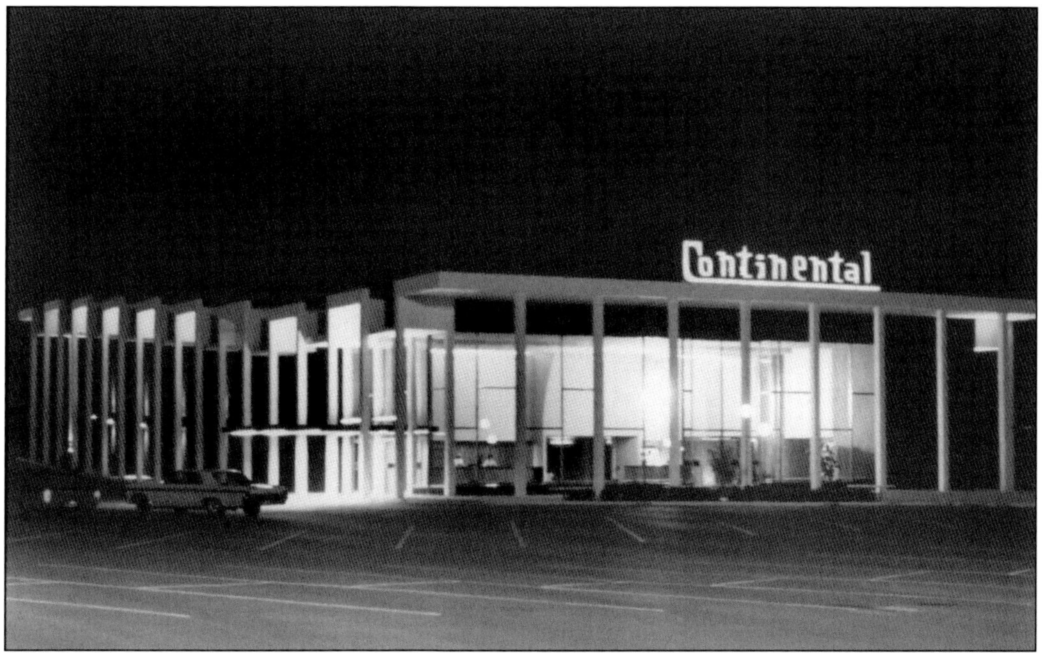

The Continental's spacious lobby was designed to accommodate crowds at intermission. Initially, instead of soft drinks, its circular concessions served juice drinks and imported candies, with no Junior Mints or Milk Duds in sight. Ultimately, the monolithic single-screen Continental could not compete with the multiplex theaters. It closed in 1981 and was demolished soon afterward.

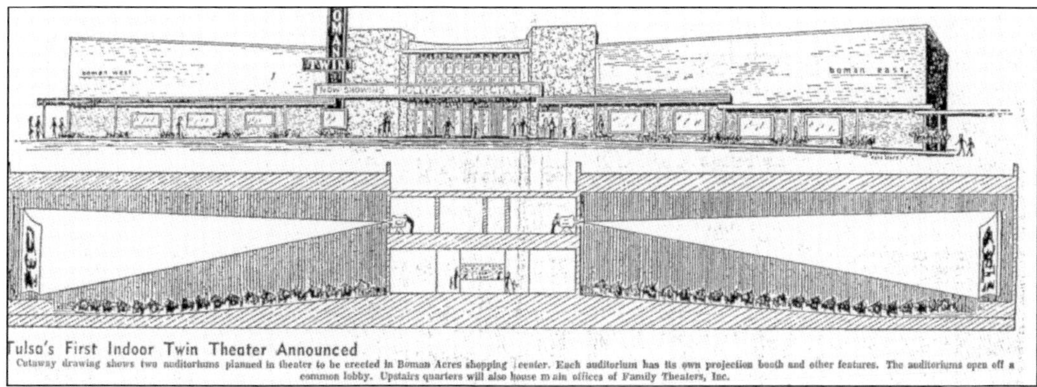

When the Boman Twin opened in 1965 on the northeast corner of East Thirty-first Street and South Sheridan Road, it ushered in the age of the multiplex in Tulsa. The screens were known as Boman West, with 800 seats, and Boman East, with 900, and they shared a common lobby. People who spent time at the Boman Twin will notice that the artist's rendition in this announcement varies from the final version that ended up being built.

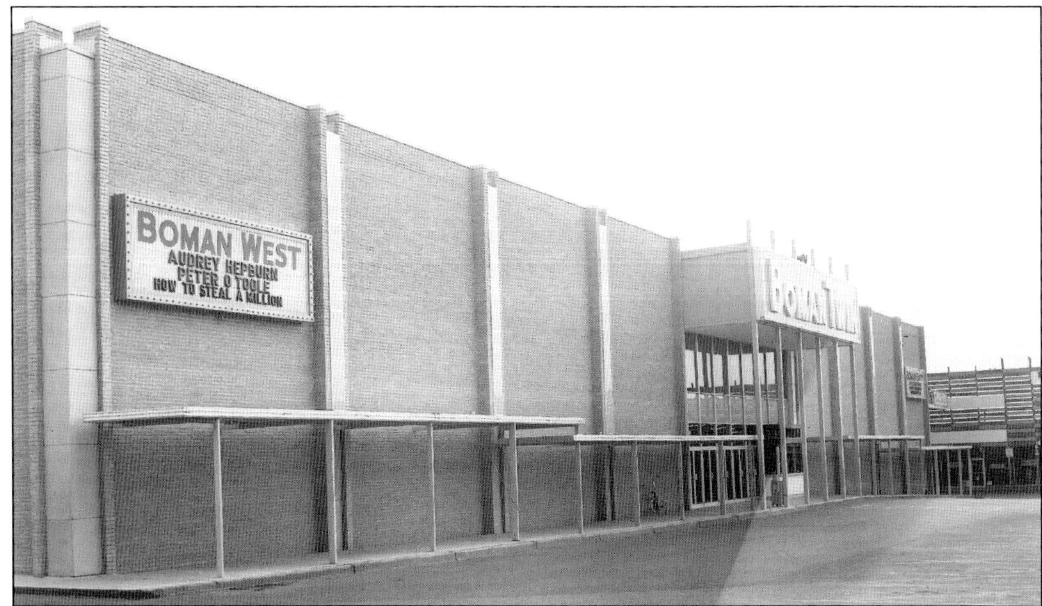

The Boman Twin was designed by the Tulsa architectural firm of Whiteside, Schultz & Chadsey, which would later design the Park Lane Theatre. Each Boman screen was 42 feet wide and 18 feet, 6 inches, high. The Boman East featured beige walls and draperies, turquoise seat upholstery, and brown waterfall curtains, while the west auditorium had turquoise walls and drapes, brown seats, and gold curtains. Each theater had Simplex projectors and Altec Lansing sound systems. The theater's surround sound was ideal for 1970s disaster films such as the *Airport* movies and *The Towering Inferno.* (Above, courtesy of Beryl Ford Collection/Rotary Club of Tulsa.)

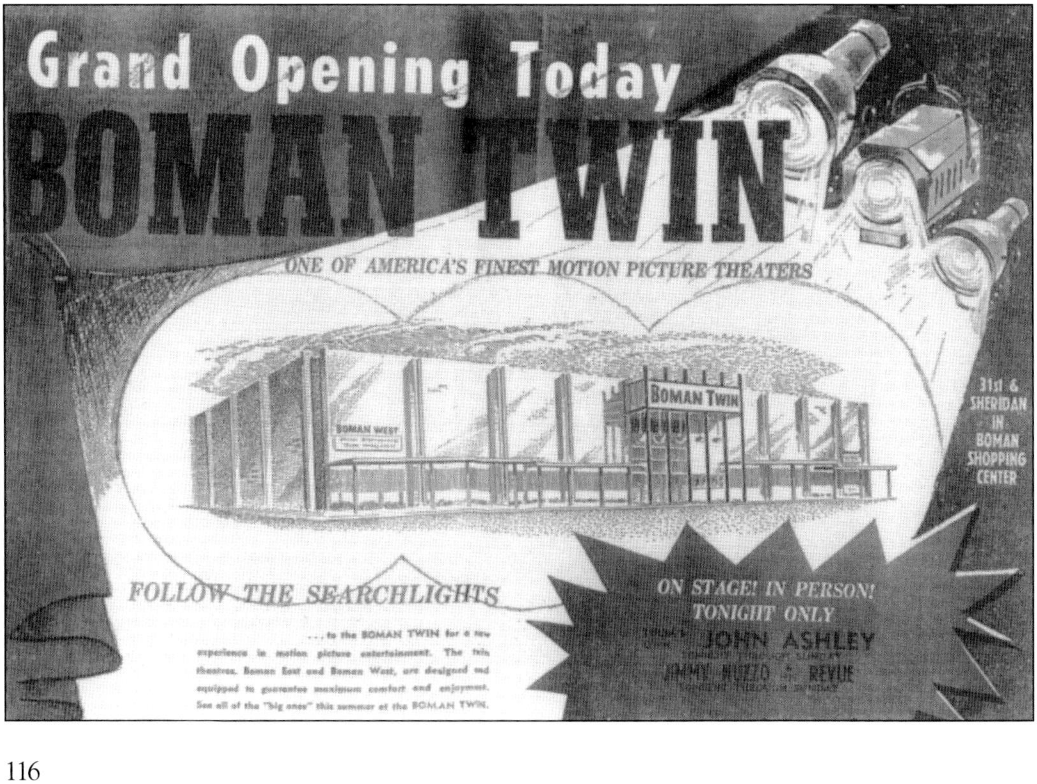

Grand Opening Today
BOMAN TWIN
ONE OF AMERICA'S FINEST MOTION PICTURE THEATERS
BOMAN TWIN
BOMAN WEST
31st & SHERIDAN IN BOMAN SHOPPING CENTER
FOLLOW THE SEARCHLIGHTS
. . . to the BOMAN TWIN for a new experience in motion picture entertainment. The twin theatres, Boman East and Boman West, are designed and equipped to guarantee maximum comfort and enjoyment. See all of the "big ones" this summer at the BOMAN TWIN.
ON STAGE! IN PERSON!
TONIGHT ONLY
JOHN ASHLEY

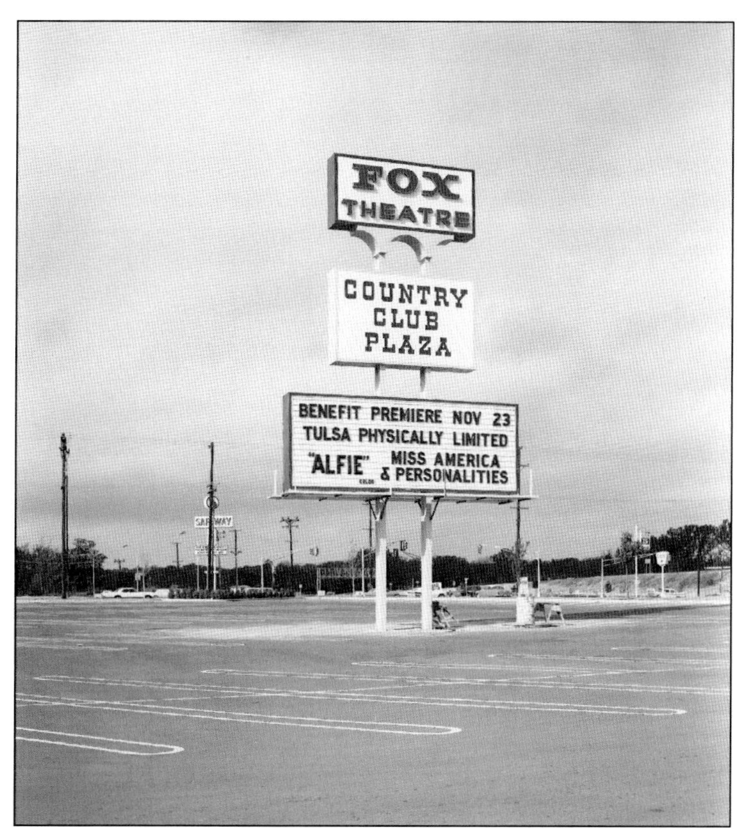

Fox Theatre, located at 3364 East Fifty-first Street, opened in 1966 with a single screen. On the southeast corner of Fifty-first Street and Harvard Avenue, the theater added three more screens to become the Fox 4. The theater was one of the first in Tulsa to feature midnight showings of the cult film *The Rocky Horror Picture Show*, for which *Rocky Horror* fans would come dressed as characters from the movie. They would act out scenes, and some attendees would throw objects at the screen—including toast, toilet paper, and rice—at specific points in the film. (Courtesy of Beryl Ford Collection/Rotary Club of Tulsa.)

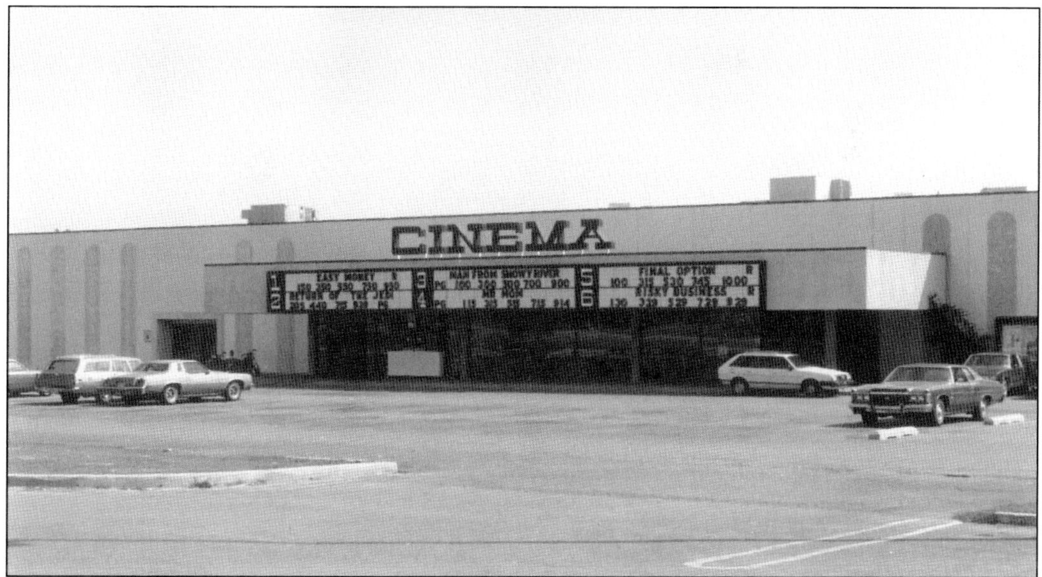

Woodland Hills Cinema, located at 8220 East Sixty-sixth Street, opened in 1977 with three screens, later doubling them to become Woodland Hills Cinema 6. For a time in the 1980s and 1990s, attending a movie in Tulsa was as simple as heading toward Woodland Hills Mall. Once Cinemark Movies 8 opened almost directly across the street, moviegoers had their choice of 14 screens within two blocks. Woodland Hills Cinema 6 closed in 2001 and was demolished.

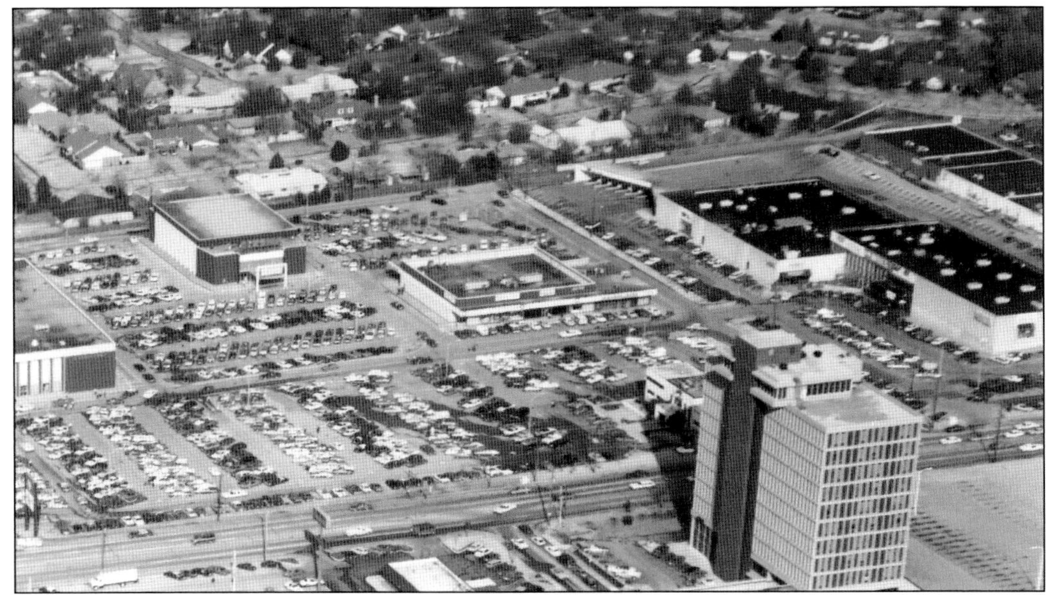

This 1984 aerial photograph of Forty-first Street between Yale and Hudson Avenues shows another clustering of multiplexes, Southroads Cinema and UA Annex 7. The freestanding building on the east end of Tulsa's first enclosed mall, Southroads Cinema (at left), opened in 1967. A second screen was added to this theater, which was where many Tulsans saw early blockbusters like *Jaws* and *Star Wars*. The theater closed in 1990 and was demolished. The UA Annex 7 appears on the right side of this image, just behind the taller building. The UA Annex 3 debuted in 1975; four smaller auditoriums were added to the larger three to make it the UA Annex 7. It closed in 1998.

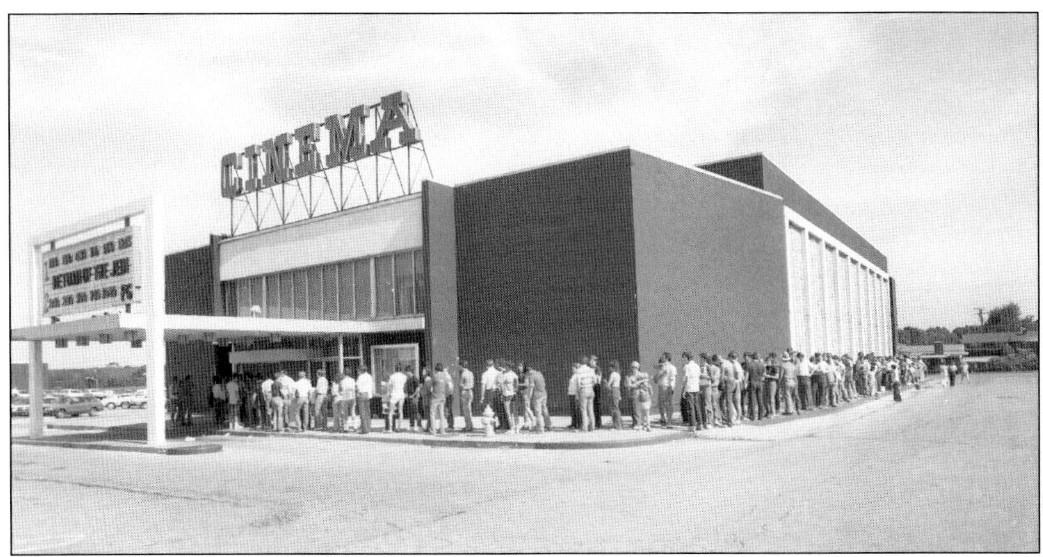

These fans were waiting in line to see the film that completed the original *Star Wars* trilogy, *Return of the Jedi*, at Southroads Cinema on May 25, 1983. The first showing was at 11:10 a.m. that day, and the line started to form at 4:30 a.m.

This newspaper advertisement from January 1984 lists the midnight movies playing at Southroads Mall and Village Cinema. *Dawn of the Dead* and *No Nukes* were playing at Southroads. Clint Eastwood's *Sudden Impact* was featured at the Village along with the film that started the midnight-movie craze, *The Rocky Horror Picture Show.* Also included in this advertisement are the dollar movies at South Side Cinema Twin on South Lewis Avenue. (Courtesy of Steve Clem.)

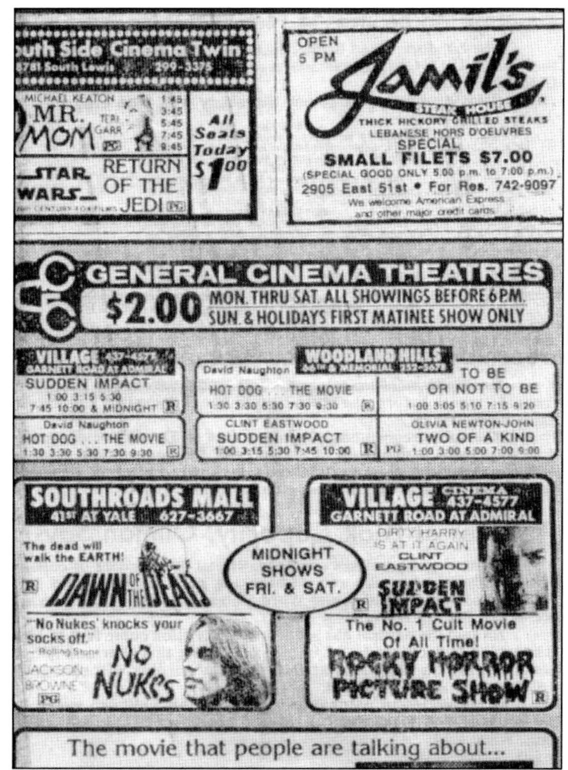

South Side Cinema Twin
6781 South Lewis 299-3375

MICHAEL KEATON
MR. MOM
TERI GARR
1:45 3:45 5:45 7:45 9:45
PG

All Seats Today $1.00

STAR WARS
RETURN OF THE JEDI
PG

OPEN 5 PM

Jamil's
STEAK HOUSE
THICK HICKORY GRILLED STEAKS
LEBANESE HORS D'OEUVRES
SPECIAL
SMALL FILETS $7.00
(SPECIAL GOOD ONLY 5:00 p.m. to 7:00 p.m.)
2905 East 51st • For Res. 742-9097
We welcome American Express and other major credit cards

GENERAL CINEMA THEATRES
$2.00 MON. THRU SAT. ALL SHOWINGS BEFORE 6 P.M.
SUN. & HOLIDAYS FIRST MATINEE SHOW ONLY

VILLAGE 437-4577
GARNETT ROAD AT ADMIRAL
SUDDEN IMPACT
1:00 3:15 5:30 7:45 10:00 & MIDNIGHT R
David Naughton
HOT DOG . . . THE MOVIE
1:30 3:30 5:30 7:30 9:30 R

WOODLAND HILLS
66th & MEMORIAL 252-3678
David Naughton
HOT DOG . . . THE MOVIE
1:30 3:30 5:30 7:30 9:30 R
CLINT EASTWOOD
SUDDEN IMPACT
1:00 3:15 5:30 7:45 10:00 R
TO BE OR NOT TO BE
1:00 3:05 5:10 7:15 9:20
OLIVIA NEWTON-JOHN
TWO OF A KIND
PG 1:00 3:00 5:00 7:00 9:00

SOUTHROADS MALL
41st AT YALE 627-3667
The dead will walk the EARTH!
R
DAWN OF THE DEAD
"No Nukes' knocks your socks off." —Rolling Stone
JACKSON BROWNE
NO NUKES
PG

MIDNIGHT SHOWS FRI. & SAT.

VILLAGE CINEMA 437-4577
GARNETT ROAD AT ADMIRAL
DIRTY HARRY IS AT IT AGAIN
CLINT EASTWOOD
R
SUDDEN IMPACT
The No. 1 Cult Movie Of All Time!
ROCKY HORROR PICTURE SHOW R

The movie that people are talking about...

Village Cinema opened in 1968 at Garnett Road and Admiral Place as a modern, single-screen theater. The Village's lobby had contemporary decor featuring leather and chrome. The auditorium had ample legroom and a massive screen. The auditorium was later split down the middle to become the twin theaters Village I and II. The theater closed in the late 1980s.

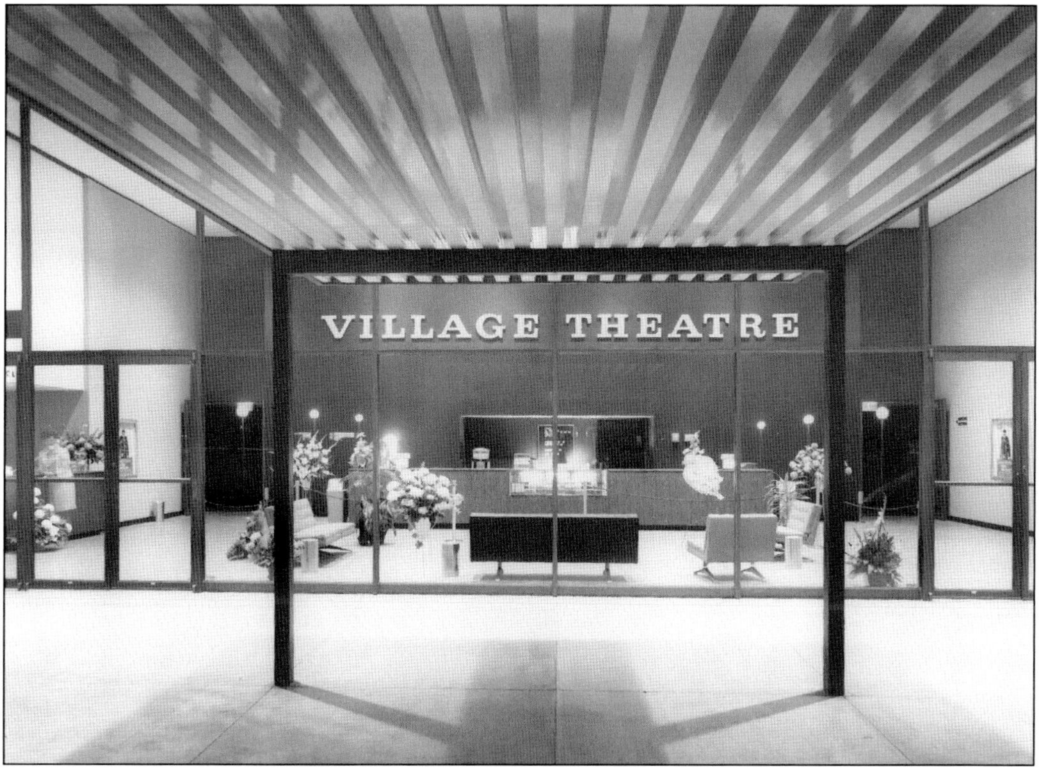

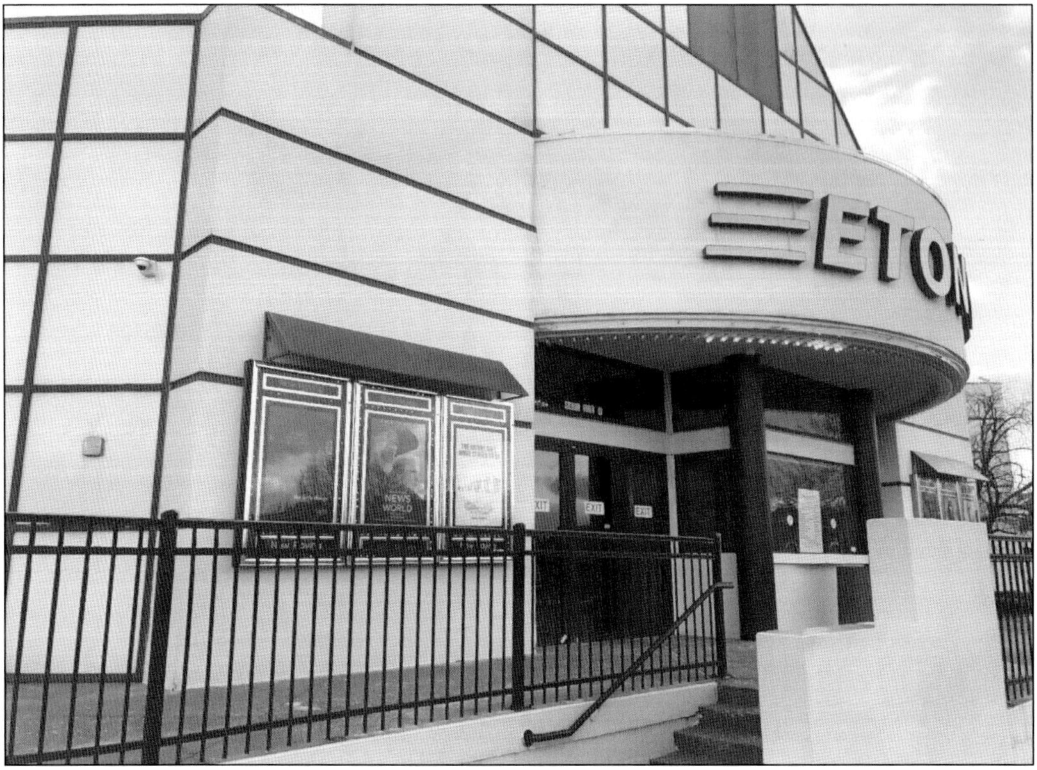

Eton Square Cinema 6 opened in 1985 at 8421 East Sixty-first Street as part of Eton Square Shopping Center. This first-run multiplex has been operated by several different companies, including General Cinema and Wallace Theaters. After closing for a time in the early 2000s, Eton Square Cinema 6 got a reboot, promoting first-run movies at affordable prices. The auditoriums feature tables in front of the seats. (Both, courtesy of Maggie Brown.)

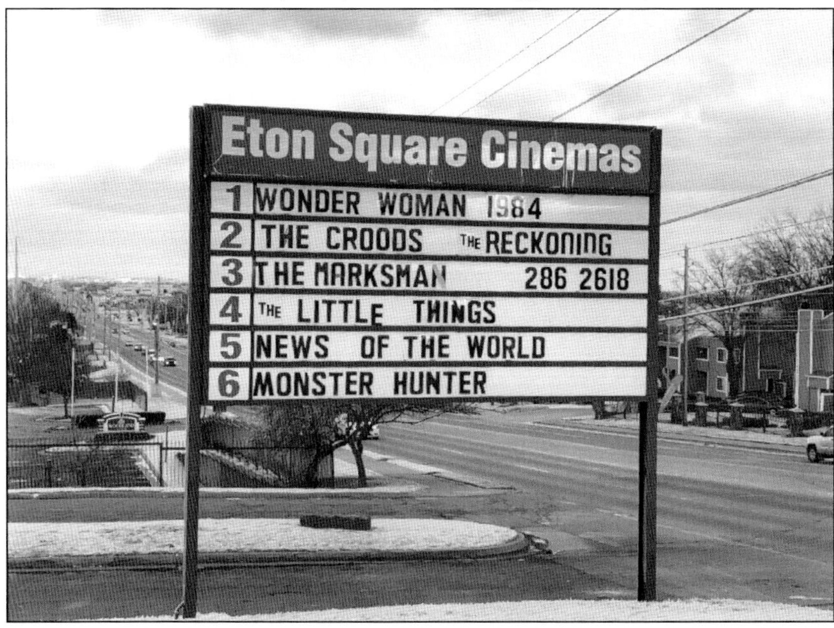

Eight

A New Millennium
Cinema in the 21st Century

By the 1990s, multiplexes had been around for a quarter century—or longer. Aging facilities and digital technology led to an emerging generation of millennials getting their own theaters. When the AMC Southroads 20 opened in Tulsa in 1997, it ushered in a new cinema experience. The key features were choice, comfort, and convenience.

These new indoor theater malls offered more screens and a wider selection of movie choices. But the major upgrade was in comfort. Stadium-style seating with big recliners quickly became the norm. The larger size of the seats reduced the capacity of each auditorium, but the plush seating was a big draw.

Convenience was enhanced by moviegoers being able to bypass the box office. Tickets could be purchased at automated kiosks or, increasingly, online, or they could be printed at home. Eventually, cell phones could be scanned for admission.

Behind the scenes, the showing of films became completely automated. Movies were distributed digitally, eliminating reels, film projectors, and a plum job in the theater trade—projectionist. Theaters made changes to concessions as well. Many, including Starworld 20 and Sapulpa's B&B Theaters, began offering alcoholic beverages. Others, like the Broken Arrow Warren Theatre, added a full menu of food items and direct service to people in their seats.

IMAX technology was another addition in mainstream theaters. Once restricted to specialty institutions like museums, technological innovations allowed existing theaters to retrofit their systems to show IMAX films. Cinemark IMAX opened in 2000, providing moviegoers with an extreme 3D experience on a screen five stories tall and 70 feet wide. The expense required to create and exhibit IMAX films still limits its use.

As new stadium-seating theaters opened, long-standing multiplexes began closing or renovating to keep up. Starworld 20 remodeled in 2014 to include new motorized recliners and wider rows. That theater's grand auditorium seating was reduced by half with this renovation.

In March 2020, the coronavirus pandemic caused theaters to close. Many were idle for several months before reopening with social distancing protocols. Only time will tell what the lasting effects of those closures will be and what the future holds for movie theaters.

With all the changes in the history of theaters, some things remain the same. The Circle Cinema still provides film entertainment for audiences, and the Admiral Twin keeps the drive-in experience alive. Wherever folks gather for the communal experience of watching movies, once the lights go down, the excitement is palpable. It's showtime!

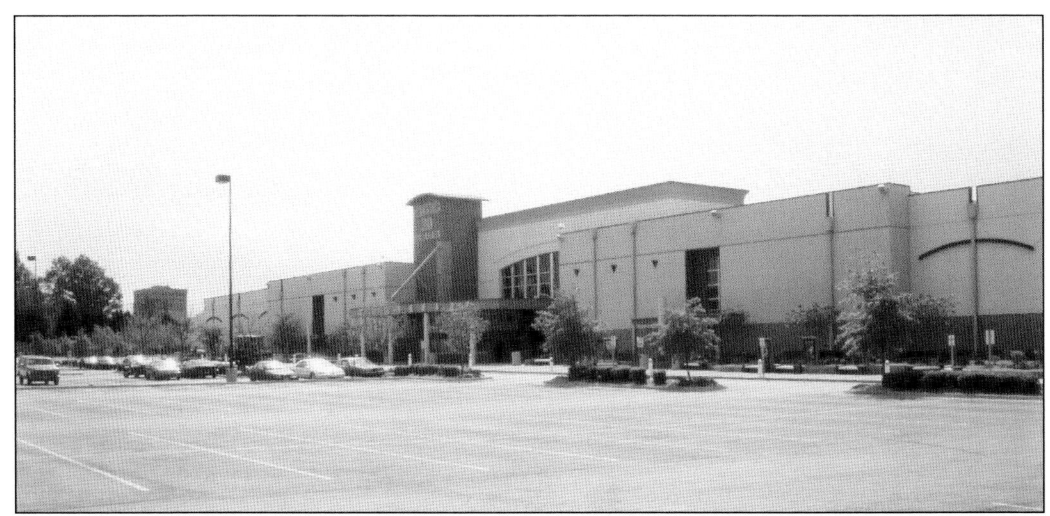

AMC Southroads 20 opened in 1997, ushering in a new era of cinema in Tulsa. The main attraction in this new kind of multiplex mall was stadium-style seating in plush recliners in each auditorium. Recliner seating quickly became the standard for new cinemas. At first, tickets could be purchased at kiosks in front of the theater, then purchasing online and printing tickets at home became the norm. Eventually, customers could simply show a barcode on their cell phones for admission. The expansive AMC theater complex is shown here in 2002.

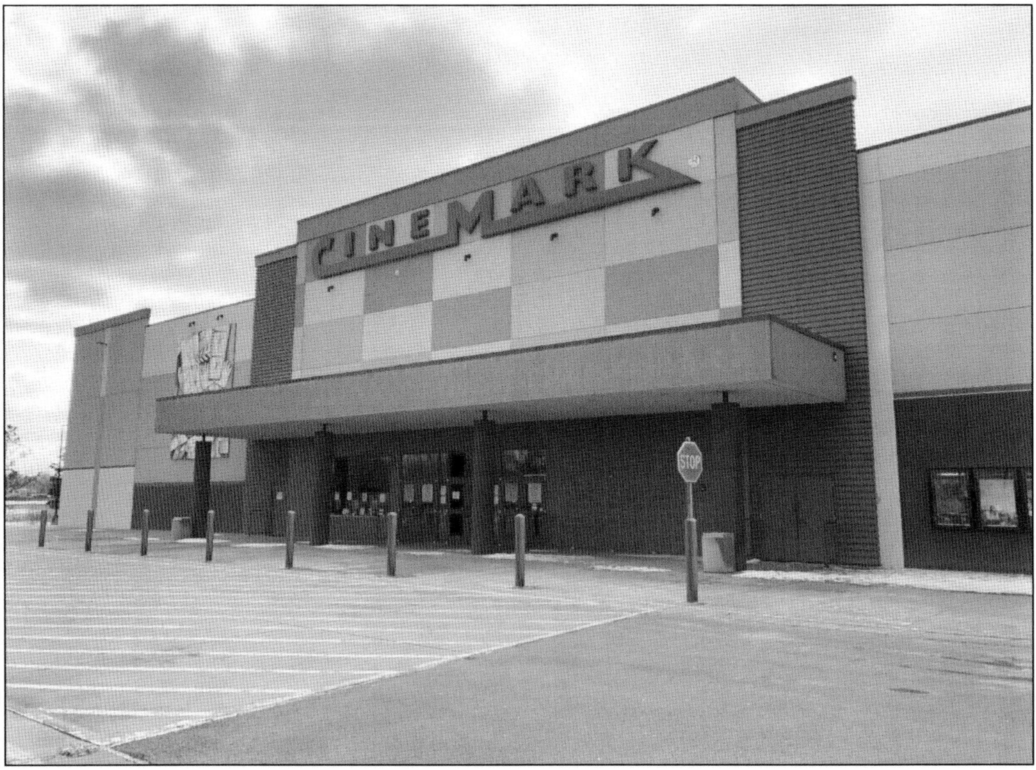

Cinemark Broken Arrow, located at 1801 Hillside Drive, opened in August 2010. This all-digital theater features stadium seating in every auditorium with seating capacities varying from 100 to 250. Six auditoriums are outfitted for RealD 3D presentations. (Courtesy of Maggie Brown.)

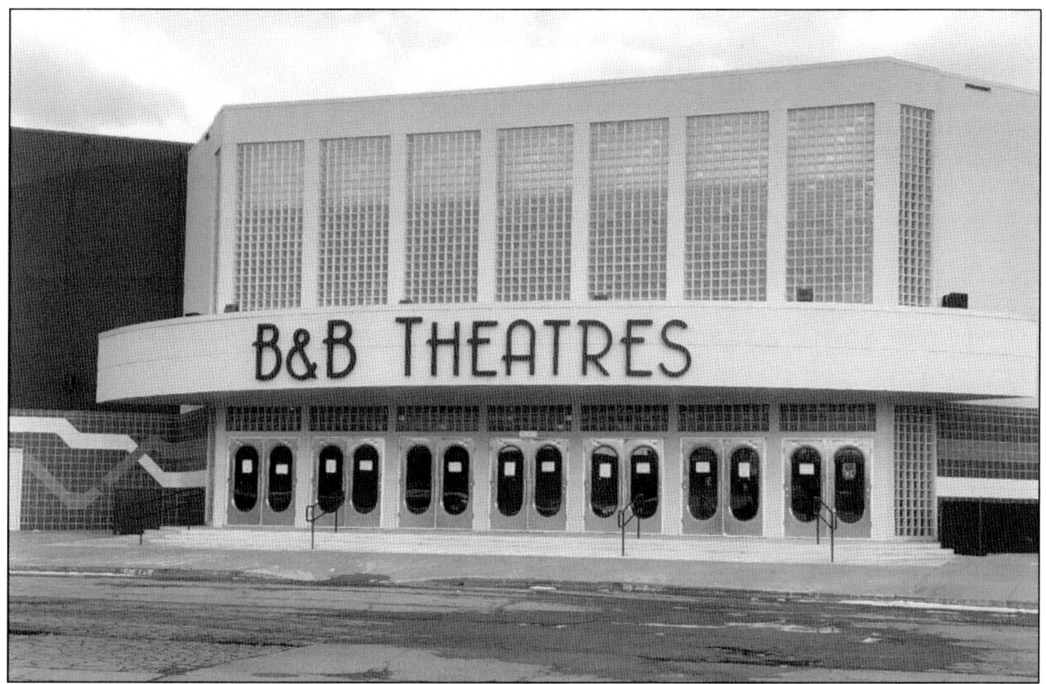

In 1998, Starworld 20 opened at 10301 South Memorial Drive. This theater had a combination of stadium-style auditoriums and more traditional seating. Arcade games were also part of the Starworld experience. In 2014, B&B Theatres purchased and remodeled the building. Upgrades included the installation of a second Grand Screen with a specialized wall-to-wall curved screen, motorized leather-style recliners, and all-digital projection with DTS:X immersive surround sound. Other new features included wider spaces between rows and a bar at the concession stand. (Courtesy of Maggie Brown.)

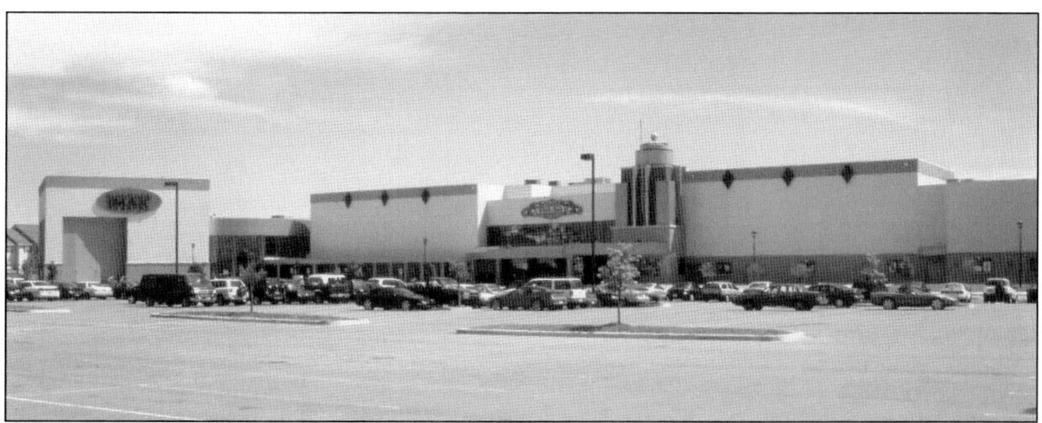

Cinemark Tulsa IMAX opened at East Seventy-first Street and Highway 169 in 2000. The complex features 16 regular theaters and 1 IMAX theater. With the IMAX format, moviegoers view the film on a five-story-high screen and receive an extreme three-dimensional experience. Producing these large format IMAX films is expensive, so the technology is only utilized for special films and occasionally for a mainstream movie. All auditoriums at this theater were upgraded to luxury recliners in 2014.

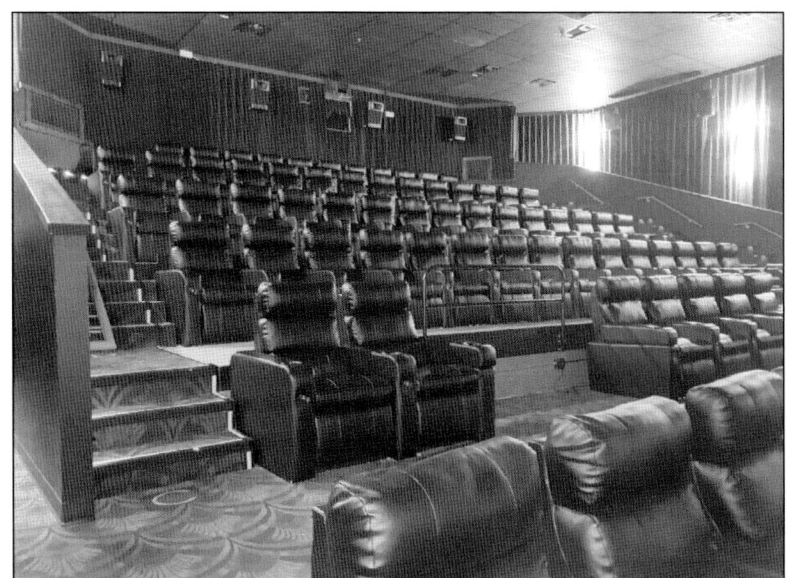

This photograph provides a view inside Sapulpa's B&B Theatres Grand Screen auditorium. The room features luxury leather-style recliners and wide rows for increased legroom. These plush oversized chairs reduced the seating capacity of the theater by half—from over 300 to 136 seats. (Courtesy of Steve Clem.)

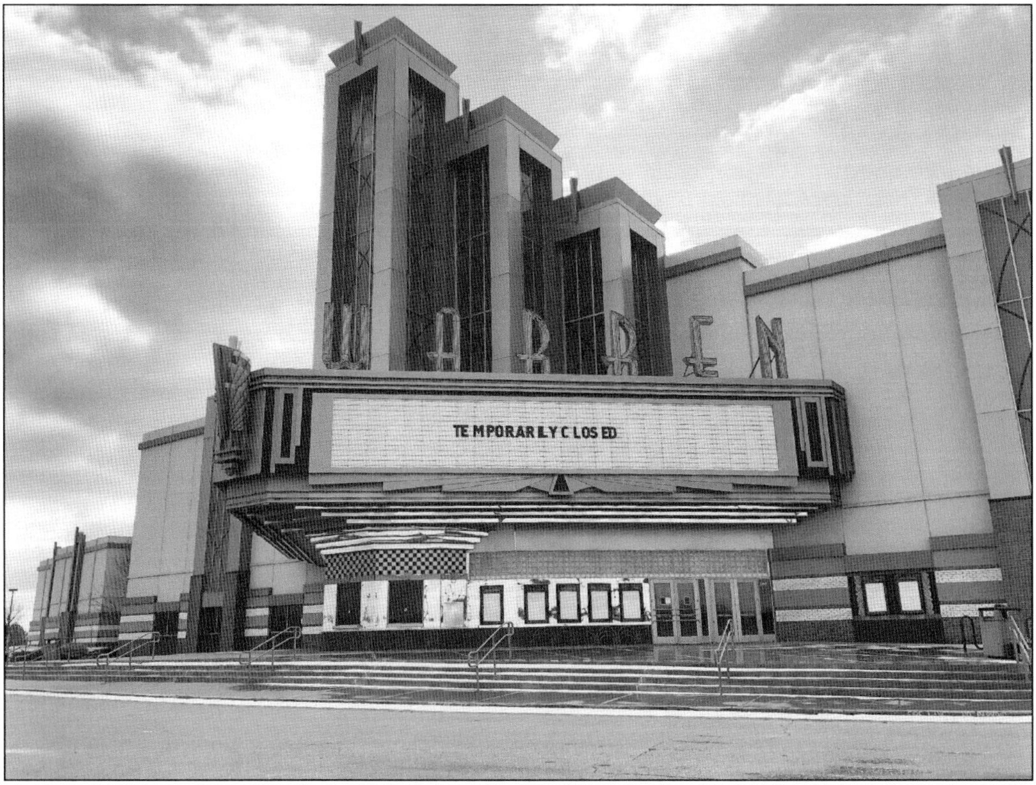

Broken Arrow Warren Theatre 18 opened at Christmastime in 2014 at 1700 West Aspen Creek Drive. With Deco stylings inside and out, this glitzy theater features five different types of auditoriums, including the screening room, grand infinity, VIP stadiums, the balcony, and director suites. Some auditoriums had full menu and cocktail service. Regal Entertainment Group acquired the theater in May 2017. The theater closed in 2020 during the coronavirus pandemic and remained closed through early 2021 before reopening. (Courtesy of Maggie Brown.)

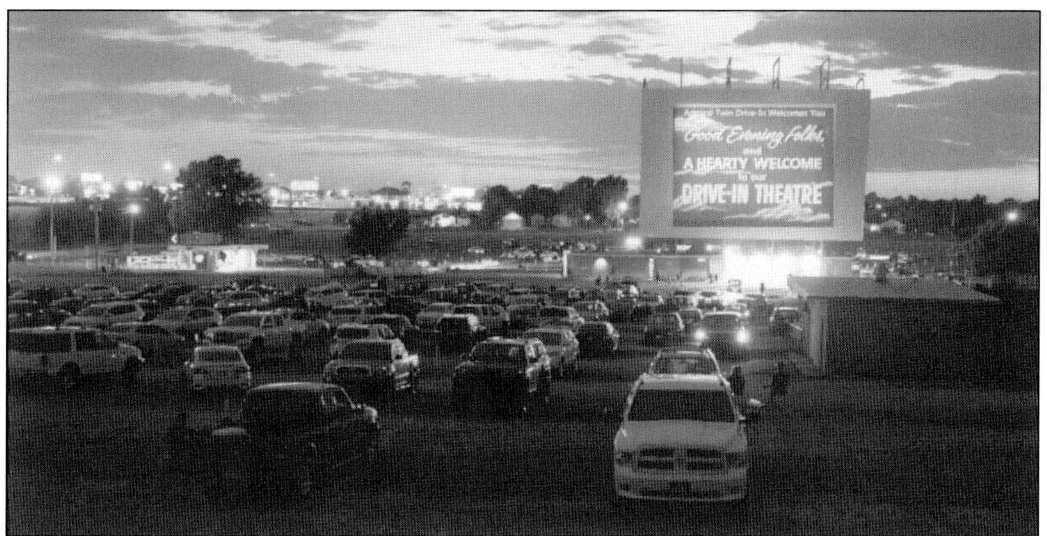

There is a saying that the more things change, the more they stay the same. That could easily apply to Tulsa's two theater mainstays, the Admiral Twin Drive-In and Circle Cinema. Both are part of the city's grand theater past, and each continues to offer innovative cinema experiences. After surviving closures in 2020 due to the COVID pandemic, in 2021, both theaters became satellite locations for the Sundance Film Festival. Moviegoers followed pandemic protocols by social distancing at the drive-in to view Sundance films, while Circle Cinema offered virtual viewings of festival fare. (Below, courtesy of Chuck Foxen/Circle Cinema.)

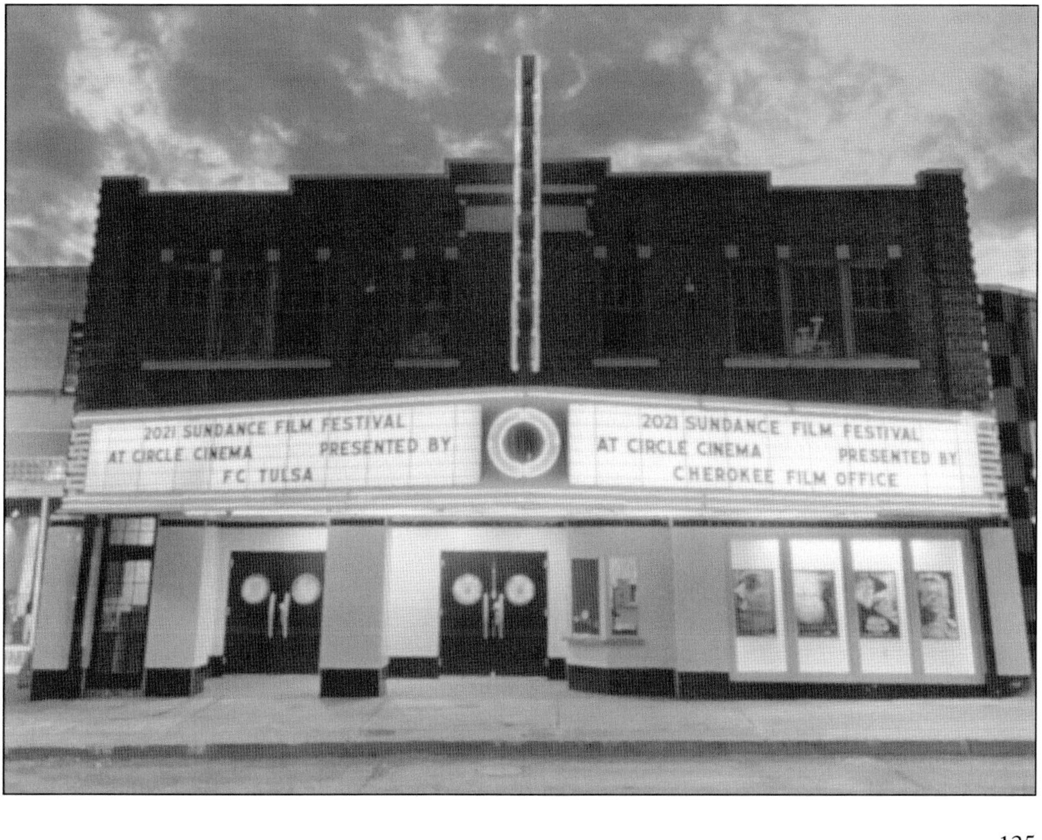

Index

About the Tulsa Historical Society and Museum

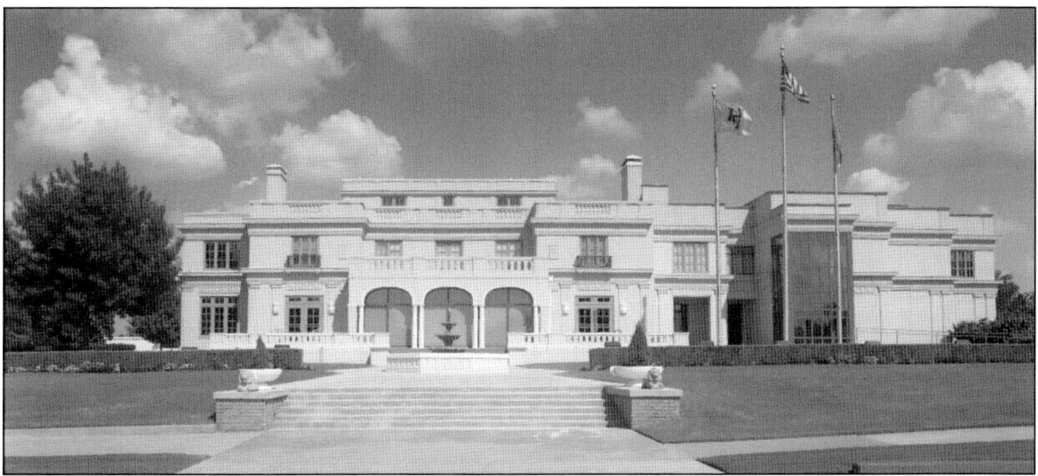

Established in 1963, the Tulsa Historical Society and Museum (THSM) holds an extensive collection of resources about the city's rich past. The collection contains nearly 200,000 photographs, books, maps, documents, textiles, architectural elements, furnishings, and personal artifacts. From 1985 until 1998, THSM had its headquarters in the Thomas Gilcrease house on the grounds of the Gilcrease Museum. In December 1997, with funds made available through the Tulsa Tribune Foundation, THSM purchased the historic Sam Travis Mansion on Peoria Avenue. The mansion has been expanded and renovated to serve as the museum's home. Featuring eight galleries, the museum collects, preserves, and exhibits artifacts and archives from Tulsa history. With frequently rotating exhibits and a variety of public programming, the museum always has new Tulsa stories to share and exciting relics and images for visitors to enjoy.

Consistent with our mission to preserve history on a local level, this book was printed in South Carolina on American-made paper and manufactured entirely in the United States. Products carrying the accredited Forest Stewardship Council (FSC) label are printed on 100 percent FSC-certified paper.

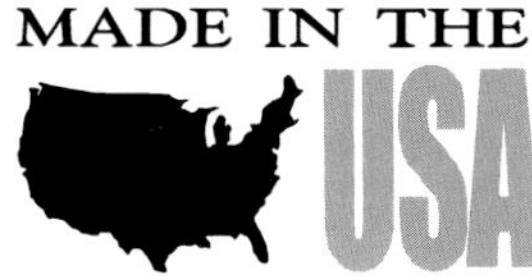